LA VERENDRYE:

Fur Trader and Explorer

D1520962

Statue of La Vérendrye, by Jan Bailleul, at Quebec.

LA VERENDRYE

Fur Trader and Explorer

NELLIS M. CROUSE

KENNIKAT PRESS
Port Washington, N. Y./London

115360

LA VERENDRYE

Copyright 1956 by Cornell University
Reissued in 1972 by Kennikat Press by arrangement
Library of Congress Catalog Card No: 79-153210
ISBN 0-8046-1520-9

Manufactured by Taylor Publishing Company   Dallas, Texas

To

Tanya and Marc, Jr.

Contents

Illustrations and Maps

LA VERENDRYE:

Fur Trader and Explorer

I

Exploration and the Fur Trade

TO THOSE who find inspiration in tales of adventure, where romance blends with history, the story of French exploration in North America will always have a peculiar fascination. It is the story of a brave, adventurous people who found at their feet a vast, unknown continent of lofty mountains, endless prairies, mighty inland seas, great rivers, and impenetrable forests, a continent of undeveloped riches, inhabited by strange savages whose ways of life were different from their own. It was the good fortune of these people to find in that portion of the continent which their explorers had pre-empted for them one of the greatest waterways in all the world—the St. Lawrence River— and by this they were able to penetrate into the very heart of the New World. No mountain barrier shut them off, as it did the English, from the great regions of the West; and so, unlike their southern neighbors, they at once struck boldly inland and took possession of a gigantic territory. In penetrating the hinterland, these French Canadians were inspired by two goals: the fur trade and the discovery of the Western Sea. It was to this dual purpose that Pierre Gaultier de Varennes de la Vérendrye devoted his life.

The reason why La Vérendrye's achievements have never been so well recognized as those of other eminent explorers is due largely to the fact that they were not spectacular and that they did not open up a territory of such importance in the history of Canada as did the discoveries of Champlain and La Salle. True, La Vérendrye penetrated regions hitherto unexplored by the white man, but as he was unable to attain his ultimate objective—the discovery of a supposedly nearby Western Sea—his work was regarded by his contemporaries as something of a failure. Later, when men began to realize that in order to reach his objective he would have had to cover the distance between Lake Superior and the Pacific Ocean, they saw the magnitude of the task to which he had unwittingly set himself and gave him credit for what he actually did accomplish. Furthermore, recent investigations have thrown more light on the circumstances of La Vérendrye's career and have disclosed many of the problems with which he had to contend. He was a fur trader turned explorer, and in both these careers, carried on simultaneously, he had to deal with almost insuperable difficulties, such as Indian warfare, the massacre of his men, and shortage of supplies, to name but a few, while he also had to face perpetual misinterpretation of his motives by an unsympathetic government at home and continual harassment by creditors who sought payment for the debts he had contracted in order to carry on his work. Yet, despite these handicaps, the man stuck courageously to his task with a stubbornness that deserved a better outcome.

During the seventeenth century the French, in developing their Canadian possessions, devoted a good part of their efforts to exploration and the organization of the fur trade. These two activities often complemented each other, for the trade lured its devotees far afield into the wilderness, and their expeditions frequently led to discoveries. Furs—usually the beaver in La Vérendrye's case—formed an important staple in the wealth of the colony; but the system employed to collect them led to grave abuses. Trading posts were set up at various strategic points, the most famous being Michilimackinac at the junction of Lakes Michigan and Huron, whence traders could proceed northward to Lake Superior or westward to Wisconsin; and at these posts they were supposed to conduct their business according to rules laid down by the government.

Meanwhile a threat had arisen to menace the French monopoly of the northwestern fur trade. In the year 1670 King Charles II of England gave the Hudson's Bay Company its famous charter, granting it a territory of vast extent and vague limits, extending westward and southward from Hudson Bay. The purpose of the new company was, of course, to obtain for England a share of the valuable fur trade. Within fifteen years of its incorporation it had established posts on James Bay at the mouths of the Rupert, Moose, and Albany Rivers and also the important station of York Factory at the mouth of the Hayes River on the western side of Hudson Bay. The mouth of this river is very near that of the Nelson, whose waters provide the principal route from Lake Winnipeg to the bay, the one by which the Indians of the more southern regions around Lake Superior had access to the British trading post. That a clash between these rival interests was inevitable is evident, and it was not long before it came to a head. The French government sent out expeditions by land and by sea to capture these posts, and for many years they changed hands according to the fortunes of war. Then, in 1713, the Treaty of Utrecht, which closed the War of the Spanish Succession, allotted the Hudson Bay district to the British in perpetuity, thus putting an end to all French efforts to capture the valuable factories situated therein. Blocked in this direction, the French inaugurated a policy of luring the

Indians away from the bay by establishing posts of their own north of Lake Superior.

There was also another attraction in the Northwest: the belief in the existence of the Western Sea. When the French first entered Canada, they heard strange reports of a great body of water, exact location unknown, which they called the Sea of the South, the Sea of the North, or the Sea of the West. By the last quarter of the seventeenth century Father Claude Dablon had found the route to Hudson Bay, and Louis Joliet, accompanied by Father Jacques Marquette, had descended the Mississippi far enough to learn that it flowed into the Gulf of Mexico. These two seas, that of the North and that of the South, being now identified, left only the third, the Sea of the West, or Western Sea, as we shall call it, to be discovered.[1] This sea might be the Pacific Ocean, but not necessarily so. A strong belief developed in the eighteenth century—we can see it on many contemporary maps—that the western coast of the North American continent was indented by a huge gulf, similar to the Gulf of Mexico, that covered roughly what are now British Columbia, Washington, and Oregon. It was connected with the Pacific by a narrow strait.

Daniel Greysolon du Lhut was in his day one of Canada's most famous pioneers and was among the first to recognize Lake Superior as a center of the fur trade. While coasting the northern shore of the lake in the summer of 1679 [2] making friendly overtures to the Indians, he stopped long enough on the northerly branch of the Kaministikwia River to build a stockade near its mouth. This river flows from the west into a large indentation of Superior known as Thunder Bay. Its mouth is just a short distance north of the Pigeon River, which forms the boundary line

[1] Jean Delanglez, "A Mirage: The Sea of the West," *Revue d'histoire de l'Amérique française*, I (1947–1948), 541–568; hereafter cited *R.H.A.F.*
[2] Date is usually given as 1678, but Du Lhut tells us that he started from Montreal in September of that year and wintered on Lake Huron.

between Canada and Minnesota. It was here, on the Kaministikwia, that Fort William, headquarters of the Northwest Company, was erected more than a hundred years later. Both these
rivers play an important part in La Vérendrye's expeditions.

The Kaministikwia itself was one of the three routes from
Lake Superior to Rainy Lake, a large body of water on the road
to Lake Winnipeg; hence the strategic importance of Du Lhut's
fort. The other two routes were the Pigeon River and the St.
Louis River. The latter empties its waters into the western ex-
tremity of Superior. The Pigeon River eventually became *the*
route to the west, the one taken by La Vérendrye when he was
building his posts; the St. Louis River was seldom used.

Like all great explorers of his time Du Lhut was interested in finding a route to the Western Sea. On his journey to
Lake Superior he had passed through the Sioux country, where
he had heard reports of a body of water called the Vermilion
Sea, distant, so the Indians said, a twenty days' journey from
their village. They even gave him some salt which they claimed
came from its shores. Anxious to visit this ocean, he humbly
requested the governor to obtain permission from the King
to establish a post among the Sioux which he could use as a base
for a voyage of exploration. Should he succeed in the enterprise,
he asked for seigniorial rights over all countries he might discover. Unfortunately for him the time was not propitious, and
he was bluntly told that the government no longer felt any interest in what it now regarded as a rather vague quest, and it
preferred to see the colonies employed in cultivating the land
already cleared. La Salle's expedition down the Mississippi,
which was about to start, was all the officials cared for in the
way of exploration.[3]

[3] Letter to Marquis de Seignelay, and Instructions of the King, May 10,
1682, in Pierre Margry, ed., *Mémoires et documents pour servir à l'histoire
des origines françaises des pays d'outre-mer* (Paris, 1879–1888), VI, 35–
37.

Foiled in this direction, Du Lhut again turned his attention to the north country. By this time Governor Lefebvre de la Barre had decided to build a more substantial post in the heart of these regions for the protection of the fur traders and missionaries who lived there and for the accommodation of the Crees and Assiniboins, who found Hudson Bay more accessible than Lake Superior. These tribes dwelt in the vicinity of Lake of the Woods (northwest of Rainy Lake) and Lake Winnipeg respectively; and as there was a water communication by the English River between these lakes and Lake Nipigon (just north of Superior) Nipigon was chosen as the proper place for a fort. For this purpose La Barre granted a commission to Du Lhut, his brother, Charles Greysolon de la Tourette, and an officer named Boisguillot.[4] The explorers started at once and in the year 1684 erected a post on the shores of Nipigon near the à la Manne River.

Shortly after Du Lhut had built his fort on Lake Nipigon, in the year 1688 to be exact, the trail up the Kaministikwia was blazed by a young man named Jacques de Noyon, a native of Three Rivers, who was the first, so far as is known, to explore the territory. De Noyon does not seem to have been sent out under government auspices; he was probably a trader traveling on his own; but he brought back a detailed account of what he had heard, and this was of considerable value when the question of finding the Western Sea was again considered by the government. The route taken by De Noyon lay up the Kaministikwia to Dog Lake, then to Lac des Milles Lacs, where he struck the route to Rainy Lake, or, as it was sometimes called, Lake of the Crees. Rainy Lake is the focal point on the road to Lake Winnipeg, as the Kaministikwia and Pigeon trails meet there, while the third route by the St. Louis River, joins this trail not far from the lake. De Noyon wintered here. While awaiting the arrival of spring, he picked up some interesting bits of

[4] Extrait d'un mémoire, *ibid.*, pp. 19–20.

geographical information from the neighboring Indians. These Indians were probably a small band of Assiniboins who had wandered far to the east of their native habitat. They told him about a river, or rather a river and a chain of lakes, that led, after a journey of some eighty leagues, to a large sheet of water (Lake of the Woods) called by them Lake of the Assiniboins. So far so good; but from here on the story becomes confused. The savages went on to tell of a river issuing from this lake which led to the Western Sea; and to prove their assertion they offered to lead him to it. On the shores of this sea he would find, so they said, a tribe of short, squat men, three and a half to four feet tall, and he could see towns and fortified places where men rode horseback with their women mounted behind them. There he would find ships and hear a great firing of cannon. The Indians also told De Noyon that if he would accompany them he would descend a beautiful river well worth seeing, and that three days before reaching the sea he would find the river's waters rising and falling like the tide. The journey, they assured him, would not take over five months. What this far-off place might be was anyone's guess. Yet, as the Indians mentioned horses, they may have heard about the Spaniards living on the Gulf of Mexico and in some way imagined that the river leading to Lake Winnipeg eventually reached some salt-water ocean. At any rate, judging by the time it would take to reach it, this sea must have been a different one from the Vermilion Sea which the Sioux told Du Lhut was a twenty days' journey from their village. It was all very intriguing.

No official attention seems to have been paid to De Noyon's discovery at the time, but in the year 1716 the governor, Philippe de Rigault, Marquis de Vaudreuil, and his intendant, Claude Michel Bégon, gave an account of it in a memoir addressed to Duke Philippe of Orleans, regent of the kingdom during the minority of Louis XV. In their comments they pointed out that an attempt had been made to find a westward passage through

Hudson Bay, though they did not favor a route so far north.[5]
On receipt of the Vaudreuil-Bégon memoir the Council of
Marine immediately took action. They agreed with the Canadian officials that it would be a waste of time to search for
a sea route through Hudson Bay and decided that the route
traced by De Noyon should be the one selected.

There was, however, another and even more important reason for establishing posts in the Northwest. The Treaty of
Utrecht, as we have said, settled for all time the ownership of
the posts on Hudson Bay in favor of the English and ushered
in an era of comparative peace between Britain and France,
both in Europe and in America, after a long period of intermittent warfare. Since the terms of the treaty made it unlawful for
the French to attack English posts on the bay, the French officials decided to revive Du Lhut's policy of luring the Indians
from the bay by means of strategically situated trading posts.
By this they hoped to capitalize on a certain weakness in the
English method of dealing with the Indians. The English had
always waited in their factories for the savages to come to
them, sometimes from a long distance; but the French, following their established policy, treated them more as customers,
bringing merchandise to places where the Indians could bring
their furs with a minimum amount of inconvenience. It was
this policy that later governed La Vérendrye in the selection
of sites for his numerous posts. Thus the French hoped to recover by strategy what they had lost in the recent war.

The Council of Marine now gave Vaudreuil definite orders
to go ahead. Since the days of De Noyon, several travelers, or
voyageurs as the French called them, had reached Lake of the

[5] E. Z. Massicotte, "Jacques de Noyon: Nouveau détails sur sa carrière,"
Bulletin des recherches historiques, XLVIII (1942), 121–125; hereafter
cited *B.R.H.* Massicotte believes that De Noyon reached Lake of the
Woods, but the memoir of Vaudreuil and Bégon of Nov. 12, 1716
(Margry, *op. cit.,* pp. 495–498), places him no farther than Rainy Lake.

Woods and confirmed the old story of a navigable river leading to the Western Sea. The Council, therefore, ordered the establishment of posts as an initial step in a voyage of discovery. The expense of founding these posts was to be financed by the fur business, for the Crown, as we have pointed out, was unwilling to underwrite the risk; but as a compromise the King offered to pay for the actual work of discovery, to be undertaken after the posts had been erected. This arrangement was an important one and shows better than anything else how the fur trade and the work of exploration were inextricably interwoven, a connection that was to plague La Vérendrye all through his life on the frontier.

Governor Vaudreuil was accordingly ordered by the Council to send out seven or eight canoes under a suitable officer to build the first fort on the Kaministikwia and, perhaps, a second one on Rainy Lake. The Council suggested to Bégon that the party should be composed of fifty men, preferably Canadians, who were after all the best people to endure the hardships of such a journey, and who understood the ways of the wilderness. Of these men twenty-four should remain at the posts while the rest should set out for the Western Sea, and this journey should take about two years.[6]

The man selected to lead this expedition was an officer named Zacharie Robutel de la Noüe, who had served with distinction in a military campaign several years before. In July, 1717, he left Montreal for the Kaministikwia, and erected a fort near its mouth. Here he learned that hostilities had broken out between the Crees and the Sioux. He therefore stopped in his tracks and turned his energies to making peace between them, fully realizing the necessity of pacifying them if he wished to pass through their territories. He is said by some to have penetrated as far as Rainy Lake where he built a second fort, but there

[6] Order of the Council, Feb. 3, 1717, and June 26, 1717, in Margry, *op. cit.*, pp. 498–507.

is no evidence that he ever constructed a post there, though he may have visited the lake itself. Several years later, after his return to Quebec, he wrote the Duke of Orleans pointing out the advisability of founding an establishment on this lake in order to lure the savages from Hudson Bay—tolerable proof that he had not built one there himself. La Noüe remained in command of the Northwest for four years; then he was replaced by Jean-Baptiste Deschaillons de Saint-Ours, who held the post until La Vérendrye became its commander.[7]

These various accounts of the Western Sea and the way thither—most of them fantastic—were sent to France, where an attempt to give them a scientific interpretation was made by an eminent geographer, Claude de Lisle, who for some time past had interested himself in the problems of American geography. Claude had a son named Guillaume, who carried on his father's work in such a way as to lead the public to believe that the son was the originator of the maps and memoirs on which the government based its plans. This was not, in all probability, an intentional plagiarism, but a natural father-and-son relationship by which the younger man expanded his father's ideas. Thus the memoir which Guillaume presented the government in 1718 was merely a copy of Claude's memoir of 1703; and the same may be said of some other maps and memoirs presented by him.[8]

According to the considered opinion of the De Lisles, *père et fils,* the stories mentioned above gave conclusive proof of the presence of a sea in the west, not to be confused with the Pacific Ocean, since it was said to be fairly near the Mississippi. As proof of this, Guillaume gives us the data sent him by Pierre Le Sueur, a trader settled on Lake Pepin, an enlargement of the Mississippi just south of the St. Croix River in Minnesota. Le Sueur told of a Sioux tribe living near his post which had at-

[7] La Noüe to the Regent, Oct. 15, 1721, *ibid.,* pp. 512–513.
[8] Delanglez, *op. cit.*

tacked a western nation living on the shores of a sea, distant only a fifteen days' journey, where there were a strange people who dwelt in forts and dressed like the French. Besides this particular report, De Lisle mentions several others that tended to confirm the theory of a gulflike western ocean, and he also mentions the expedition of Coronado into modern Kansas, where, according to the historian Lopez de Gomara, the Spaniards saw an ocean in a locality believed by De Lisle to be near the fortieth parallel.[9]

The government now decided to make a thorough examination of all geographical features pertaining to this matter and to appraise the possibilities of finding a route to this mysterious sea by sending an agent to make a personal survey of the situation and advise them accordingly. The agent chosen was a Jesuit priest named François-Xavier Charlevoix. Father Charlevoix left France for Quebec in July 1720 and reached his destination in September. The season being then too far advanced for travel, he remained in Quebec for the winter; but during this time he improved his knowledge by cross-examining travelers who could give him information on the subject, and he even went to Montreal and Three Rivers in search of further information. In this, he tells us, he met with little success, as the *voyageurs* seldom took the trouble to make intelligent observations of the regions they traversed; and to make matters worse, they often gave their imaginations full rein in order to cover up their ignorance.

Leaving Montreal in the spring, Charlevoix made his way to Michilimackinac. Here he learned that La Noüe, on his return from Kaministikwia, had just left for Montreal. Hastening after him—for he believed that here was an opportunity to get the latest news—he presently overtook him, only to learn what he had already heard before. As Charlevoix had no time to go in

[9] De Lisle's memoir is in Philippe Buache, *Considérations géographiques* (Paris, 1753).

person to Lake Superior, he contented himself with sending a messenger to Jacques Legardeur de Saint-Pierre, commander at Chequamegon, a post on the southern shore of the lake, asking him to question the Sioux when they came there; and he also sent word to Saint-Ours at Kaministikwia urging him to continue the good work of his predecessor, La Nouë, in obtaining information about the Western Sea. While staying at Michilimackinac, he interviewed Father Joseph Marest, an aged missionary who had spent considerable time among the Sioux, as well as many others who, he believed, might give him pertinent information. This done, he descended the Mississippi, making careful note of all he saw, and presently reached New Orleans. On the way he questioned Canadians who had been up the Missouri, but found too many contradictions in their stories to make them trustworthy.

As a result of his observations, or rather from his analysis of the rumors he had collected, Father Charlevoix concluded that from the fortieth parallel or possibly from somewhere south of it, up to the fiftieth, the western lands ended at a sea situated perhaps near to, perhaps far from, Louisiana. By this sea he meant, of course, the hypothetical gulf we have mentioned. He was confirmed in this opinion by the stories of two Pawnees who told him they had reached it after a three months' march along the forty-third parallel,[10] going always toward the setting sun. This sea, thought Charlevoix, would be found west and southwest of Lake of the Woods, which is in latitude fifty degrees; for the country about this lake, though farther north than eastern Canada, is more temperate, an indication of the proximity of salt water. In regard to the accessibility of such an ocean Charlevoix informs us that he learned from the Indians of rivers flowing westward from the sources of the Mississippi, Missouri, and St. Pierre, by which, presumably, one could reach it. In concluding his remarks, he points out two ways

[10] That is, the latitude estimated by Charlevoix as 43° N.

of making the discovery: one, by ascending the Missouri and making a drive to the sea; the other, by founding a mission among the Sioux and using it as an outpost where more detailed information could be gathered from Assiniboins who were occasionally captured by them. Furthermore, as the Sioux traded with the Iowas dwelling along the Missouri, they could learn much about the upper reaches of that river.[11]

A change of great importance now took place in the personnel of the French government both at home and abroad. Certain officials, who for some time past had been in charge of affairs, disappear, and their places are taken by three men destined to play an important part in the career of La Vérendrye. During Louis XV's minority the Ministry of Marine and Colonies was nominally in the hands of a youth named Jean-Frédéric Phélippeaux, Comte de Maurepas. He was born in 1701, and at the age of fourteen he was given his father's position as head of this ministry; but owing to his extreme youth, the actual administration of the post was conducted by the Marquis de Vrillières, whose daughter he subsequently married. Maurepas began his active duties in 1725, shortly after the death of the Regent and the coming of age of Louis XV. He was interested in science, and since his position as Minister of Marine naturally put him in touch with exploration and geography, he helped advance these sciences by sending out expeditions headed by such men as La Condamine and Moreau de Maupertuis. Philippe Buache, the royal geographer, was also attached to his department. With such qualifications, then, one can easily understand why he took such interest in the discovery of the Western Sea.

Maurepas is described by those who knew him as a man of superficial nature, incapable of steady concentration, but endowed with a cleverness that enabled him to solve intricate problems with little effort. In his estimate of La Vérendrye's

[11] For Charlevoix's correspondence, see Margry, *op. cit.*, pp. 521–538.

achievements he seemed unable, as we shall see, to comprehend the difficulties that beset the explorer and for this reason continuously accused him of using his position in the Northwest as a blind for furthering his private interests in the fur trade. Maurepas held his post until 1749, when he was dismissed because of an obscene pasquinade he had written about Mme. de Pompadour.

In Canada important changes also took place at this time. Governor Vaudreuil died on October 10, 1725. The administrative duties of his office were discharged temporarily by Charles Lemoyne de Longueuil, who aspired to the governorship of the colony. But the authorities at home felt otherwise and allowed this officer to hold the position only until a permanent official could be sent to Canada. The man selected for this all-important post was Charles de la Boische, Marquis de Beauharnois, a naval officer well along in middle life.

Governor Beauharnois' administration was on the whole a peaceful one, punctuated occasionally by petty warfare with the Indians. Since the peace treaty signed at Utrecht put an end to clashes along the northern frontier, the governor was able to devote his time to domestic affairs, and it was thus that he became an enthusiastic backer of La Vérendrye, who, he believed, would solve the fur problem in the Northwest, even if he did not discover the Western Sea. His administration lasted until 1747.

Governor Beauharnois landed in Canada in August, 1726, bringing with him orders and plans for the discovery of the sea.[12] He also brought as his intendant Claude-Thomas du Puy; but this official did not prove to be efficient and was soon replaced by Gilles Hocquart, a man of considerable ability, under whose management the colony's affairs prospered. Hocquart arrived in Quebec toward the end of August, 1728, and imme-

[12] Antoine d'Eschambault, "Le Voyage de la Vérendrye au pays des Mandannes," *R.H.A.F.*, II (1948–1949), 424–431.

diately took up his duties, though he was not formally inducted into office until three years later. His tenure ended in 1748. On his return to France the government was so impressed with his services that he was given the important post of Intendant of Brest.[13] Thus, during the twenty years of La Vérendrye's activities in the Northwest, the three principal offices controlling Canadian affairs, the Ministry of Marine and Colonies, the governorship, and the intendancy, remained in the charge of the same men; they were occupied respectively by Maurepas, Beauharnois, and Hocquart.

The government, with Charlevoix's report before it, now had the opportunity of choosing between the two plans for discovering the Western Sea, and it chose the plan of establishing a post among the Sioux. For this purpose the King issued an order on May 14, 1726, providing for an establishment consisting of an officer and his subordinates, together with two Jesuit missionaries; and, as the government was anxious to avoid expense, a company of merchants was organized to pay the cost of the venture from the profits of the fur trade. Beauharnois, therefore, drew up an agreement on June 6, 1727, with this group, which was called the Company of the Sioux.

The officer selected as leader of this undertaking was René Boucher de la Perrière, an uncle of La Vérendrye. The two missionaries detailed to look after the spiritual needs of the Indians were the Jesuit fathers Michel Guignas and Nicolas Flavien Degonnor. These two men were greatly interested in the discovery of the Western Sea and were well fitted to carry out the geographical investigations assigned to them as part of their duties. Guignas was a man of about fifty years of age who had been in Canada for a decade, most of the time at Michilimackinac. Degonnor, ten years younger, had just arrived from France, and this expedition was to be his first as-

[13] W. B. Munro, *Documents Relating to the Seigniorial Tenure in Canada 1598–1854* (Toronto, 1908), p. 169n.

signment. A man of powerful build—the Indians called him
Saranhès, the big tree—he was just the man to take part in any
enterprise that called for strength and endurance.

The party left Montreal in June and reached Michilimackinac
five weeks later. Stopping there for a few days, they then proceeded to Lake Pepin, arriving there on September 17; they
looked about for a suitable site and selected a spot on its western side about two miles below modern Frontenac. The name
given the station was Fort Beauharnois, while the mission was
called St. Michael the Archangel. Here the party remained
throughout the winter and learned to their sorrow that the
place they had selected was entirely unsuitable, for in the spring
a flood inundated the buildings, causing great damage.[14] Fort
Beauharnois also proved untenable for other reasons. It was
situated in the territory of the Fox tribe, whose chief had
grandiose plans for expelling the French from North America.
Scarcely had La Perrière settled on Lake Pepin when trouble
broke out, and despite the military assistance sent him by the
governor, his men were obliged to abandon the place the following year. Foiled in this direction, Beauharnois turned his
attention to the Nipigon post, and to this he appointed Pierre de
la Vérendrye.

[14] Guignas to Beauharnois, May 29, 1728, in Margry, *op. cit.*, pp. 552–
558.

II

Early Life of La Vérendrye

RENÉ GAULTIER DE VARENNES, the father of Pierre de la Vérendrye, and ancestor of the family in Canada, was born in 1634 in the village of Bécon near Angers, France, in the modern department of Maine et Loire. He was the son of Adam Pierre Gaultier and his wife, Bertrande Gourdeau, people of position in the community, though it is doubtful if they were related to the Marquis de Varennes who figures in the reign of Louis XIV.[1] A record has been found of one Gaultier de Varennes who was given a patent of nobility in 1354, and René may have been one of his descendants. Suffice it to say that René was an *écuyer* of good family. The name "Varennes," it is interesting to note, was one given to uncultivated tracts of land inhabited only by game, while "Vérendrye" (variously spelled) meant a specific portion of a landed estate called "Varennes." Varennes de la

---

[1] Aegidius Fauteux, "Les Gaultiers de Varennes et de la Vérendrye," *B.R.H.*, XXIII (1917), 244–249.

Vérendrye—not an inappropriate name for one destined to carve out his fortune in the wilds of Canada.

When René was nearly thirty years of age there came to France a prominent Canadian colonist named Pierre Boucher de Grosbois, then governor of Three Rivers, an important settlement founded in 1634 at the mouth of the St. Maurice River. Boucher had been sent by his fellow citizens to secure from the King sufficient military assistance to protect them from the Iroquois, who were then pushing their attacks as far as the St. Lawrence River and at one time had even reached the walls of Three Rivers itself. Boucher also had a plan of his own, which was to collect six hundred colonists and transport them to Canada at the King's expense. In the main his mission was successful. He succeeded in impressing the King with the military needs of Canada, and while awaiting a favorable reply he managed to get together some two hundred prospective settlers whom he took back to Canada with him the following spring.

At the same time he did not do so badly for himself, as he was able to obtain, thanks to an old acquaintance, Jean de Lauzon, sometime governor of Canada, two valuable tracts of land on the south shore of Lake St. Peter, an enlargement of the St. Lawrence, just above Three Rivers. On April 20, 1662, a deed was handed him conveying the seigniory of Saint-François-du-Lac, situated at the mouth of the St. Francis River, and also the fief of Yamaska adjacent to it. These properties were given him as a reward for his projects of colonization.[2]

Meanwhile, preparation for the protection of the colony were proceeding with exasperating slowness in France. The King felt unable, because of troubles in Italy, to furnish the colonists with adequate military defense. A few soldiers were indeed sent out; but their numbers were insufficient for the business at hand. At last, during the summer of 1665, the King managed

[2] Benjamin Sulté, "Pierre Boucher et son livre," *Proceedings and Transactions of the Royal Society of Canada*, 2d ser., II (1896), 99–115.

to detach from his army a regiment of about one thousand men under the command of Alexandre de Prouville, Marquis de Tracy, and to send it to Canada, where it became famous in local annals as the Regiment of Carignan-Salières. The troops were sent over in three detachments which reached Quebec in June, August, and September. In the last division was a company commanded by Arnoult de Loubias, and in this company, serving as a lieutenant, went René de Varennes.[3]

Though the season was well advanced when the last of the troops had landed, it was decided to press on into the Iroquois country as soon as the ground had frozen over. Meanwhile, the men were quartered in various places; and, as there were not sufficient accommodations for all in Quebec, some were obliged to seek lodgings elsewhere. By chance the company of Loubias came to Three Rivers, where Pierre Boucher was still ruling as governor. There is little doubt that René and Boucher met at this time, and that in all probability the governor tried to induce the promising officer to settle in his district, for at the close of the campaign we find him back at Three Rivers, ready to take up the life of a Canadian colonist.

As Governor Boucher was a man of considerable importance in Canada, René quickly saw the advantage of forming an alliance with him cemented by stronger ties than those of friend- ship. Boucher had among his numerous progeny a daughter named Marie-Ursule, a young girl but twelve years of age, yet old enough to be deemed marriageable in those days when matrimony and religion were the only careers open to women in Canada. To this young lady René paid his court. His suit found favor in the eyes of his prospective father-in-law, as well as in those of Marie herself, and after a brief courtship the pair

[3] Régis Roy and Gérard Malchelosse, *Le Régiment de Carignan, son organisation et son expédition au Canada* (Montreal, 1925); Benjamin Sulté, "Le Régiment de Carignan," *Mélanges historiques* (Montreal, 1922).

were married on September 26, 1667. The bridegroom was then past his youth, being thirty-three years old. Mme. de Varennes settled down at Three Rivers with her husband, who, despite the adventurous disposition of his youth, became thoroughly domesticated, while she, like most colonial wives, bore him a large family. She lived to a ripe old age, her last years being relieved, let us hope, by a pension for which the governor applied to Maurepas.[4]

Pierre Boucher evidently had a high opinion of his son-in-law. In the marriage contract signed a few days before the wedding it was stipulated that he should support his daughter for six months in order to give the young couple a start in life; and the following year, when he resigned his office, he transferred the governorship of Three Rivers to René. This position René held until his death. He lived with his family on a farm just outside of Three Rivers, and here his children were born. But as the gubernatorial office paid only 1,200 *livres* a year, on which its incumbent was expected to keep open house for the many travelers who journeyed back and forth between Montreal and Quebec, René was obliged to look about for some other source of income.

At this time the intendant, Jean-Baptiste Talon, was inaugurating a policy of settling soldiers in certain strategic positions, so that they would be able to protect the colony from Iroquois raids. This policy had the warm approval of the King. Talon selected as recipients of these land grants the officers of the Carignan-Salières regiment, and he gave them seigniories situated along the Richelieu River, highway of the Iroquois, and along the south shore of the St. Lawrence below the Richelieu's mouth. The King also appropriated 12,000 *livres* to finance the undertaking, and this sum was to be divided among the *seigneurs*

---

[4] Beauharnois and Hocquart to Maurepas, Oct. 15, 1730, Archives des colonies, Correspondance générale, C[11]A-52, 63–65.

as the intendant saw fit.[5] It was expected that the beneficiaries of this policy would bring tenant farmers to their lands; and in this way a sort of landed gentry was formed which played an important part in Canadian history.

Pierre Boucher and René de Varennes were, of course, among those favored, the former in recognition of his services in bringing over settlers, the latter as an officer of the famous regiment. On November 3, 1672, Talon signed a deed giving Pierre Boucher a tract on the south shore of the St. Lawrence opposite the eastern part of the Island of Montreal. It had a river frontage of 114 *arpents* [6] with a depth of two leagues. To this Pierre gave the name of Boucherville. On the same day Boucher received another tract, one and one-half leagues frontage by two leagues in depth, on the north shore of Lake St. Peter. It was divided into two equal parts by the Yamachiche River.[7] It was to Boucherville that Pierre retired after he surrendered the governorship of Three Rivers.

At the same time René de Varennes received, by a deed signed on October 29, 1672, an estate adjacent to the eastern boundary of Boucherville. It had a river frontage of twenty-eight *arpents* by a depth of one and one-half leagues. This property René was to hold "in fief and seigniory with jurisdiction, himself, his heirs and assigns, under condition of paying fealty and homage which the Sieur de Varennes, his heirs and assigns, shall be held to do at the Castle of Quebec." [8] As a matter of course René called the place "Varennes." As a gesture of good will Boucher now gave his son-in-law part of his Boucherville property, a tract of similar dimensions to Varennes, adjacent to

[5] W. B. Munro, *The Seigniorial System in Canada* (New York, 1907), pp. 68–70.

[6] The lineal *arpent* is 12 rods; the square *arpent* .85 of an acre.

[7] *Titles and Documents Relating to the Seigniorial Tenure* (Quebec, 1852), pp. 56–57, 76–77.

[8] *Ibid.*, p. 33.

the western boundary of Boucherville. It was named "Trem-blay."

Varennes and Tremblay, unfortunately, brought their lord little or nothing, though he did manage to settle on them a fair number of tenants, as the census of 1681 shows that Varennes had seventy-one tenants and Tremblay thirty. This at first blush seems a fairly good showing, but the appearance is deceiving, for the net profit accruing to the lord of the manor, after the tenants had taken their livelihood, was usually small.[9] Needy in purse, the new governor of Three Rivers therefore took up fur trading at La Gabelle, a post he had founded on the St. Maurice River about thirteen miles above its mouth. This gave him first call on the furs brought down from the north, to the great disadvantage of the traders at Three Rivers. He called this place "La Vérendrye," perhaps because a brother of his who bore that name sent him goods from France to keep him in business. Trade of this sort, it so happened, was forbidden except at Three Rivers, but Governor La Barre, who understood the needs of his subordinate, winked at his transgressions. Though La Barre was tolerant, his intendant was not. The lat-ter in his complaint to the government at home pointed out that he had repeatedly called Varennes' attention to the law; but as the governor of Three Rivers was under the protection of the governor of Canada nothing could be done.

René de Varennes held his position as governor of Three Rivers until his death on June 4, 1689. During the twenty-two years of his married life he was blessed with thirteen children, though none of them save Pierre attained much prominence in Canadian affairs. The following, however, should be mentioned. Louis, the first child to reach maturity, was born in 1673, and at the age of twelve took the name of La Vérendrye, doubtless because, as the oldest, a certain portion of the family estate

[9] Benjamin Sulté, "La Vérendrye avant ses voyages au nord-ouest," B.R.H., XXI (1915), 95–111.

was set aside for him. Madeleine was born the following year, and in 1677 came the twins: Jacques-René, who married a lady of the prominent Lemoyne family, and Jean-Baptiste, who took Holy orders. In 1690 was born Marie-Renée, destined to become the wife of Christophe Dufrost de la Jemeraye and the mother of a son of the same name, for several years La Vérendrye's right-hand man in the Northwest. Then, on November 17, 1685, there were born in Three Rivers in a house situated at what is now the intersection of Boulevard Turcotte and Rue Saint-François Xavier, Pierre, the subject of this biography.[10]

Pierre was baptized the day after his birth in the parish church of Nôtre-Dame by Father Jean-Gaultier de Brullon. He had as godparents his distinguished grandfather, Pierre Boucher, whose son Lambert acted as proxy, and his oldest sister, Madeleine. As soon as he was able to write, Pierre took the name, not of La Vérendrye, for this had been pre-empted by his brother Louis, but of Boumois, a name which means a homestead or large property. The name of La Vérendrye which he acquired later came to him after the death of Louis in accordance with the custom of transferring the title to the next in line of succession then in force in houses of nobility. When Mme. de Varennes divided her property in the year 1707, Jacques-René received the seigniory of Varennes, and in the document recording the transaction Pierre is referred to as "Sieur de Boumois et de la Vérendrye." On this occasion his mother deeded to him the seigniory of Tremblay, reserving for herself the property at La Gabelle. By this time Louis was serving in the army overseas (he died two or three years later) and

---

[10] Cyprien Tanguay, *Dictionnaire généalogique des familles canadiennes* (Montreal, 1871–1890), I, 258, gives the complete list as follows: René, 1669; Jeanne, 1671; Louis, 1673; Madeleine, 1674; Pierre (died young), 1675; Jacques-René, 1677; Jean-Baptiste, 1677; Marie-Marguerite, 1680; Marie-Renée, 1682; Anne-Marguerite, 1684; Pierre, 1685; Philippe, 1687; Jean, 1688. Sulté ("La Vérendrye avant ses voyages," *op. cit.*) mentions only the eight children who reached maturity.

may have left Canada with the intention of never returning;
hence the property was divided without reference to him. Jean-
Baptiste, being a clergyman, received neither land nor title.

Shortly after the birth of his last child René de Varennes died
on his estate at Three Rivers. An inventory of his property, in
which every item of his personal possessions was duly appraised,
shows livestock consisting of four oxen, four cows, three sheep,
a pig, and some assorted poultry. Then, of course, there was the
usual household equipment, the most valuable item therein being some flat silver valued at 350 *livres*.[11] Thus, despite his real-
estate holdings and his prominent position, he left his widow
in rather straitened circumstances. Fortunately, the governor
who succeeded him, Claude de Ramezay, was induced to pay
the widow 3,000 *livres* for the privilege of occupying the office,
and this took care of her immediate needs. Yet, in the course
of time she again seems to have fallen into want, for we find
in a letter written by Governor Vaudreuil to the Minister of
Marine in 1714 a complaint that the pension accorded her by
the King was never received by her, and to make matters worse
she was obliged to help out her three daughters.[12]

Though by no means well off, Mme. de Varennes managed to
give her children a good start in life. Her problem was partly
solved by moving to Boucherville, where she took up residence
on her father's estate. Here she lived in the manor, called Fort
St. Louis, which Pierre Boucher had built at the mouth of the
little Sabrevois River. It consisted of a few houses surrounded
by a palisade and protected by a redoubt on the banks of the
St. Lawrence. When Mme. de Varennes arrived there, a school
for boys had just been established which took care of the educa-
tional needs of her sons. In the year 1695 she moved to her

[11] *Rapport de l'archiviste de la province de Quebec, 1949–1950*, pp.
40–49; hereafter cited *R.A.Q.*
[12] *Ibid.*, p. 273.

own property of Varennes and built a home only five miles distant from her father's manor.[13]

At Boucherville young Pierre had a distinct advantage for one who was to follow the career of an explorer, for he grew up in an atmosphere conducive to a love of adventure. The travelers who came to visit his grandfather brought with them a wealth of stories, exaggerated, no doubt, of the mysterious regions far to the west, stories from which the boy learned of the opportunities that lay open out there for a man of spirit. Surrounded by this influence in his early life he soon developed those tendencies that drove him continually forward and later led him to forsake the comparatively quiet life of a fur trader for that of an explorer of the Far West.

Pierre, like his brother Louis, at first took up the profession of arms, and at the early age of twelve was appointed a cadet in the militia. This organization had been founded by order of the King's great minister, Jean-Baptiste Colbert, probably in the days of Governor Frontenac, to meet the pressing needs of the colony. The King, as we have seen when he organized the Carignan-Salières Regiment, often found it difficult to spare troops for the overseas service necessary to defend his subjects against the Iroquois; hence it was deemed highly advisable to have a citizen army capable of protecting the settlers. Every man able to bear arms was enrolled in the militia, and a captain was chosen for each parish, the parishes in time of war being grouped together in detachments under garrison commanders. The various districts were independent, each wearing a distinctive dress, that of Three Rivers being a uniform of white *capotes*, or cloaks, and white caps. The highest grade in this organization was that of captain, and the possessor of such rank held a prominent position in the community. The rank of cadet was one

[13] Donatien Frémont, "L'Enfance de La Vérendrye," *Le Canada français*, 2d ser., XXV (1937), 5–21.

specially designed to give young men experience in military training without binding them too closely to the work; thus the cadets who were appointed on the recommendation of some important person served without being enrolled in the organization and also without pay. It was in a company of this militia that the youthful Pierre enlisted.[14]

The war of the Spanish Succession (or Queen Anne's War, as it was called in America) broke out in 1701, and Pierre was assigned to a unit under Jean-Baptiste Hertel de Rouville, which waged a brief campaign against New England three years later. One would suppose that the logical target for such an attack would have been Fort Orange (Albany), but the French had no desire to stir up their hereditary enemies, the Iroquois, who lived in the vicinity of this settlement. The object chosen, therefore, was a little village of forty-one houses called Deerfield, situated in the northwestern part of Massachusetts. Success in this quarter, it was felt, would have the desired effect of preventing the Abnakis from declaring in favor of Queen Anne. Rouville's command consisted of some three hundred Indians officered by some twenty or thirty Canadians. It was more of an Indian expedition under French supervision than a French expedition with Indian allies.

The party reached a spot two miles from Deerfield on the afternoon of February 28, 1704. Here they halted to await nightfall, for it was their purpose to make a surprise attack, not to conduct a siege. Just before dawn the little army fell upon the town. The inhabitants offered a stout resistance, but they were no match for the Indians, who had the advantage of numbers and of a surprise attack. Within a few hours nearly all resistance had been crushed. The captives were rounded up and Rouville started back to Canada with the main body. Since it was the policy of the French to take as many captives as pos-

[14] Benjamin Sulté, "The Early History of the Militia, 1636–1700," *Mélanges historiques*, I, 127–146.

sible—they had a marketable value in Canada—there does not appear to have been much wanton slaughter. Meanwhile, the light from the burning houses had roused the neighboring villagers, who hurried to the rescue. They found the fortified house of one Jonathan Wells the center of resistance and, joining forces with the inmates, delivered a counterattack on some Indian stragglers who had remained behind. These they succeeded in driving from the village. In this engagement the French and Indians lost fifty men, took eighty prisoners, while the English killed numbered fifty-two.[15] Such was young La Vérendrye's introduction to warfare; it was to serve him in good stead.

A year later we find Pierre in Newfoundland. The French at this time held the settlement of Placentia Harbor, on the western shore of the Avalon Peninsula, whose inhabitants were commanded by Daniel de Subercase, while the English lived in numerous fishing villages on the Atlantic coast. The capital and principal settlement of these villages was St. John's. For some time past there had been considerable ill feeling between the two groups, the English accusing the French of having ravaged their settlements on Trinity Bay and tortured the inhabitants to force them to disclose their possessions. This had been reported to the home government, and the Council of Trade and Plantations had expressed the opinion that the complete reduction of Placentia would benefit the fishing business.

Whether the Canadian officials knew this or not we have no means of knowing, but at any rate they saw fit to launch an expedition aimed at destroying the English villages. Early in January 1705, Subercase assembled his army and crossed the Avalon Peninsula with a motley force of one hundred soldiers, ninety Indians, and between two and three hundred inhabitants of Placentia, the whole commanded by thirty officers. Among these officers Pierre held a subordinate post. Subercase's first

15 An excellent account of this expedition may be found in Francis Parkman, *A Half-Century of Conflict* (Boston, 1900), I, 52–72.

stop was Bay Bulls on the Atlantic coast; then he turned northward, reaching Petty Harbor, seven miles south of St. John's, on
January 19.

St. John's at this time was protected by Fort William, manned
by ninety-two officers and men under the command of Lieutenant John Moody. This post does not seem to have been in
good enough condition to withstand a siege; its gun-carriages
were in disrepair, its garrison in a sullen mood. Subercase
launched his attack at 3 A.M. on the morning of the twenty-first.
He seems to have met with but little opposition. There were no
guards protecting the harbor. Nor were there any at the north
battery, which the French promptly took; and they amused
themselves by firing its thirteen guns at the south battery. The
fort, however, held out for five weeks when the French gave
up any attempt to take it and returned to Placentia. Meanwhile,
Subercase sent out detachments to ravage the fishing villages,
going as far south as Renews and as far west as the settlements
on Trinity Bay. Unfortunately we know nothing of Pierre's
personal exploits in this campaign, but we do know that it added
to his previous experience in New England, so that by now he
could consider himself a seasoned veteran. When the campaign
ended he returned to Three Rivers where he settled down to a
quiet life for the next two years.[16]

It was now a question of a suitable marriage for Pierre, and
the lady selected was Marie-Anne Dandonneau du Sablé, a girl
about twelve years of age.[17] Mlle. Dandonneau was the youngest child of Louis Dandonneau, a native of the settlement of
Champlain near Three Rivers. The Dandonneau family was

[16] For details of this campaign see *Calendar of State Papers, Colonial
Series, America & West Indies, 1704–1705*, nos. 315, 686, 749, 812, 836,
1056, 1185, 1187. Pierre Margry was the first to gather information about
La Vérendrye's early life. See *Moniteur Universel*, Sept. 14, 1852, pp.
1408–1410.

[17] Exact date of birth unknown. Tanguay (*op. cit.*, I, 155) does not give
it but places her after her brother, Joseph, born in 1694.

one of substance and worthy of alliance with a descendant of Pierre Boucher. Many years before, Louis Dandonneau and one Jacques Brisset had purchased the Isle Dupas, not far from Three Rivers, and the fief of Chicot near it, from the original owner, Pierre Dupas, at a bankruptcy sale. The two men divided the property between them; Dandonneau settled on his share of the Isle Dupas, thus becoming one of the landed gentry of Canada. When Marie-Anne was still a child, her father gave her a portion of his property, thereby supplying her with a suitable dowry.[18]

At this time Pierre had decided to join the army in France —for the campaigns of the Duke of Marlborough were then at their height—and it was therefore deemed advisable for him not to marry until later. Moreover, the youth of the bride-to-be may have been a factor in postponing the ceremony. It was considered best, however, to bind the young couple together by a *contrat de fiançailles* and await the bridegroom's return before celebrating the marriage. Accordingly, a formal betrothal took place in Quebec on November 9, 1707; and the prominence of the families may be judged by the presence of Governor Vaudreuil, his wife, and the intendants Raudot, father and son. By this agreement Pierre and Marie promised to marry in the Holy Catholic Church as soon as their parents thought it wise for them to do so. They were then to own their property in common according to the custom of Paris, even though they might live in some place where this custom was not in force; but neither one was to be held responsible for any debts the other might contract before the marriage took place. The bride's mother, in behalf of her husband, who was absent, promised to give their daughter 2,000 *livres* and several parcels of real estate on her marriage—all of which made her a very desirable bride. Mme. de Varennes, it appears from the *contrat*, approved the betrothal and signified her readiness to give her consent in

[18] *R.A.Q., 1949–1950*, p. 65.

writing if there were time to do so before her son left for France —reasonable evidence that the matter had been decided on rather hurriedly.[19]

Immediately after signing the contract, Pierre left for France, where he joined the Regiment of Brittany, in which his brother was serving, and entered the campaign in Flanders. At the battle of Malplaquet, fought in September 1709, he was seriously wounded by a shot and four saber cuts and left for dead on the field. Taken prisoner by the enemy, he remained with them until his release fifteen months later.[20] At the end of the war he returned to Canada. His military career had been a creditable one, and he brought with him proofs of valor in the form of certificates of meritorious conduct from his colonel, his *maréchal de camp,* and Marshal de Contades. There was one injustice, however—at least he deemed it such—that rankled within him for many years and which he tried many times to have righted. It was the custom in Louis XIV's reign to create during a war a number of lieutenancies which were canceled at its termination, when the army was placed on a peace footing. Pierre, together with a number of others, had been promoted after Malplaquet to the rank of lieutenant, but at the end of the war, when he returned to Canada, he found himself deprived of his rank. To make matters worse, the cadetship in the Canadian militia, which he held when he went to France, was also taken away from him, and he arrived home minus all military rank. Fortunately, he had an influential friend, no less a person than Governor Vaudreuil, who had acted as godfather for his youngest brother. Mme. de Vaudreuil had sailed for France just before Pierre landed in Canada, and on her arrival she was appointed governess to the Duc de Berry's children. This, of course, placed her in a position where she could ob-

[19] *Ibid., 1921–1922,* p. 88.

[20] La Vérendrye's petition of Feb. 15, 1712, Archives des colonies, Correspondance générale, $C^{11}A$-33, 378.

tain a small favor from the government. At the request of her husband she managed to secure for Pierre an ensign's commission in the troops kept by the King in Canada. Yet it was years before Pierre was able to recover his rank of lieutenant.

La Vérendrye, as we shall now call him, returned to Canada in 1711 and made straightway for Three Rivers, where he found his bride awaiting him. The long-delayed marriage took place the following year, and on October 29, 1712, Pierre de la Vérendrye and Marie-Anne were married in Quebec. Louis Dandonneau had died, meanwhile, leaving his property to his wife. She ceded his estate, Chicot and Isle Dupas, to her sons, Louis-Adrien and Joseph, who in turn transferred a portion of their holdings to their new brother-in-law; and it was to the Isle Dupas that he took his bride. Here they established their home.

La Vérendrye lived for many years on this seigniory, perhaps until his departure for the Northwest, cultivating the land and managing his business at La Gabelle. His children were born here, four of them sons who were to play a conspicuous part in their father's work of exploration. The eldest, Jean-Baptiste, was baptized on September 5, 1713; the next, Pierre, on December 26, 1714; then came François on December 22, 1715, and Louis-Joseph on November 9, 1717. Two girls were born later: Marie-Anne, baptized on June 12, 1721, and Marie-Catherine on May 26, 1724. They play no part in their father's career.[21]

To support this growing family, La Vérendrye seems to have been in better circumstances than his father. He had considerable property, he had his pay as ensign, and he stood in well with the authorities. Claude de Ramezay, who for a year was acting-governor of Canada, granted him in 1715 a *congé* or license to trade with the Indians at La Gabelle. This, as in the case of his father, brought a howl of protest from the merchants at Three Rivers; but their objections were overruled, and the

[21] Tanguay, *op. cit.*, IV, 208.

son was thus able to do legitimately what the father had done illegally.[22]

Still intent on recovering his lieutenancy, La Vérendrye now decided to go to France and obtain it in person. At his request the governor wrote the government asking permission to allow his protégé to make the journey. This was promptly granted,[23] but before starting La Vérendrye fortunately wrote Maurepas, the then Minister of Marine,[24] and from the answer he received he learned that his request for the restoration of his rank would in all probability not be granted; in fact, the Minister, while he still allowed the petitioner to come to France, politely suggested that he remain in Canada unless the matter were imperative; [25] and La Vérendrye had the good sense to take the hint.

While carrying on his fur business at La Gabelle, La Vérendrye had come under the spell of adventurous traders whose tales of the Far West had so stirred him during his boyhood. Though no longer a young man, and now living in easy circumstances with a wife and growing family to support, he still felt burning within him a desire to expand his business on a much larger scale. His life at Isle Dupas, with occasional excursions to La Gabelle, was not exciting enough for a man of his temperament; the humdrum routine of daily existence was beginning to bore him, and he was ripe for a change. It was at this time that Governor Beauharnois offered him the Nipigon post.

La Vérendrye accepted the offer with alacrity; but in doing

[22] Memoir of the King to Vaudreuil, Moreau de Saint-Méry Collections, F³-10, 172.

[23] Archives des colonies, B 48-2, 344.

[24] This was Jerome de Maurepas, who took office in 1699 when he dropped the name of Maurepas and took that of his father, Pontchartrain, though he is sometimes referred to by the former. It was his son, Jean-Frédéric Phélippeaux, Comte de Maurepas, who took office in 1725 and became the Minister of Marine during La Vérendrye's career in the Northwest.

[25] Maurepas to Beauharnois, *ibid.*, B 50-2, 344.

so it cannot be said that he did so from a desire to discover the
Western Sea; this ambition came later. He was then merely
looking for an opportunity to enlarge his fur business, and the
great fur regions of the Northwest offered just such an opportunity. Yet the eagerness with which he seized upon the reports
of a route to the Western Sea by way of the Kaministikwia,
which he gathered during his first visit to the Nipigon River,
and the eagerness with which the governor devoured them,
show that the work of discovery was never far from their minds.
And so, with this boundless field of discovery before him, La
Vérendrye bade farewell to his family and started for Lake Superior. On this his first venture, as in his subsequent ones, he
received no financial assistance from the government, but provided his own supplies on a credit basis, to be repaid from
prospective profits from the fur trade. On this occasion he obtained 330 *livres* from one Paul Marin de Maugras, who later
appears in the Northwest.[26]

[26] Archives des colonies, Séminaire de St. Sulpice, 10-5-E.

III

News of the Western Sea

THAT portion of France's Canadian empire to which La Vérendrye was now assigned is a vast district lying north and west of Lake Superior. It is a territory broken by lakes and rivers so numerous that they almost defy computation. Over such a terrain one can reach nearly any point by a continuous water route broken only by portages around various rapids and across strips of land separating the lakes. There were, of course, main thoroughfares in this wilderness, trails long ago mapped out by the Indians, by which one could reach the principal bodies of water that form landmarks in this labyrinth of lakes and rivers. Yet, for the most part, the country was not too well known even to the savages living there. Each tribe was familiar with its own domains and to a certain extent with those of its neighbors; but for knowledge of the lands stretching far to the west the Indians were obliged to rely on accounts that were often misunderstood, usually misinterpreted, and therefore unreliable. It was this that handicapped the French when they began to make inquiries about a route to the Western Sea.

The Indians living in these regions were divided into three principal tribes, and, as we shall find them cropping up continually in our narrative, we shall pause here to describe them briefly. The Crees, or Cristinaux as the French called them, were a branch of the mighty Algonquin family that ranged over much of modern Canada, extending down through New England and westward to the states east of the Mississippi, thus completely surrounding the warlike Iroquois. The Crees themselves dwelt principally between the Red and Saskatchewan Rivers, but they were also to be found on the Nelson as far as Hudson Bay and to the northwest as far as Lake Athabasca. La Vérendrye later had them as neighbors on Lake of the Woods. Generally speaking, this nation was divided into three groups: the Crees of the Plains, living on the prairies of Alberta and Saskatchewan; the Crees of the Woods, whose habitat was the northern part of these provinces; and the Swampy Crees between the Red River, Hudson Bay, and Lake Superior. These savages were of moderate stature, well built and active. Their complexion, like that of most Indians, was copper colored; their hair was black, their eyes dark and penetrating. Of a mild and affable disposition, they treated strangers who entered their territory with generosity and hospitality.

The second tribe was the Monsonis, who were also of Algonquin stock, closely related to the Crees with whom they are sometimes classified. They were a small tribe dwelling about Rainy Lake, and their connection with the Crees is shown by the fact that this body of water was first called Lake of the Crees and not Lake of the Monsonis. La Vérendrye, however, treats them as a separate tribe.

The third tribe was the Assiniboins, who belonged to an entirely different family. They were a branch of the Sioux, the great nation of the prairies, and lived around the southern part

of Lake Winnipeg. About the year 1640 they separated from
the parent nation and formed an alliance with the Crees, settling first on Lake of the Woods, though by the time La Vérendrye met them they had migrated to Lake Winnipeg. For this
reason we find Lake of the Woods called Lake of the Assiniboins in the first reports concerning it. The Assiniboins did not
live in fixed villages but roamed about the country in search
of food, a habit that frequently brought them into conflict with
neighboring tribes.

The fur trade at this time was carried on by merchants in
Montreal and was based on a system of credit. The merchants
bought the goods imported from France and turned them over
to licensed traders or *bourgeois,* who in turn enlisted men,
known as *engagés,* to carry them to the western posts, there to
be exchanged for furs. The *bourgeois* supplied his men with
canoes, provisions, and merchandise. When a consignment of
furs was brought down to Montreal it was not put on the open
market but sold to a commercial company which held a monopoly from the government. In this way those who had backed
the venture were reimbursed.[1] In the year 1717 the Compagnie
d'Occident received a royal charter for this purpose, and among
its many provisions was a clause granting it exclusive right to
trade in Canada and Louisiana for a period of twenty-five years.
All others were, of course, forbidden to encroach on these privileges.[2] Five years later the Compagnie des Indes succeeded
the Compagnie d'Occident and held the monopoly until 1760.
This monopoly, however, covered only the beaver skins, leaving the other furs—marten, lynx, fox, and so on—to be dis-
posed of as the owner wished. These furs, the *menus pelleteries*
as they were called, formed more than half of the total ex-

[1] Louise P. Kellogg, *The French Regime in Wisconsin and the Northwest* (Madison, 1925), pp. 364–371.

[2] For copy of the charter see *Edicts, Ordinances, Declarations and
Decrees Relative to the Seigniorial Tenure* (Quebec, 1852), pp. 29–40.

port. While the amount of beaver, both *sec* and *gras*, exceeded that of any other single fur, these furs, taken in the aggregate, amounted to 60 per cent of the total between the years 1713 and 1761.[3]

In La Vérendrye's day it was easy enough to obtain *engagés* for this business. Canada lacked the industries necessary to provide work for the growing population; hence the young men, unable to get employment, and probably bored by the monotony of farm life, flocked to Montreal, headquarters of the fur trade, eager to sign up for a more adventurous career. The professions had little to offer, especially to the ambitious; the Church naturally appealed only to a few, and there was little chance of promotion in the army, while the higher governmental posts were filled by officials from France. Between the years 1670 and 1760 some fifteen thousand men took to the woods to earn a livelihood.[4]

The applicant for a voyage to the west was obliged to sign a complicated document couched in proper legal phraseology —the gist of which was probably explained to him in words of one syllable—engaging himself to the sponsor of the expedition for a specified length of time, in return for a specified remuneration to be paid him when the furs arrived in Montreal. Some *engagés* signed merely for the trip to and from a certain post, the same to be accomplished in a few months; others remained in the West for several years and became adept in woodcraft, frequently adopting the Indian mode of life. In general the *engagés* thus employed may be roughly divided into two classes: the legitimate traders who kept within governmental regulations and were known as *voyageurs,* and the free-lances who broke away from restraint and were called *coureurs de bois.*

The merchants who financed these undertakings were drawn

---

[3] E. R. Adair, "Anglo-French Rivalry in the Fur Trade during the 18th Century," *Culture,* VIII (1947), 434–456.

[4] *R.A.Q., 1929–1930,* pp. 191–192.

from the leading families of Canada. They were persons of means, many of whom owned the fiefs and seigniories along the St. Lawrence River. Being members of the upper class, they naturally intermarried. Thus we find La Vérendrye's sister, Marie-Renée, married to Christophe Dufrost de la Jemeraye, and her daughters, Marie-Clémence and Marie-Louise, married to Pierre Gamelin Maugras and Ignace Gamelin, the younger, respectively; while Pierre's sister, Geneviève, took Jean-Baptiste Legras for a husband. During La Vérendrye's time these men were continually engaged in traffic with the western posts.

When Pierre de la Vérendrye left Montreal on this his first journey to the Northwest, he was forty-two years of age, a mature man by any standard. He had been surrounded during his boyhood by influences calling him to a life of adventure. His youth and early manhood had been spent in military campaigns, where he had gained the toughness necessary to withstand the hardships of a pioneer's life in the wilderness. After his marriage he had settled down as a fur trader and had thus obtained the experience so needful to one who was to earn his livelihood by dealing with the Indians. Thus we see him in early middle life starting on his great adventure well equipped for the business at hand.

As a husband and father La Vérendrye had done well by his family, thanks to his properties at Isle Dupas and La Gabelle, but now his domestic life with Marie-Anne came to an abrupt end. For the next seventeen years we find him trading and exploring west of Lake Superior, returning from time to time to the East, where he stayed only for a few months, arranging his business affairs and conferring with the governor. After his departure in 1727 Marie-Anne tok up her residence in Montreal, where she attended to her husband's affairs during his absence, sending him provisions and discharging various duties for which she seems to have had some sort of power of attorney.

Her three older sons followed their father four years later, her youngest shortly afterward, while she remained to console herself with the society of her daughters, like so many Canadian women of her day. When La Vérendrye returned from his next-to-the-last expedition she was no longer living.

In the autumn of 1727 La Vérendrye arrived at the mouth of the Nipigon River, where he took command of the fort already there. It was called Ste. Anne. Many Indians were gathered at this post, and during the winter he had ample opportunity to question them about the regions lying far to the west. In answer to his questions they told him many things, drawing on their picturesque imaginations to fill the gaps in their knowledge; and of the tales they told him the one that held his attention best was the story of the route to the Western Sea. That these accounts were at variance with the actual facts is not surprising, nor must the Indians be accused of a deliberate attempt to mislead; for it must be constantly borne in mind that, with the exception of a few who had gone to Hudson Bay, these children of the western prairies had not the slightest conception of an ocean, nor could it be described to them save as a "great body of water," and this they naturally interpreted as some large lake or river.

When La Vérendrye heard of the Western Sea from his savage neighbors he saw his opportunity. His duties as a commander were at once subordinated to his ambition as an explorer; and so, after collecting all the information he could, he hastened down to Michilimackinac in the spring of 1728 with the intention of forwarding a report to Governor Beauharnois by the fastest means possible. By a stroke of good fortune he met Father Degonnor at this post, who was just then returning to Montreal from Fort Beauharnois, where, as we have pointed out, he had been engaged in missionary work and in picking up what information he could about western geography. Father Degonnor was greatly interested in the news

brought him by La Vérendrye. He offered to carry the report
to the governor and to do all in his power to push forward any
scheme for exploring the region west of Lake Superior. La
Vérendrye asked for nothing better. He handed his report to
the Jesuit, together with a map given him by the Indians, while
he himself returned to his post to obtain additional information.
Here he found awaiting him a detachment of sixteen men with
three canoes of merchandise, the first consignment sent him
by his wife, under a permit issued by the governor.[5]

Father Degonnor at once hastened to Quebec, where he laid
La Vérendrye's report before Governor Beauharnois. The latter
was not slow in grasping its significance; but as the settlement
on Lake Pepin had not yet been abandoned he felt it impossible
for him to order an expedition to discover the Western Sea by
way of Lake Superior when the home government had committed itself to a policy of founding a post among the Sioux as
a preliminary step toward such a discovery. Hence, the governor did nothing with the report at this time, at least we can
find no traces of what became of La Vérendrye's manuscript.
Father Degonnor, on the other hand, felt strongly that the authorities in France should be apprized of the situation, and he
therefore wrote Maurepas on November 3, 1728, expressing
his own opinion and embodying the gist of the information he
had received from La Vérendrye. Maurepas was sufficiently
impressed to write the governor the following spring, requesting additional information; and since he did this before he received the news of the abandonment of Fort Beauharnois in
October 1728, he must have been influenced by the merits of
the proposition rather than by any belief in the impracticability
of finding a route through the Sioux country.[6] The additional
information he asked for was sent him in the autumn of 1729
in a memoir by Father Degonnor. This he acknowledged the

[5] *Ibid.*, 1921–1922, p. 214.
[6] Maurepas to Beauharnois, Archives des colonies, B 53-2, 399.

following April, including in his letter to Governor Beauharnois instructions ordering him to pursue his inquiries. The Minister also asked the governor to advise him when he had formulated a plan of discovery and estimated its cost.[7] In this exchange of correspondence Maurepas does not seem to have had La Vérendrye's memorandum before him; he refers only to the memoir of Father Degonnor. Evidently Beauharnois kept La Vérendrye's papers for the purpose of studying them; at least he kept the map, for the Minister complains of not having received it. Thus Degonnor deserves the credit of being the first to urge La Vérendrye's project on the government and to pave the way for the favorable manner in which Maurepas eventually came to regard the scheme.

La Vérendrye, on his return to the Nipigon River after bidding farewell to Father Degonnor, pursued his inquiries with renewed vigor. The lure of the West was now upon him, far outweighing, so it seems, his interest in the fur trade. We have, fortunately, the substance of the findings he now made, embodied in a report he brought personally to Beauharnois in 1730, and which the latter promptly forwarded to Maurepas. In this report the Minister was told that an Indian named Pako, chief of the Crees on Lake Nipigon, accompanied by his fellow chiefs, Lefoye and Petit-Jour, had journeyed westward beyond a height of land to a great river flowing toward the setting sun, its width increasing as it gathered volume. It drained a level country covered with groves of hardwoods interspersed with fruit trees and inhabited by all sorts of wild animals. Wandering over these plains were tribes of Sioux and Assiniboins, moving from place to place without any fixed home, but stopping now and then to form a village. Three hundred leagues farther down this river one came upon sedentary, crop-raising nations who from lack of wood lived in mud houses. The forest lands came to an end on the shores of a great lake into which flowed the

[7] *Ibid.*, B 54-2, 424.

stream, which was some two hundred leagues long. Going westward the traveler came to the mouth of a river whose waters looked "red like vermilion," and near it was a small mountain "the stones of which sparkle night and day." It was called the Dwelling of the Spirit, and no one dared approach it. The river was also said to contain gold-colored sand which seemed precious to all the tribes of this region.

The geographical picture now begins to take shape. To identify this river flowing into a great lake is a fairly simple matter—setting aside the question of distances expressed in leagues—for we know from information later obtained by La Vérendrye that this account relates to the route from Lake Superior to Lake of the Woods, which latter may be considered the source of the Indians' westward flowing river. The height of land mentioned was, in all probability, the divide situated fifty-six miles from the mouth of the Pigeon River. At Lake of the Woods the Winnipeg River leaves the lake at Rat Portage on the northern shore, and after running a course of 145 miles over rapids that cause the traveler to make some thirty portages, falls into Lake Winnipeg. Westward from its mouth, so the Indians said, they came to a stream whose waters look "red like vermilion," and this, of course, would be the Red River, flowing into Lake Winnipeg from the south. After this all is rather vague and nebulous. The savages living in mud houses were probably the Hidatsas (Gros Ventres), dwelling on the banks of the Missouri, later called by La Vérendrye the Ouachipouennes or Mantannes.

Shortly after obtaining this information, La Vérendrye left the Nipigon post, never to return, for the one on the Kaministikwia River. Governor Beauharnois approved of this—if, indeed, he did not actually order it—for on June 2, 1729, he gave the Nipigon command to Jean-Baptiste Jarret de Verchères, one of Canada's landed gentry, authorizing him to take two canoes and ten men with him.[8] Verchères remained at Nipigon for several years, doing a brisk fur trade with the Indians.

While wintering at Kaministikwia, La Vérendrye received a visit from a Cree chief named Tacchigis who had been as far as Lake Winnipeg and whose story corroborated what the explorer had already learned. Tacchigis told him of several rivers he had found on his travels, but the River of the West, he said, was by far the greatest. He had seen four rivers from a height of land somewhere south of Rainy Lake. To identify these streams is by no means an easy task, and different interpretations of the Indian's statement have been offered, none of which is entirely satisfactory. According to Tacchigis one of these streams ran to the lake of the River of the West, a description that suggests the Red River flowing into Lake Winnipeg. Another, he said, ran northeast into a stream flowing west-northwest into the same lake; it may have been the Big Elk River. The last two flowed south; they were probably tributaries of the Mississippi.[9] To make his geographical descriptions clearer, Tacchigis drew a map of these regions and gave it to La Vérendrye.

While awaiting the arrival of some Indians who had been far down the River of the West and who, he believed, could supply him with a more accurate account of these regions, La Vérendrye conversed with a slave belonging to an aged chief named Vieux Crapaud. This slave came from a country south of the river; possibly he was a Hidatsa or a Mandan. He had been captured by the Assiniboins, presumably in the general locality of the Assiniboine River, turned over to the Crees by them, and finally given by the Crees to Crapaud. The savage told La Vérendrye

[8] *R.A.Q., 1921–1922*, p. 217.

[9] *Journals and Letters of Pierre Gaultier de Varennes de la Vérendrye and His Sons*, ed. by L. J. Burpee, Publications of the Champlain Society (Toronto, 1927); hereafter cited *J. & L.* Footnote on p. 49 gives the most plausible explanation. The Champlain Society has graciously granted me permission to quote extensively from this book.

that the Indians of his country were people of sedentary habits, devoted to the business of raising grain and fruit and of hunting with bows and arrows the plentiful game with which the region abounded. In this country there was little wood, so that they had no canoes for water transportation; in fact, they were obliged to use the dung of animals for fuel, which the French called, appropriately enough, *bois de vache*. This description appears to conform with the country between the Saskatchewan and the Missouri, for there the Indians used boats made of buffalo skin stretched over frames (bullboats) instead of the regular birchbark canoes. There can be no doubt, then, that the slave came from the country around the Missouri River where it passes through Dakota. Not only do the features he mentions point to such a conclusion, but the sedentary occupations of the Indian people show them to have been one of the tribes who built their villages on that river. La Vérendrye, when he visited the nation he called the Mantannes, discovered the same characteristics as those mentioned by Crapaud's slave. The slave also told La Vérendrye that he had often passed in sight of a mountain of shining stones and at this point had noticed in the river a rise and fall of the tide. How great was the distance between the lake (Winnipeg) and the sea he could not say, but he did not think that there was a man bold enough to pass through the different tribes along the lower part of the river. He further confirmed all the points in the memorandum La Vérendrye had sent Governor Beauharnois the previous year, and he also repeated that strange rumor about the tribe of dwarfs three feet high (they had evidently shrunk since De Noyon's time) we find so often mentioned in the documents of this period.

Anxious to secure a guide to the western country, La Vérendrye selected a savage named Ochagach—though whether or not he ever served as a guide we cannot say—a man who was devoted to the French and in whose care the explorer felt safe from desertion and treachery. La Vérendrye wrote the governor:

I gave him a collar [of wampum] by which, after their manner of speaking, I took possession of his will, telling him that he was to hold himself in readiness for such a time as I might need of him, and indicating to him the season of the year when I might be in the flat country [10] for the purpose of proceeding to the discovery of the Western Sea; if, Monsieur, I should have the honor of receiving your orders to do so.

La Vérendrye at this time also made inquiries as to the best route for reaching the River of the West and learned from various sources, particularly from a map drawn by Ochagach, that there were three distinct trails leading there. The first was the one discovered by De Noyon when he ascended the Kaministikwia River, a circuitous route broken by rapids and portages. The second, called by the Indians "Nantouagan," lay up the Pigeon River along the international boundary line. The mouth of the Pigeon is blocked by rapids, but one may gain the river by a ten-mile carry over what was known later as the Grand Portage. This route La Vérendrye considered the more practical of the two and used it exclusively when he came to make his numerous voyages to Rainy Lake; for while it had forty-two carries as against twenty-two on the Kaministikwia River, there are no rapids to hold back the canoes, save one at the mouth of the Pigeon, and, moreover, the distance is one-third shorter. To go by this road, the Indians said, would take twenty-two days to Rainy Lake, four more to Lake of the Woods, and ten more to Lake Winnipeg. The third route was the St. Louis River, sometimes called Fond du Lac.

There presently came to Kaministikwia a party of Crees under the leadership of the venerable centenarian, Marteblanche. These people lived at the outlet of Lake of the Woods. They

[10] Flat country was the region about the mouth of the Nipigon River.

gave the French commander a map which resembles so closely
the one drawn by Ochagach that both must have had the same
origin.[11] In particular, the Crees mentioned the metals to be
found south of the River of the West, especially lead and copper and a peculiar metal they thought might be silver, for the
French, although they were primarily interested in the fur trade,
had also inquired about the mineral products of the country.
The Indians said further that there were white people at the
mouth of the river, though they could not say to what nation
they belonged. The journey from Lake of the Woods to the
Western Sea would, in their opinion, be a long one; it would
take from March to November to make the round trip, a length
of time coinciding roughly with the five months' journey of De
Noyon's Indians. But who were these far-distant white people,
and where did they live? This was the question that constantly
puzzled La Vérendrye during his many wanderings, and it was
one to which the Indians could give no satisfactory answer.
Now we can only guess that the savages had probably at some
time or other been in touch with the Spanish settlements on the
Gulf of Mexico or the French in Louisiana, through contact with
more southerly tribes. Thus, influenced perhaps unconsciously
by a desire to give the French a favorable answer to their repeated queries, they had become confused in their orientation
and described these white men as living to the west of them
instead of to the south. They frankly admitted never having
journeyed to the sea themselves, for once when they had gone
far to the west they lost two canoes in the ice, a misfortune
that discouraged them from further attempts; but the principal
reason that deterred them was, in all probability, the comparative ease with which they could trade with the English on Hudson Bay, distant but a twenty days' journey. La Vérendrye was
led to believe from his interpretation of the map that there were

[11] One has but to compare the reproductions of these maps in *J. & L.*,
pp. 53, 192, to see that one must be a copy of the other.

several rivers flowing to the Western Sea in the latitude of Lake Winnipeg, and he therefore urged the establishment of a post on that body of water.

In his reports to the governor, La Vérendrye, in addition to his comments on discovery, pointed out the natural wealth of the country between Lake of the Woods and Lake Winnipeg; this region, he had been told, abounded in moose and marten, while beaver was so plentiful that the Indians had little regard for it. In fact, they gathered only the best skins for the English trade; the others they used themselves during the winter and threw them away in the spring. As a result there was grave danger of the Crees falling under English influence and giving the Hudson Bay traders the same information about the western country they had given the French, thus enabling the English to forge ahead and control the territory. It was the same old problem that had bedeviled the French many years before. But if, on the other hand, the French could push forward the work of discovery, they would be able to secure a large share of the furs now going to waste among the Sioux and Assiniboins or being carried to Hudson Bay by the Crees.[12]

In order to drive home his point La Vérendrye went down to Quebec and presented his maps to the governor in person. Beauharnois was much impressed; and since the government's plan of founding a post among the Sioux seemed to have failed, at least for the time being, he seized the opportunity to send Maurepas letters urging the adoption of La Vérendrye's scheme of pushing into the northwest territory. To enlighten the Minister more fully he also forwarded the explorer's report and a copy of the map Degonnor had brought down two years before, together with a sketch drawn from charts made by Chief Ochagach and the Crees.[13] He also expressed in a letter the conclu-

[12] Report of La Veréndrye, *J. & L.*, pp. 43–63.
[13] Beauharnois to Maurepas, Archives des colonies, Correspondance générale, C[11]A-52, 160.

sions forced upon him by an analysis made by the engineer
Gaspard Chaussegros de Léry, who had taken Guillaume de
Lisle's map of North America and superimposed thereon the
outline of the Indians' River of the West. De Léry, said the
governor, had voiced the opinion that this stream must dis-
charge into the Western Sea near the inlet discovered on the
Pacific coast by the Spanish explorer, Martin Daguilar, which
bore his name on many maps and was supposed to connect this
mythical sea with the Pacific. As the Indians in their drawings
showed the Mississippi rising just south of Lake Winnipeg,
Beauharnois believed that such a large country as North America, traversed as it was by two great rivers, the St. Lawrence
and the Mississippi, must also be drained to the westward by
a stream of similar size, otherwise there would be an extent of
territory with an area seven or eight hundred leagues square
entirely devoid of drainage, a condition hitherto unknown in
the science of geography. It seemed reasonable, then, that the
Indians were correct in their reports of a great river running
westward, and this, Maurepas believed, must empty into the
Pacific through Daguilar's inlet.[14]

Maurepas was now informed of a scheme La Vérendrye had
concocted for building a post on Lake Winnipeg and from there
making a dash for the Western Sea with a band of sixty *voyageurs*. All this he would do without expense to the King, save
for a modest sum with which to buy presents for any tribes he
might meet on the way. Convinced of the plan's feasibility,
Beauharnois had already decided to send forth La Vérendrye
in the spring of 1731 with orders to establish himself on the
shores of Lake Winnipeg, it being understood that he would
then allow himself to be guided by the government in matters
pertaining to discovery. The governor hoped that Maurepas
would not criticize him for this, since the venture might result
in the discovery of a route to the sea, if not the sea itself, and

[14] Beauharnois to Maurepas, Oct. 15, 1730, *J. & L.*, pp. 63–66.

in getting peltries now going to the English through the Crees. His hope for success, in the first of these objectives, was based on La Vérendrye's statement that the Western Sea was only a ten days' journey from the proposed post on Lake Winnipeg, or fifteen to twenty if one went west-northwest. This was indeed a strange statement when we remember that La Marteblanche said it would take from March to November to go from Lake of the Woods to the sea and back; but the geographical information gathered by these Indians is so confused that we must expect such glaring inconsistencies. No doubt they were speaking of entirely different bodies of water.[15]

It was, perhaps, this alleged proximity of the sea that became fixed in Maurepas' mind when he showed such impatience at the explorer's failure to reach it. For the present, at any rate, Beauharnois acceded to La Vérendrye's request to supply him with presents for the Indians to the value of 2,000 *livres,* which he was to give the savages under the supervision of Father Jean-Baptiste Saint-Pé, missionary of the coming expedition.[16] In concluding his correspondence for the year with the Minister, Beauharnois promised to inform him of the results of the expedition, and he said that if there were any favorable developments he would make arrangements with the local merchants to send additional goods to La Vérendrye to secure the Indian trade.

Maurepas, meanwhile, had been carrying on an investigation of his own in France. In seeking advice he turned to the one person capable of giving it, namely, Father Charlevoix. But events moved rapidly in Canada, and Charlevoix's report, which Maurepas forwarded as quickly as possible, did not reach Beau-

[15] Mr. Burpee suggests that it is not altogether impossible for the Indians to have been describing the Nelson River which flows from Lake Winnipeg to Hudson Bay, when they spoke of the great river flowing westward to the sea. They would in this case, of course, have been completely confused in their sense of compass direction, or La Vérendrye might have misunderstood them (*ibid.,* p. 49n.).

[16] Beauharnois to Maurepas, Oct. 15, 1730, *ibid.,* pp. 66–69.

harnois until after La Vérendrye had signed the contract and
left for the Northwest. Fortunately for all concerned the report
was favorable.

In his report Charlevoix began by saying that La Vérendrye
was a man well regarded in Canada and therefore trustworthy.
Though many of La Vérendrye's ideas coincided with his own
opinions, he did not think .well of the plan of building posts in
the Northwest, if by posts the explorer meant permanent stations; for he could not regard the information about the route to
the Western Sea submitted by La Vérendrye as more reliable
than the data he himself had collected. Such posts, he felt,
would be expensive, would delay the work of exploration, and
might possibly degenerate into mere trading stations. He pointed
out that while it might be inadvisable for the French to penetrate too far into the lands of the Sioux and Assiniboins, they
should not on the other hand avoid these savages entirely, since
they had an excellent knowledge of the Northwest. Moreover,
it was very necessary to obtain all possible information about
Lake of the Woods for it was there, so Charlevoix believed, that
lay the height of land whence the explorer must take his bearings
to reach the Western Sea. The work of discovery, he advised,
should be carried through without a stop; but the actual route to
be followed need not be decided upon until the men engaged in
the business had spent a year or two exploring the country west
of Lake Superior. Above all, they should be supplied with proper
charts and all available information, lest by mistake they stum-
ble into the Vermilion Sea (Gulf of California), for there was
every indication that the Vermilion (Red) River, mentioned by
La Vérendrye, flowed into it! Supplies for such an expedition
must be confined to portable provisions, arms, ammunition, and,
of course, presents. The men employed should have everything
to hope for from the Court; and in this connection Charlevoix
suggested that the party consist of young men, or rather officers,
who could be encouraged to hope for advancement. A small

number of trading permits, judiciously distributed, would enable these people to finance themselves and thus relieve the King from the expense of providing them. Indians should be employed as guides to prevent the party from failing into the hands of the Spaniards; for Charlevoix on his last journey had, like La Vérendrye, heard of a distant people different from the Indians, and they might be hostile to the French colonists. Whether the sea was far away or close at hand Charlevoix was not prepared to say, but the attempt to find it was, he believed, well worth the effort. "Besides," he wisely added, "in our search for it that may happen which has often happened in like circumstances, namely, that in searching for what we are not destined to find, we may find what we are not looking for, and what would be quite as advantageous to us as the object of our search." [17] Charlevoix closed his remarks with the pious hope that a missionary would be sent with the expedition to preach the Gospel to the Indians.

Governor Beauharnois replied to Charlevoix in the following manner. It was an error, he said, to suppose that La Vérendrye intended to build permanent trading stations in the Northwest; he merely wished to erect temporary posts—*entrepots*, he called them—where he might find shelter, and which he could use as rendezvous with the Assiniboins and other savages who could enlighten him on the subject of western geography. Since these posts were to be erected solely to facilitate the work of discovery, there was no danger of their becoming permanent; they would be promptly abandoned unless the explorers could assure themselves of some chance of success. As to trade, it was necessary, absolutely necessary, that La Vérendrye engage in it, since the King, in contradiction to his former attitude, now refused to bear any share of the expenses. That a post among the Assiniboins was justifiable was proved by the success of the French in weaning the Sioux away from the Fox tribe during the recent

[17] Charlevoix to Maurepas, n.d., *ibid.*, pp. 73–81.

115´360

clash between these two nations, a success due largely to settlements which they had among the former. Friendship with the
tribes through whose territory the French must pass was essen-
tial, and doubly so when it was a question of going far beyond
their territory, for it would be dangerous for the explorers to
leave a hostile people between them and home. Furthermore, a
thorough reconnaissance of the region around Lake of the
Woods was necessary, as it was there, so reports said, that the
height of land was to be found. Then, taking up Charlevoix's
statement that the undertaking should be pushed through without a stop, Beauharnois interpreted it as meaning that the main
object of the expedition was not to be lost sight of, for it would
be impossible to make a drive to the sea without a certain
amount of preliminary work, such as getting acquainted with
the natives. La Vérendrye, so the governor said, would take with
him the very best men for the purpose, enlisting them under an
arrangement that would cost the King nothing. Should he succeed in founding a post, he intended to settle there some young
Canadians who would devote their time to learning the dialects
of the new tribes with whom they would have to deal.[18]

We have given the gist of Charlevoix's criticisms and Beauharnois' comments on them at some length to show the conditions
under which La Vérendrye labored, for out of these conditions
arose the misunderstandings of his aims on the part of the government at Versailles, which led to such bitter prejudices against
him and to the refusals which met his appeals for assistance.
La Vérendrye had expressed his belief that the Western Sea was
not far from Lake Winnipeg, and he had committed himself by
promising not to linger in the northern posts but to use them
merely as winter quarters on his dash to the sea; that is, his
object was exploration, not trade. Yet, as he was given no financial support by the government, he was obliged to engage in
trade, at least enough to pay for the supplies advanced him by

[18] Beauharnois and Hocquart, Oct. 10, 1731, *ibid.*, pp. 83–90.

private individuals. As the years went by and he failed to cross the supposedly short gap between his westernmost post and the sea, while he carried on his fur business with the Indians in order to repay the sums he had borrowed, the government concluded, not unnaturally under the circumstances, that he was using the proposed discovery as a blind to cover up his commercial ventures. What the government, through no fault of its own, failed to realize, and what La Vérendrye himself did not fully understand, was that the great gulf or Western Sea simply did not exist, and that the Pacific was far, far away. La Vérendrye, in fact, had unwittingly promised to perform in a few months what could be accomplished only in two or three years. Moreover, once he had established his forts in the Northwest, he met with various misfortunes, so that for several years he did not even attempt to force his way westward. Though the government's treatment of the explorer was niggardly, its suspicions of his motives were, all things considered, not altogether inexcusable.

Returning now to the main thread of our narrative, we find the Marquis de Beauharnois in the midst of arrangements for dispatching La Vérendrye on his journey. He felt, after considering the various phases of the matter, that since there seemed to be difficulties in the way it would be well to establish an outpost in the far country where the French could become better acquainted with the conditions they would have to face; then the explorer could speak with more precise knowledge and, perhaps, obtain the King's unqualified approval of his venture. It was therefore decided that La Vérendrye should build a fort on Lake of the Woods and other posts in different localities, if he thought it advisable to do so; and for this purpose he was to have a monopoly of the fur trade in the upper country. To this end an agreement was signed on May 19, 1731, at Montreal in the presence of its governor, Jean Bouillet de la Chassaigne, by which La Vérendrye associated himself with certain local merchants who were to advance him the necessary supplies on credit. The posts to be built by the explorer were expected to facilitate the trade by which the merchants were to recoup themselves; hence a clause was inserted in the contract giving specific details for the erection of the principal one, probably the one built on Lake of the Woods, where La Vérendrye made his headquarters during the early part of his sojourn in the Northwest. It was to consist of a chapel, a house for the missionary, a building for the commander, and one for the men, the whole to be surrounded by a wall made of several rows of stakes.[19] In order to get the expedition under way, Maurepas approved all these arrangements, and since he could offer no financial aid at this time, save presents for the Indians, he authorized Beauharnois to grant the explorer whatever trading privileges were necessary for financing the enterprise. Then, in order to protect the expedition from the dangers of Indian warfare, the governor ordered the re-establishment of the post among the Sioux on Lake Pepin.[20] This was effected the following year by René de Linctot. La Vérendrye, once he had signed the agreement, made ready to set forth on his journey.

[19] L. A. Prud'homme, "Pierre de Varennes," *Bulletin de la société historique de St. Boniface*, V, 35.

[20] Beauharnois to Maurepas, Oct. 1, 1731, *Wisconsin Historical Collections*, XVII (1906), 230–233.

IV

At Fort St. Charles

WHEN day broke on the morning of June 8, 1731, the town of Montreal was a scene of great activity. Accustomed as the townsfolk were to the work of launching expeditions of fur traders, there was something in the present undertaking that made it of special interest. News had spread abroad that a chain of posts was to be established in a hitherto unknown portion of the far Northwest, and that these posts were to serve as bases for the discovery of the mysterious ocean whose very existence had intrigued the Canadians for many years. The big canoes were drawn up alongside the shore, while details of men passed to and fro filling their capacious holds with provisions and supplies under the careful supervision of Pierre de la Vérendrye. Guns, ammunition, clothing, food, and an infinite variety of tools and trinkets were brought on board and stowed away. On the shore stood the commander surrounded by his three sons, Jean-Baptiste, Pierre, and François—Louis-

Joseph, then but a boy, was to be left behind to complete his studies. Christophe Dufrost de la Jemeraye stood near his uncle to assist him in superintending the work of the fifty *voyageurs* who were to make up the party. These men were signed up by La Vérendrye, his son, Jean-Baptiste, La Jemeraye, and some Montreal merchants who were interested in the venture but did not accompany it.[1]

Christophe de la Jemeraye, who now appears for the first time in our narrative, was but twenty-three years of age. He was the youngest of six children, and like his brothers and sisters was brought up in comparative poverty. His father had left his widow with very little, and it took the combined efforts of her friends, assisted by Mme. de Vaudreuil, to obtain for her a modest pension of fifty *écus*. Poverty, however, did no harm to young Christophe, for by the time he joined his uncle he had gained considerable experience by serving as a cadet in the local militia and by wintering among the Sioux on the upper reaches of the Mississippi, where he had made himself familiar with the various tribes in this locality. Being older than his cousins, he took precedence over them in their father's counsels and was well qualified to act as second-in-command of the expedition.

La Vérendrye, like the other travelers of his day, used canoes. as the chief means of water transportation. These boats were thirty-five feet long and four and one-half feet wide. The shell was made of birchbark one-quarter of an inch thick, laid over a cedar frame and held in place by stout bars laid across from gunwale to gunwale. The sheets of bark were sewn together with small roots of the spruce tree, called wattap, and the seams were stopped with a gum made from the sap of pinetrees. These canoes carried sails as well as paddles to propel them in a favorable wind. A canoe of this type was manned by eight men; the one stationed in the bow and the one in the stern were se-

[1] *R.A.Q., 1929–1930*, pp. 278–283.

lected because they were experts in their craft and were given a higher wage. Three or four canoes constituted a brigade under command of a guide, who was responsible for the loss of any goods under his care and answerable for the wages of his men. The carrying capacity of these craft was estimated at sixty packages weighing ninety to one hundred pounds each, besides which each man could take for his own needs a bag weighing forty pounds, so that the total weight of both cargo and crew was about four tons.[2]

When all was ready, La Vérendrye bade farewell to M. de Chassaigne and stepped aboard his boat. The canoemen sprang to their posts, and soon the little fleet was speeding over the waters of the St. Lawrence under the rhythmic beat of the paddles. The route taken was the usual one for those going to the northern lakes. The commander piloted his boats up the Ottawa River, now aided by favorable breezes, now stopping to carry his craft around impassable rapids, until after many days of arduous toil he came to the little stream called Mattawan that leads to Lake Nipissing. From this lake the route lay down the French River along the course marked out long ago by the Jesuit fathers when they set forth into the wilderness to found the mission of Old Huronia. Down this stream the canoes glided until they reached Georgian Bay, then turning northward they sped along the shores of Lake Huron to the station of Michilimackinac. Here the commander found awaiting him the Jesuit father, Michel Mesaiger, a man forty years of age who had been in Canada nine years serving an apprenticeship which fitted him to undertake the labors connected with a new mission. He replaced Father Saint-Pé, who for some reason did not follow the expedition.

The station of Michilimackinac, which we have had occasion to mention before, was situated at this time on the south shore

[2] Alexander Henry, *Travels and Adventures in Canada and the Indian Territories*, ed. by James Bain (Boston, 1901), pp. 13 ff.

of Mackinac Strait at the junction of Lakes Huron and Michigan, just west of modern Mackinac City. The post was originally a mission founded by Father Jacques Marquette in 1670 at Point St. Ignace on the northern side of the strait. The mission soon became a center of trade, a rendezvous for *coureurs de bois* and Indians, who built their dwellings around the place. When the post at Detroit was established, Michilimackinac was abandoned in its favor; but it was not long before the value of a trading station in the strait was recognized, and Governor Vaudreuil sent Louis de Laporte Louvigny to rebuild it. Louvigny, however, instead of returning to St. Ignace, erected his post on the south side of the strait. This was indeed a strategic position, the best in the upper lakes; for besides commanding both Huron and Michigan it was also situated not far from the spot where the St. Mary's River tumbles the waters of Lake Superior into those of its southern neighbor. It was here that La Vérendrye now landed.

The explorer paused at this station only long enough to write Maurepas, apprizing him of his success thus far and assuring him of his readiness to proceed the following year to the unexplored regions of the Far West as soon as he received orders to do so. So far so good; but since the object of the expedition was to carry the King's arms to the western country, he requested for this purpose a grant of trading privileges in the regions about the Kaministikwia post and Lake Nipigon for five years beginning with 1732, as his expenses up to date were considerable.[3] What he wanted was a monopoly of the district which would forbid others to trade there.

This letter must have appeared almost self-contradictory to the Minister, since the writer expressed great enthusiasm for exploring the Far West and at the same time asked for a monopoly of the fur business around the northern part of Lake

[3] La Vérendrye to Maurepas, Aug 1, 1731, *J. & L.*, pp. 70–72.

Superior; it gave the impression that the writer was more interested in the latter than in the former activity.

The French now ascended the St. Mary's River and, coasting along the eastern shore of Lake Superior, presently turned their canoes westward and reached Grand Portage at the mouth of the Pigeon River on August 26. Here the *voyageurs* became discouraged and refused to go any farther. These men, according to some contemporary authorities, were paid by the merchants of Montreal to stir up trouble and prevent La Vérendrye from going farther west, as they wanted him to remain near Lake Superior and develop the fur trade. Be this as it may, the explorer, with the aid of Father Mesaiger, was able to induce some of the mutineers to accompany La Jemeraye and one of his sons in three medium-size canoes to Rainy Lake, while the rest of the party retired to Kaministikwia for the winter.[4]

La Jemeraye set out for Rainy Lake.[5] The route he followed was along the Pigeon River through the concatenation of lakes that marks the present international boundary line. It was reached by a carry of ten miles from Lake Superior, called the Grand Portage. After crossing this carry, La Jemeraye followed the Pigeon to a height of land that separates the waters of the Great Lakes from those flowing into Hudson Bay. Then a few more portages brought him to Gunflint Lake. From there to Sagnagou Lake, the next body of water of any importance, the route is simply a succession of little lakes with intervening narrows. Then come Lakes Knife, Basswood, and Crooked, and finally the large La Croix. This last is important, for the Maligne River flowing into it from the northeast connects with Lac des Mille Lacs and the Kaministikwia trail. Furthermore, a short cut may here be taken by the Namakan River to Namakan Lake,

[4] Summary Journal, *ibid.*, p. 437.
[5] The account of La Jemeraye's journey is found in Report of Beauharnois, Sept. 8, 1733, *ibid.*, pp. 102–110.

but La Jemeraye presumably followed the usual route along the boundary line, that is, south through Loon Lake, then north to Namakan, after passing through Little Vermilion Lake, a connecting link with the St. Louis trail.[6] From Namakan one enters Rainy Lake.

La Jemeraye crossed Rainy Lake to its outlet in the Rainy River. Here he stopped on the north bank of the stream just inside a little peninsula, known today as Pither's Point, that separates river from lake, and selecting a beautiful spot in a meadow surrounded by a grove of oaks he erected a post which he named St. Pierre in honor of his uncle. It was a happy selection, for during the next 150 years there was always a post on this site or very near it. In the year 1830 the Hudson's Bay Company erected a structure about two miles west of it which was called Fort Frances. This grew into a settlement, until to-day it has reached the size of a town.[7]

The fort La Jemeraye now constructed consisted of two main buildings with double chimneys, each house having two rooms. Surrounding the buildings was a roadway seven feet wide, the whole being enclosed by a wall of double pickets projecting thirteen feet above ground. In a bastion of this rampart were placed a storehouse and a powder magazine.

When the work was completed, La Jemeraye invited the Crees and Assiniboins to visit him, for it was part of his uncle's program to establish friendly relations with the savages and discourage them from making war on each other. These tribes, however, failed to put in an appearance. They did not dwell near Rainy Lake, and as the winter was a severe one they did not feel inclined to brave its rigors to meet the French chief; but La Jemeraye was able to use his influence to promote peace by stopping several war parties of the neighboring Monsonis, who

[6] For a careful analysis of the route see Elliott Coues, *New Light on the Early History of the Greater Northwest* (New York, 1897), I, 6 ff.

[7] Grace L. Nute, *The Rainy River Country* (St. Paul, 1950), p. 7.

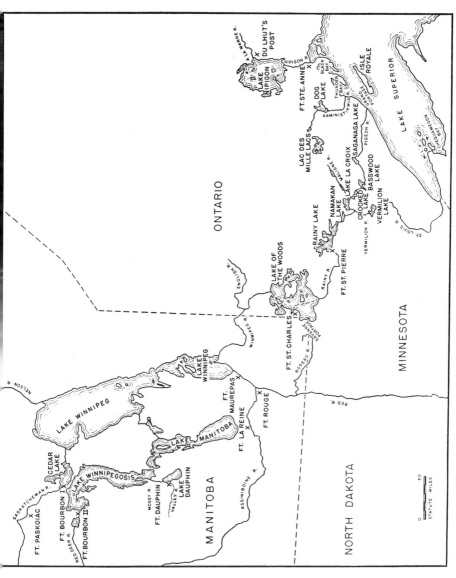

The region explored and posts established, by members of the La Vérendrye family, between Lake Superior and Cedar Lake.

were preparing to attack the Sioux of the Prairies.[8] The hostility that existed between these Sioux and the three tribes amongst whom La Vérendrye was to dwell, namely, the Monsonis, the Crees, and the Assiniboins, was to prove a stumbling block to his progress in the Northwest; and the work of pacification now begun by La Jemeraye was one to which his uncle was later to devote considerable effort; for during the entire time the French occupied this region, war between these tribes was continually smoldering, ready to break out at the slightest provocation. La Jemeraye, after spending the winter at this post, returned to Lake Superior, probably in the early spring, and rejoined the main party at Kaministikwia.

During the winter La Vérendrye received his first check, one that caused him considerable embarrassment. The Indians had failed to show up at Kaministikwia in as great numbers as he had expected, thus making it impossible for him to obtain enough furs to pay for the supplies advanced him by the Montreal merchants and also to meet his payroll. It was the old trouble of the lure of Hudson Bay. Some relief was obtained by sending out a few canoes, which returned in the latter part of May with a small supply of skins. These were at once dispatched to Michilimackinac in charge of Jean-Baptiste, who was told to pick up some supplies which his father had ordered from Montreal, supplies which he was to bring to Lake of the Woods, where the principal post was to be erected. This merchandise, amounting to 3,789 *livres,* had been obtained on credit from Ignace Gamelin by Mme. de la Vérendrye and one Louis Hamelin.[9]

While Jean-Baptiste was thus occupied, La Vérendrye, accompanied by his two other sons, La Jemeraye, Father Mesaiger, and the rest of the party, left Kaministikwia on June 8, the anniversary of the day on which they had left Montreal the previ-

---

[8] Beauharnois to Maurepas, Oct. 15, 1732, *J. & L.,* pp. 91–94.
[9] *R.A.Q., 1929–1930,* p. 293.

ous year, and with seven canoes proceeded to Fort St. Pierre. The course he took was the same as that followed by his nephew the preceding autumn; and as there were a great many portages —forty-seven, according to La Jemeraye—La Vérendrye had his men clear the trails to make them easier in the future. This work delayed the expedition, so that it did not reach St. Pierre until July 14. Here the French were joined by a large group of friendly Indians who came in fifty canoes to visit the white chief and to be received under the protection of the Great Father, Governor Beauharnois. La Vérendrye was overjoyed at the arrival of this host; not only could they act as guides to Lake of the Woods, but it gave him the opportunity to get acquainted with his future allies.

Eager to be on his way, La Vérendrye gave the signal to depart. The *voyageurs* stepped briskly into their canoes, thrust their paddles into the turbid waters of the Rainy River and, accompanied by their colorful escort, began the journey to Lake of the Woods. The voyage downstream was in the nature of a triumphal procession. To the fifty canoes of Indian braves, clad in their motley colors and accompanied by their squaws and children, were added those of the French *voyageurs*, loaded down with merchandise. The little flotilla spread itself out over the surface of the river, forming a pageant as if to celebrate the coming of the white man. At night both Indians and Frenchmen landed, and when gathered about the camp fire the former listened to the white chief's plea for friendship and answered as best they could his queries about the route to the Far West.

At last the journey came to an end, and La Vérendrye stood on the shores of the famous Lake of the Assiniboins, whence, according to rumor, flowed the river that was to lead him to the Western Sea. This lake, he found, was a great body of water heavily studded with islands in its northern part, while its southern portion, which first presented itself to his view, spread out before him in a vast expanse of open water. The surrounding country, as well as the islands, was covered with virgin forests of fir, pine, and oak in such profusion as to give the lake its descriptive name. Here it was that the explorer built the post that was to be his headquarters.

Crossing the lake to its western side, La Vérendrye selected for the site of his fort a spot about forty miles from the mouth of the Rainy River. The exact place was a tiny headland projecting from the southern shore of a bay known as Northwest Angle Inlet, the location of the fort being about two miles west of American Point, as the headland that marks the entrance to the inlet is called. The international boundary line now runs from the mouth of the Rainy River to the head of this inlet, whence it drops south to the forty-ninth parallel, thus cutting off from Canadian territory the peninsula which forms the southern shore of the inlet and leaving the place where the fort was situated in the state of Minnesota. The location selected was, roughly speaking, on a direct line from the Rainy River to Rat Portage, a point of vantage on the route to Lake Winnipeg.

In constructing his fort, La Vérendrye laid out a rectangle one hundred feet on each side and sixty on each end, placed in such a manner that one of the ends flanked the inlet. The palisade erected on this rectangle consisted of a double row of pickets, fifteen feet in height, reinforced by four bastions. Within this enclosure were built a house for the missionary, a chapel, and a dwelling for the commander, all in accordance with the agreement signed at Montreal. In addition to these there were also four structures for the *voyageurs*, a powder magazine, and a storehouse. The buildings were made of logs laid one above the other, the interstices being stopped with clay and the whole covered with bark, thus securing for the inmates protection against rain and cold. Two gates were cut in the opposite sides of the surrounding wall, and the place was surmounted by a watch-tower.[10] The post was completed in the autumn of 1732 and given the name of Fort St. Charles in honor of the Marquis de Beauharnois; and perhaps the commander also intended to remember Father Mesaiger, as it was he who selected the site.

It was La Vérendrye's intention, when he reached Lake of the Woods, to push his way down the Winnipeg River to Lake Winnipeg as soon as possible—in fact during the current autumn—and there erect his westernmost fort, but unforeseen events prevented him. In the first place, the Indians whom he had engaged as guides objected to the route; then his own men began to express fears of starvation, as their provisions were low and Jean-Baptiste had not yet arrived with the supplies he had gone to seek at Michilimackinac. Consequently, La Vérendrye thought it wise to postpone further exploration until the following spring. Meanwhile, as he was preparing to anticipate any possibility of famine by sowing some of the grain he had with him, the food problem solved itself unexpectedly. The wild rice that grew abundantly in these regions soon became available for harvesting and by good fortune yielded an ample crop; and this enabled the French to save for future planting the corn they had brought with them. Then, too, the lake was well stocked with fish, and the countryside abounded in game, while the land was so well suited for cultivation that La Vérendrye made a clearing near the fort to be ready for spring planting.

The winter passed none too quickly for the explorers, who were eagerly awaiting the coming of spring to begin the work of discovery. During the cold weather they improved their time by working on the buildings, for this post was to be an elaborate one, not a mere stockade set up in the wilderness, and

---

[10] Report of Beauharnois, *J. & L.*, p. 103. Complete account of the discovery of the remains of the fort is found in *Bulletin de la société historique de St. Boniface*, VII, 205–234. See also T. C. Blegen, "Fort St. Charles and the Northwest Angle," *Minnesota History* XVIII (1937), 231–248.

it did not receive its finishing touches until the following summer. La Vérendrye for his part busied himself in cultivating friendly relations with the neighboring Crees. His policy toward the Indians had a twofold object: first, there was the necessity of maintaining peace among the tribes if he was to succeed in his undertaking, and he therefore bent his efforts to keep them from flying at each other's throats; secondly, since the financial success of the enterprise depended entirely on friendly trade relations, he set himself to the task of discouraging their intercourse with Hudson Bay. In this latter problem he was aided somewhat by the preference which the savages felt toward the French over the English, as the former were accustomed to treat their Indian customers on a plane of equality, admitting them to their posts and bargaining with them in an amicable fashion, while the English, on the contrary, did not permit them to come within their fortifications, but held them at arm's length and selected what they wanted from their stock of furs, giving them in return what *they* thought was a fair price. La Vérendrye not only dealt with the Indians in a friendly manner, but, be it said to his credit, sternly refused to ply them with liquor, a common practice among the *coureurs*, in order to drive a more advantageous bargain.

To attain his first object La Vérendrye called a meeting of the Cree chiefs the following spring when the ice on the lake had broken up. They came in goodly numbers, eager to hear what the white leader had to say. As the braves gathered around the campfire, the commander stepped forth and presented them with a ceremonial collar of wampum in the governor's name, telling them that he did so to bar their way to the Sioux country, where the French were dwelling on Lake Pepin. The White Father in Quebec, he said, wanted no war with the Indians of the prairie and urged his children to remain at peace with them. The leader of the Crees replied in a friendly manner. Handing a collar to La Vérendrye, he agreed to respect the Father's

wishes, promising to obey him in all things, and he urged the
explorer to accept the wampum as a pledge that the Crees
would not attack the Sioux and would always keep the road to
Kaministikwia open. The chief then gave a second collar to
show the pleasure the Indians felt in having the French in their
country and to express the hope that the Assiniboins would join
them in their allegiance to the White Father in Quebec. He also
begged the Father to receive the Cree people as his children
and always maintain St. Charles as a depot to supply their
needs and shelter their families.[11] Then, in closing his remarks,
the chief promised to remain at the fort during the summer to
help and protect his white brethren. When the council broke
up, La Vérendrye, greatly pleased with the results, wrote the
Sieur de Linctot at Lake Pepin urging him to take similar
steps with the Sioux so that they would maintain peace with the
Crees.

    Early in the spring of 1733 La Vérendrye, who had been wait-
ing impatiently for the opportunity, dispatched Jean-Baptiste
and La Jemeraye to explore Lake Winnipeg and find, if possible, a suitable location for the fort he intended to erect there.[12]
Unfortunately the party started too soon and found the ice as
yet unbroken by the warmth of the coming spring. After descending the Winnipeg River to within fifteen or twenty leagues
of the lake, they were obliged to call a halt, and La Jemeraye,
seeing no prospect of an early advance, decided to return to
Fort St. Charles, as the commander was awaiting his return to
send him to Quebec with a message to the governor. Young La
Vérendrye, it seems, remained to continue the voyage as soon
as conditions permitted, but we do not know the details of his
further efforts.

    [11] La Vérendrye to Maurepas, May 21, 1733, *J. & L.*, pp. 95–102.
    [12] The report of Beauharnois which covers this incident does not give
Jean-Baptiste's name, but speaks of the young Sieur de la Vérendrye. As
Jean-Baptiste was the eldest son he was probably the one referred to by
this title (*ibid.*, p. 105).

La Jemeraye left the fort on May 27 carrying with him the two collars of wampum given by the Indians and the letters of his uncle, together with a map showing the results of the expedition thus far. With him went Father Mesaiger. The reasons for the missionary's return are not known, but as he was presently entered in the registry at Quebec as being ill, it is probable that poor health rendered him incapable of discharging his duties. The two men reached Montreal on September 20 and from there went to Quebec.

On being ushered into the governor's presence La Jemeraye first presented him with the two collars, one, as he explained, being a token of submission on the part of the Crees, the other, a sign of joy at the presence of the French among them. Then turning to the more pressing business of discovery, he handed him his uncle's letters, which he supplemented by verbal explanations. La Jemeraye's report regarding the proximity of the Western Sea was reassuring. Prevailing winds on Lake of the Woods, he said, were westerly; and as these brought copious showers the sea could not be far off. Encouraged by this phenomenon, he now planned to start the following spring to discover this sea, or at least to penetrate as far westward as he could. He intended to leave Quebec when the ice melted, and hoped to reach Lake of the Woods in August. The following month he would start for the west, and after a journey of 150 leagues go into winter quarters. Next year he would proceed to the country of a tribe called Ouachipouennes, or Sioux-Who-Live-Underground,[13] who were also known as Mantannes. These people dwelt on the River of the West, so the Crees said, some three hundred leagues from Lake of the Woods. They lived in eight villages surrounded by fields of Indian corn, melons, and pumpkins. Their houses were built of wood and earth like the

[13] Ouachipouennes were later called Kouathéattes and Mantannes. As La Vérendrye uses all three names, we shall refer to them hereafter as Mantannes without regard to the name used in the text. This will prevent confusion.

houses of the French. These Mantannes, of whom we now have the first description, were, according to reports, a nation different in appearance from any La Jemeraye had ever seen, for although of the same stature and proportions as other savages (not three or four feet high, as some had contended) the color of their hair, unlike the jet black of the Indian scalplock, was light and sometimes red. They spoke a language similar to French. As a rule they were peacefully inclined and refrained from making war on their neighbors, though they were ready enough to defend themselves when attacked. The Crees and Assiniboins occasionally waged war on them; but recently peace had been made, and the Crees had promised to lead La Jemeraye to these villages, where he would find the river which discharged into the Western Sea. Here we have the first inkling that the River of the West was not one flowing from Lake of the Woods or Lake Winnipeg, but an entirely different stream that rose in a western country, whence it flowed to the western Sea or the Pacific Ocean.

Such is the first description of that important tribe, the Mantannes, through whose territory, so La Vérendrye was led to believe, lay the route to the sea, and from whose members he expected to obtain the necessary guides. In regard to the River of the West, the map which La Jemeraye now handed the governor, and also the one brought him by La Vérendrye the following year, show a grasp of geographical features that corresponds fairly closely to the actual facts.[14] Here we see a river (the Winnipeg) flowing from Lake of the Woods to Lake Winnipeg. At the southern end of Winnipeg is the Red River flowing north into it, and a short distance from its mouth is the Assiniboine coming into the Red from the west, and referred to as the St. Charles. Somewhat to the south of the Assiniboine is shown a section of a river coming from the forty-sixth parallel

[14] Chaussegros de Léry made a map in 1734 based on the information now brought to the governor. For copy see *J. & L.*, p. 98.

and curving westward at the Mantanne villages. If the reader will glance at a map of North Dakota he will see in the Fort Berthold Reservation a point where the Missouri turns southwestward. Here it was that the French explorers later found a village of the Mantannes and were lead to believe that they had discovered the River of the West.[15]

La Jemeraye also discussed with the governor the financial condition of his uncle's enterprise. Forty-three thousand *livres* had already been spent, and the returns thus far had been insufficient to cover the sum. Assistance from the Crown was therefore necessary if the work was to be continued. The amount needed would not exceed 30,000 *livres,* which amount would cover wages and the supplies obtained from the King's stores.[16] That La Vérendrye was eager to undertake a voyage of discovery at this time is shown by a letter he wrote to Maurepas, expressing the hope that he would be allowed to do so and requesting that two canoes manned by twelve men, with a consignment of supplies and presents, be sent him forthwith from Montreal.[17]

Beauharnois at once transmitted La Jemeraye's report to Maurepas, putting the situation in as favorable a light as possible, for he was greatly interested in the outcome of the venture and he believed strongly in his protégé's integrity. But the answers he received the following year were not encouraging. Maurepas placed the substance of the governor's letter, as well as the report, before the King and obtained his approval of the forts on Rainy Lake and Lake of the Woods. Louis was likewise

[15] Whether La Vérendrye in 1738 visited the Hidatsas or Gros Ventres in the Fort Berthold Reservation or the Mandans much lower down the Missouri is a matter of controversy. The question is discussed in Appendix C.

[16] Beauharnois and Hocquart to Maurepas, Archives des colonies, Correspondance générale, C¹¹F-16, 295–297.

[17] "Dossier de la Vérendrye," no. 18, Archives des colonies, ser. E, carton no. 263.

pleased with the friendliness shown by the Crees, and he hoped
for the same results from the Assiniboins; but even though he
harbored no suspicion of the explorer's good faith he was em-
phatic in his refusal to finance the expedition. He did not care
to carry out the suggestion formerly made by the Regent that
the Crown should contribute to the actual journey of discovery
as distinguished from the business of founding posts and organizing the fur trade. Those interested in the venture, he felt,
should be in a position to continue it, paying their way by the
profits of the trade; then, if the undertaking proved successful,
he would grant rewards to those deserving them.[18]

Meanwhile, La Vérendrye at Fort St. Charles was having his
own troubles. For some time past the Sioux and Chippewas had
been carrying an intermittent warfare with the Crees, Monsonis, and Assiniboins, the tribes invading each other's territories
and creating a state of affairs decidedly inimical to the peaceful development of trade. At this particular time the Crees, in
spite of their promise, and Monsonis were planning to attack
the Sioux of the River, as the Sioux living around Lake Pepin
were called, and also the Chippewas at Chequamegon Point
where the French had a station. For this purpose they had divided themselves into two bands. To the Monsonis who formed
the first group was delegated the business of attacking the
Chippewas. They arrived at Fort St. Charles on June 15, 1733,
three hundred strong.[19] At first they concealed their purpose
from the French, knowing that La Vérendrye would regard it
with displeasure, and asked for ammunition, under the pretext
of planning an attack on the Sioux of the Prairies, a different
group from those at Lake Pepin. But La Vérendrye quickly
realized what was taking place when one of the chiefs, who
did not share his colleagues' views, whispered a few words in

[18] Council of Marine to Beauharnois and Hocquart, *ibid.*, ser. B, 61-1,
78.
[19] La Vérendrye's Journal from May 27, 1733, to July 12, 1734, is the
principal source for the events in this period (*J. & L.*, pp. 133–192).

his ear. He saw that once hostilities began the entire region
would be involved, and all the work he had done and was in-
tending to do would be ruined. Realizing that there was no
time to lose, he called the chiefs to a council, for the Monsonis,
unlike the Crees, had not exchanged wampum with him to bar
the road to war. Perhaps he could persuade them to renounce
their plans at the last moment. At least it was worth a try. When
the chiefs had gathered about him, he bluntly accused them of
plotting war against the Chippewas and showed them that he
had not been deceived by their talk about the Sioux of the
Prairies. Then he handed them a collar in the name of the Great
Father at Quebec, who, he said, forbade them from making
war on his children the Chippewas, at the same time promising
them anything they wanted if only they would obey. He evidently played his part well, showing force without betraying
his anxiety, for, impressed by his firm stand, the Indians
promptly yielded and agreed to respect his wishes.

There was a feeling at this time among the several tribes
that the presence of the French in the Northwest would bring
them certain advantages in the way of trading facilities, such
as convenient posts where they could trade their furs without
making the long journey to Hudson Bay. For this reason they
were quite willing to enroll themselves under the banner of the
Great Father and be guided by his wishes. Yet, anxious to do
something now that they were mobilized for war, they invited
La Vérendrye to accompany them up the Rainy River [20] to a
place whence led a trail southward to the prairies where the

[20] La Vérendrye in his journal speaks of the Rainy River as the St.
Pierre, a name which appears on contemporary maps. A few miles from its
mouth is a small stream coming from the south, called on modern maps the
Winter Warroad. Evidently this was the route taken by the Indians when
on the warpath. A small creek emptying into the southwesterly part of
Lake of the Woods has been suggested as the river in question, as it is
a path to the Sioux country and is called the Warroad today; but as La
Vérendrye speaks of the St. Pierre and the St. Pierre was the name given
the Rainy, the Indians doubtless referred to the Rainy in this particular
case.

Crees were to meet them; but the commander declined the invitation with thanks and left the Indians to their own devices. They departed, fully resolved to keep their rendezvous. Ascending the Rainy, they did not go far before they met with trouble. On reaching a fork in the stream they suddenly came upon three scouts who were ranging ahead of a body of one hundred Sioux and Chippewas. Instinct was too strong for the Monsoni braves and they opened fire on the trio, killing one man and allowing the others to escape. Somewhat confused by what they had done, or perhaps fearing to face the main body, they hastened to Fort St. Charles to lay before the commander their complaint against the Sioux and Chippewas, who, so they said, had attacked them despite the commands of the Great Father. Evidently they interpreted the presence of these tribes near their homes as an invasion, and equivalent to an act of war. Seeing that what well might have been a serious conflict had been avoided, La Vérendrye seized the occasion to congratulate them on their self-restraint in not firing on the main body, and after loading them with presents he sent them home with his blessing, well pleased with the outcome of the excursion. At any rate war had been prevented.

The day after the Monsonis left, the second group consisting of five hundred Crees arrived at Fort St. Charles, ready to march against the Sioux of the River. This was, if anything, more serious, yet La Vérendrye had little difficulty in coping with the situation, since he had so recently exchanged wampum with them to bar the road to war. Reminding them of this, he now managed by his eloquence, accompanied by a generous distribution of gifts, to persuade them to abandon their plans, or rather to change them, for they presently left to attack the Sioux of the Prairies instead of those of the River.

After a twenty-days' march the Crees reached at nightfall the village they had planned to attack. While waiting for daylight, their rearguard was assaulted by thirty Sioux of the River who had mistaken them for Assiniboins. Those comprising the main body immediately doubled back to assist their companions. Surprised at seeing such large numbers, the Sioux now retreated and took refuge in a wood, where they kept up a continual fire on the Crees until darkness put an end to the conflict. When the firing ceased, a Cree chief emboldened by the lull determined to learn the identity of his enemies. "Who is it that is killing us?" he inquired, advancing toward the wood; and the Sioux answered: "French Sioux." The chief was nonplussed by the answer, for now, despite his promise to La Vérendrye, he had unwittingly clashed with the very tribe he had agreed to respect, thus endangering the safety of the French traders on the Mississippi. Anxious to make amends he called out: "We are French Cree. Why are you killing us? We are brothers and children of the same father." This declaration fortunately had the desired effect, for it put an end to the trouble; the Sioux came forth from the wood and mingled freely with their foes, exchanging presents and making friendly demonstrations to them. Satisfied that the misunderstanding had been cleared up, the Crees retraced their steps to Fort St. Charles and arrived there on July 18, greatly upset by the loss of their chief's son, who was among the casualties. Their unexpected clash with the Sioux of the River, who called themselves French Sioux was enough for the Crees, and they now abandoned all intention of attacking the Sioux of the Prairies, to the great relief of La Vérendrye.[21]

On the whole La Vérendrye's experiences with the various war parties had been satisfactory, for while the tribes had come to blows, a serious clash had been avoided. It seemed that the various alliances which the French commanders at St. Charles, Chequamegon, and Lake Pepin had made with the tribes in their respective neighborhoods had stood the test and that La Vérendrye could now go forward with his plans of discovery, confident that no trouble would arise when he was gone.

In August the canoes which La Jemeraye had taken with him

[21] Journal of 1733–1734, *J. & L.*, pp. 135–139.

to Montreal returned, bringing a quantity of supplies. Toward the end of the month the Crees and Monsonis arrived at the fort in great numbers with 150 canoes loaded with meat and wild rice. It was their purpose to obtain from the French a certain amount of goods on credit to be paid for later when they should have accumulated a supply of beaver. To make such an arrangement was not altogether in La Vérendrye's power, for the goods belonged to the traders who were with him; but after a consultation all agreed to take a chance and advance merchandise to the savages.

La Vérendrye now received an unpleasant surprise. He had sent four canoes of merchandise to his people at Kaministikwia for safe keeping and was anxiously awaiting their return when a trader came to the fort with news that the garrison had used up all the supplies for their own needs. Fortunately La Vérendrye had an additional consignment coming from Montreal by way of Michilimackinac, so he dispatched one of his sons and six men to Fort St. Pierre, there to await the arrival of the convoy and place it in the hands of a responsible person. The young man met the party at Rainy Lake, and hurrying forward the canoes to his father, he set himself to the task of reorganizing the garrison, which consisted of twelve men under command of a trader named Marin Heurtebise, who had just left his newly wedded wife to seek his fortune in the Northwest.

Young La Vérendrye saw to it that the garrison had enough to last them through the winter, then returned to Fort St. Charles, which he reached on October 12. Here he found his father in high dudgeon. He was greatly displeased with the supplies he had just received, both as to quality and quantity; in fact so poor was the quality that he despaired of carrying on the trade he had anticipated.[22] In addition to this there was yet another cause for worry. The heavy rains of the previous spring had damaged the wild rice, and now that the expected supplies

[22] Summary Journal, *ibid.*, p. 440; Journal of 1733–1734, *ibid.*, p. 140.

had failed him he felt obliged to take some drastic measures to forestall a famine; for in addition to his own people the vast horde of savages that had come in the 150 canoes informed him of their intention to spend the winter encamped around the fort, and the meat and wild rice they had brought with them were not enough to see them through. To make matters worse, a rainy spell in early September had so discolored the waters of the lake that the Indians could not see well enough to spear the sturgeon, which formed a staple diet for them during the winter months. To relieve the situation La Vérendrye sent ten of his people across the lake, where they built a shelter, and here they managed to eke out a living until spring. Then he turned over to the savages a field of Indian corn he had planted the previous spring. In this way all managed to pass the winter with no greater hardship than a slightly reduced diet.

The autumn passed quickly enough. After the rains came a beautiful Indian summer, warm and bright, turning to crispness when frost appeared in mid-November. At Christmastide two Crees and two Assiniboins arrived as ambassadors of six chiefs who wished to be enrolled with their followers under the aegis of the Great Father. The group in question consisted of ninety Assiniboins and ten Crees, and as they were encamped only a half-day's march from the fort they requested La Vérendrye to send them some Indian corn and tobacco as a mark of good will. The commander was only too delighted to add these people to his allies; he immediately dispatched one of his sons with a suitable retinue to do everything possible to secure their friendship.

Trouble among the Tribes

IN THE late fall of 1733 the old trouble of Indian hostilities broke out afresh, and La Vérendrye was obliged to use all his skill to keep the peace. Two Monsoni messengers had arrived post-haste from Rainy Lake with a letter from Heurtebise saying that a war party of this tribe, three hundred strong, was preparing to march on the Sioux and Chippewas, and that although he had done what he could to quiet them, they refused to listen to reason. La Vérendrye's first impulse was to start at once to ward off the threatened calamity; but on second thought he decided to remain at St. Charles to receive the Assiniboins who were expected at any moment, for he could not afford to miss this chance to extend his influence over them. To gain time he sent the Monsonis back to their tribe, promising to join them in a fortnight at St. Pierre and sing the war songs with them. This, of course, was a subterfuge, for his real intention was to discourage them from making war; but the trick proved successful, and the Monsonis agreed to postpone their preparations until his arrival.[1]

On December 30 the Crees and Assiniboins arrived at St. Charles in the early afternoon, heralding their approach by a threefold volley of guns to which the twenty men comprising the French forces replied in kind. The gates of the fort were thrown open, and, preceded by their leaders, six chiefs, two Crees and four Assiniboins, entered the enclosure amid the cheers of the garrison. A royal welcome was given these men whose friendship was deemed so valuable to the French. At the meeting held next day the nephew of a Cree chief spoke in the name of his tribe which, he said, consisted of seven villages, the smallest comprising one hundred cabins, the largest eight or nine hundred. In the name of his people he implored the French commander to receive his fellow tribesmen as children of the Great Father and provide them with supplies, particularly axes, knives, and guns, of which they were almost destitute. To accompany this request he gave, as was the Indian custom, a package of beaver skins and one hundred pounds of beaver fat. Then La Vérendrye stepped forward and addressed them. "My children," he said, "I will tell you tomorrow what are our Father's orders to me regarding you, and shall let you know his will." Pleased with this assurance, the braves withdrew for the night.

On New Year's Day, 1734, a general council was held. La Vérendrye, who knew the value of theatrical effect as a means of impressing the savage, left nothing undone that would add to the solemnity of the occasion. The conference was held within the enclosure of the fort. When the gates were opened the Indians filed in and arranged themselves in a semicircle before the commander, their colorful costumes standing out in bold relief against the dark background of the palisade. Cree braves,

[1] The chief source for the following account is the Journal of 1733–1734, J. & L., pp. 146–164.

their scalp-locks twisted into long queues encased in otter skins and their bodies painted a rich vermilion color, over which were thrown jackets of fur, stood shoulder to shoulder beside young men wearing head-dresses ornamented with feathers, quill work, and ermine tails. In another group were gathered the short, well-formed Assiniboins, clad in their tanned deerskin garments, highly adorned with every device of Indian art. They wore rings, necklaces, and earrings, while on their heads were bunches of colored porcupine quills, skillfully worked into the hair. The chiefs occupied prominent positions in front of their respective followers, while the squaws and children were placed inconspicuously in the rear. Opposite this picturesque group stood La Vérendrye, flanked by his lieutenants and surrounded by his men, who bore in their hands banners emblazoned with the arms of France and flags embroidered with the fleur-de-lis. Between the white men and the savages were heaped the gifts which the French, in compliance with time-honored custom, were about to offer their Indian friends. There were thirty pounds of gunpowder, forty of ball, two hundred gun-flints, thirty fathoms of tobacco, twenty axes, sixty knives, sixty ram-rods, and sixty awls, together with beads, needles, and vermilion.

After an impressive pause the French commander, well versed in the art of dealing with Indians, began his harangue. He spoke of the power of the French, of their great numbers, and of the vast extent of their worldly dominions which spread to all corners of the earth. Then, with pardonable exaggeration, he described the head of this mighty nation, the King, overlord of the Great Father at Quebec, his wealth, his fleets, and his unconquerable armies; and as he warmed up to his subject he drew, perhaps from memory, a picture of magnificent Versailles, the wigwam of the mighty chief. His audience listened spell-bound, scarcely able to understand what the speaker was telling them, but impressed, at any rate, as he expected them to be, by the fact that back of this little group of French traders was a chieftain whom they might well accept as master. Then, coming down to the business at hand, La Vérendrye proceeded to tell them that the Great Father (Beauharnois) would be glad to learn of their coming to the French; and in the Father's name he received the tribes as his children. He warned them, however, never to listen to the words of anyone save the Great Father which he (La Vérendrye), or someone in his place, would make known to them from time to time. If they obeyed the Father, supplies would be sent them every year. Dazzled by this eloquence, the savages agreed to accept the commander's conditions, and when the meeting broke up they departed loaded with gifts—all save the six chiefs, who were told to return the next day when the details of an alliance would be discussed.

On the following day, when the chiefs were again assembled, some moderate gifts were placed before them, and La Vérendrye spoke. "I am ashamed," he said, "to have only that to give you today, but, if you are clever, you will come back to see me with all the people of your villages after their hunting, so that you may be in a position to have your wants supplied by the trader. Don't come with empty hands as you did the first time." Then, after impressing upon them that they were the children of the French, and not of the English, he continued:

My children, I have with me a blacksmith who knows how to make axes, guns, knives, kettles and everything else; but he lacks iron; it is difficult to bring it from Montreal on account of the length of the journey. Is there no one amongst you who has some knowledge of iron? The color of it does not matter; iron of any color would be good to work.

After a long deliberation the Indians answered through an interpreter that they knew of many mines yielding ores of different colors and that there was one five days' journey from the fort. Then, taking an iron shovel, the interpreter struck it and said that the iron of their mine gave forth an even clearer sound. He also told the French that there was another mine farther away that produced large pieces of metal from which they made bracelets. Then near the River of the West there was yet another "of ore which is yellow, hard, in grains and in flakes sparkling like the sun." A stream of water passed through this mine and deposited sands of the same color. Then the Indian told a curious story, current in these parts, of a large opening in the bank of the River of the West whence issued fire (probably lignite fire), which gave rise to the rumor that a French smith was busy inside making guns. La Vérendrye, of course, was anxious to learn something about this mine, whose deposits he thought might be gold, so he urged the savages to bring him samples of its ores; but they declined to do so, saying that even if they did procure the metal they would be unable to return until the following winter, as they were going to a far-off country to buy corn from the Mantannes.

Here we have the second mention of the curious tribe living on the Missouri, the first report of which had been taken down to Quebec by La Jemeraye. La Vérendrye, as may be expected, spared no pains in cross-examining the interpreter, for the Assiniboins had frequently been in touch with these people, and were in a position to give an accurate account of them. At least this is what the commander believed. He now learned for the first time that the Mantannes were not only different from the other aborigines but had characteristics that resembled the French; hence arose the legend of a race of white men living on the River of the West. Who were these white people? La Vérendrye was inclined to regard them as Europeans, probably Spaniards, who had ventured up the river to found a settlement; and news of such a colony confirmed him in his belief that he was on the track of a river flowing into the Western Sea. As a matter of fact, as we shall see when we come to discuss the explorer's journey to the Mantannes, the Assiniboins had heard of white men living farther south, and now they conveyed to the French their information in such a manner as to cause them to believe that these Europeans were the Mantannes. These white people, said the interpreter, were tall, well proportioned, and white in complexion. Unlike the Indians with whom the French had come in contact, they, or rather a large number of them, grew beards. Their clothing was made of leather or skins, worked in different colors, and consisted of a jacket with breeches and stockings for the men, while the women wore long gowns reaching to the ankles, trimmed with a girdle or apron, the whole being made of leather finely worked. The tribe was much given to agriculture and raised quantities of corn, beans, peas, and oats, which they used in trading with whatever Indians came to visit them, and thus they furnished their savage neighbors with vegetable food. They also raised considerable livestock, such as horses, turkeys, poultry, and ducks.

The houses wherein these people dwelt were much like those of the French, so La Vérendrye was told, save that the roofs were flat and covered with earth and stones. These dwellings were large and adjoined a palisade which formed the surrounding wall of the fortified village, so that one could easily make a tour of the place on the housetops. The palisade consisted of a double row of stakes with bastions at opposite corners. In these enclosures the Mantannes lived, seldom leaving them save to work in the fields, a labor in which the women joined as well as the men. The smallest fort was square, measuring five or six *arpents* on a side. Each fort was encircled by a ditch and had a large double gate. These villages were all situated on the bank of a westward-flowing river with a subterranean passage leading from a square in the center to the river's edge, so that the inhabitants could embark in their boats without being seen by an enemy. La Vérendrye's informant said that he knew of but nine of these settlements, though he had heard of others situated along the river, both above and below the principal one. Each village had its own leader, subject, of course, to the jurisdiction of the head chief. All were united for defense, and when an alarm was sounded they warned each other by trumpet calls and other signals. The head chief's residence was a large affair that occupied the whole side of the fort opposite the main gate. One side was reserved for his personal use and for the accommodation of his slaves, the other for his family, while the middle section served as a reception hall. The river at this point was said to be eighteen or twenty *arpents* wide and to water a vast, mountainless country, partly bare and partly wooded like the forests of Canada.

La Vérendrye, anxious to learn if these people were really Europeans, questioned the interpreter about their language; but the savage sidestepped the question, saying that he had not stayed with them long enough to learn it, though from what he had heard of their dialect he believed them to be French. The commander, then trying another tack, asked what kind of implements they used, and he was told that they had no iron tools such as the French used, but only a few axes made of a metal somewhat harder than copper. Their weapons, i.e., lances, arrowheads, etc., were made of the same copperlike substance, while their kettles and kitchen vessels were made of earthenware.

Eager to learn more about this river, which might indeed be the one he was seeking, La Vérendrye asked the interpreter if he knew how far it extended and into what body of water it flowed. The man replied that the Mantannes knew of no tribe but their own along its banks and that apparently the villages did not extend to the sea. Unable to get any satisfaction on this point, La Vérendrye then inquired if the Mantannes knew anything of the French. To this a group of three Assiniboins, who were listening to the conversation, replied:

It is a year since we got the message which you sent on behalf of our Father. It gave us so much pleasure that we mentioned it to everyone we met. It was only four moons ago that we left the settlements of the Mantannes, and we did not fail to speak to them of the Frenchman and the word we had received in his name. They were so pleased that the great chief said to us: "You are going to see the French. I request you to tell the chief from me that it would give me a great pleasure to see him or any of his people, in order that we may establish a friendship with him. If he comes himself, or if he sends one of his men, I beg him to let me know beforehand in order that I may send to meet him as he deserves."

La Vérendrye listened with unflagging interest to this account of the strange Mantannes who might be a white people living far to the west. If this were so, their river might indeed lead to the Western Sea—or so he thought. He would have liked to go at once to visit them, but as his precarious condition prevented him from leaving the fort he decided to postpone the undertaking for at least another year. The merchandise sent him from Montreal was, as we have said, disappointing; so before engaging in any further exploration he felt he must return to Montreal to replenish his stock and report the results of his activities to the governor.

A few days later La Vérendrye dismissed his new friends with the usual presents and the gift of a few French flags. He said in bidding them Godspeed:

My children, take courage, keep well in mind the word of our Father, the great chief, fly your flags when you arrive in your villages, spread out your collars on the mats so that everyone may see them, speak of the honorable manner in which I have received you in his name and of the presents he has sent you. Come next year as you have promised; you will then have new words from our Father.

He then requested the privilege of taking with him two chiefs that they might see and speak to the Great Father themselves. This the Assiniboins promised to consider if they for their part might take with them two Cree chiefs and one of the commander's sons who spoke the Cree dialect. La Vérendrye ap-

proved the bargain, and the savages departed on January 5
highly pleased with their reception, particularly with the business side of it, for liberal rates had been given them to prevent
their going to the English. Jean-Baptiste was later chosen by his
father to accompany them. On their departure they left a few
Cree families under the venerable chief, La Marteblanche,
whose household the commander supported during the winter.

During the conference with the Crees and Assiniboins we
have just described—a conference very important in La Vérendrye's eyes—matters had been coming to a head at Rainy Lake.[2]
The commander had urged the Monsonis to delay their attack,
and now, a week after the departure of the Assiniboins, there
came to Fort St. Charles three Frenchmen and four savages,
bringing a communication from Marin Heurtebise which told
that the three hundred Monsonis encamped about him were
ready to march at a moment's notice, against the Sioux of the
River. Apparently they had decided not to attack the Chippewas. To do the Monsonis justice, however, it must be said that
the more intelligent chiefs were not willing to set out before
they had obtained La Vérendrye's permission; but the messengers who brought the news feared that the little army might be
persuaded to start at any time, owing to the pressure brought
on its members by the squaws who had lost relatives in the
recent war. The following day a Cree, accompanied by a dozen
Monsonis, appeared at the post and urged La Vérendrye to take
immediate action, or, at least, to send one of his sons to Fort
St. Pierre, if he could not go himself. Realizing the gravity of
the situation, he promised to start in two days. In the meantime
he called his neighbors together and explained to them the reasons for his journey. They expressed approval and offered the
commander a detachment of their own braves as a sort of body-

[2] For an account of the events up to June, 1734, see La Vérendrye's
Journal, 1733–1734, J. & L., pp. 164–192.

guard to back him up if the Monsonis should prove difficult to handle. Above all, they urged him to take a firm stand, reminding him how he had thwarted their own warlike schemes the previous year.

The time had now come for La Vérendrye to put his influence with the Indians to the test. A crisis had arisen wherein the question of war or peace between the natives dwelling about the various French settlements and the powerful Sioux nation must be decided one way or another. The case was one requiring all of La Vérendrye's skill in handling Indian affairs. Fortunately, the Crees had promised to stand back of him. He accordingly made up a party consisting of Jean-Baptiste, five Frenchmen, a Cree, a Monsoni guide, and a small group of miscellaneous savages to carry his supplies and, placing himself at their head, left St. Charles for Rainy Lake.

Progress up the Rainy River was slow, for the midwinter cold held the stream in its icy grip and threw a blanket of snow over the forest trails. After a weary journey of seven days the explorer saw in the distance columns of smoke arising from the Monsoni lodges. His men hurried forward and, on reaching the cabins, threw aside their burdens and sat themselves down to enjoy a well-earned rest. That evening three Frenchmen arrived from St. Pierre, and La Vérendrye at once dispatched them with Monsoni guides to summon all tribes to a meeting at the fort. Then, placing himself at the head of his little band, he proceeded to St. Pierre, arriving there after a two days' march.

January 29 was the day set for the meeting, the place, the house of Marin Heurtebise. La Vérendrye, in preparing his opening address, gave careful thought to the situation. He had previously received from the Monsonis a solemn promise not to wage war on the Sioux of the River; hence any move on their part to engage in strife was virtually a breach of good faith. He therefore determined to shame them into submission by a frontal attack.

When the tribes had gathered around the council fire, La Vérendrye, after presenting them with a collar to bar the road to the Sioux, stepped in front of the assembled chiefs and addressed them with reproaches:

Have you then forgotten the word that was sent last spring to our Father and to the Saulteur [Chippewas] and the Sioux from the Cree and the Monsoni? Why don't you wait for an answer? Peace is proposed, yet you seek to trouble the land. Do you want to strike the Saulteur and the Sioux? You needn't leave the fort; here are some [pointing to the Frenchmen], eat if you are bold enough, you and your warriors.

Then presenting a second collar, he invited them all to Fort St. Charles the coming spring. At this a Cree chief, who had accompanied the French from Lake of the Woods, sprang forward to back up the commander. He pointed out that the French Sioux (i.e., Sioux of the River) and Chippewas were their brothers, that all were children of the same Father, and that their present actions in the face of their promises to the governor would brand them as liars before the French and the other Indians. In concluding, he urged them to abandon their warlike plans and accept La Vérendrye's invitation to meet at Fort St. Charles.

The Monsonis, struck by the force of this argument, assented, but only on condition that the explorer would not oppose their going to war with the Sioux of the Prairies and would send one of his sons with them to bear witness to their promise. For the sake of peace La Vérendrye agreed to this, for, after all, his principal object was to prevent an outbreak of hostilities dangerous to the French on the Mississippi; and as the savages evidently needed some outlet for their warlike propensities, he decided that if the worse came to the worst, a war with the Sioux of the Prairies would be less harmful to French interests than one waged with the Indian tribes near their settlements. At any rate, his compliance, feigned as it doubtless was, insured peace for the time being, and much might happen before the Monsonis gathered at Fort St. Charles.

But there was also another matter, a question of trade, to be settled at this meeting. As rumor had it, the Monsonis were again trading with the English at Hudson Bay. To block this traffic, La Vérendrye now gave the savages a collar to bar the road to the bay, warning them at the same time that they must be entirely French or entirely English, for the French brought their wares from a great distance and could little afford to take this trouble unless assured of the undivided loyalty of their customers. The chiefs saw the point, and endeavored to persuade their people to devote themselves to the French alone. In closing the conference the Indians promised to postpone all hostilities until spring.

By the middle of February, La Vérendrye was back at Fort St. Charles, where he reported the result of his negotiations to the Crees assembled there. At this time there came to the post four Crees, sent by a chief living on the shores of Lake Winnipeg, with a request that the French build an establishment on his lake. As La Vérendrye's plans included building a post there, he was overjoyed to learn that his project had the warm approbation of the natives living in the vicinity. Such a station, he knew, would be of great advantage to the French in securing the fur business from the Crees and Assiniboins, for it would be situated well within their territory at a strategic point in the struggle between the French and the English; and, besides, it could be used later in the drive for the Western Sea. The request was at once granted, or at least the commander promised faithfully to comply with it as soon as possible, and the messengers were sent back with the usual presents. La Vérendrye also seized the occasion to ask for guides to aid him in selecting a site for the proposed fort. Three weeks later the guides arrived; and on March 9 Pierre, the commander's second son, accompanied by one or two Canadians, left for Lake Winnipeg with

a complete set of instructions for his guidance. He was to choose
a suitable site for the fort, to note the location of mines, and
to compile a list of the various woods different from those
around Fort St. Charles.[3]

While Pierre was busy on his tour of exploration, seven
Frenchmen arrived from Fort St. Pierre, together with four
hundred Monsonis all eager for war, and in this they were
joined by the Crees. Faced with this situation, the explorer held
a council with the savages, hoping to avert the crisis by a frank
discussion of the vexing questions of war and trade. The Monsoni chieftain opened the meeting by reminding the French
commander that the Indians had come to the fort at his invitation; then passing on to the matter that was uppermost in everyone's mind, he bluntly asked him which of the enemy tribes
they would be permitted to attack, for several chiefs, it seemed,
were bitter against the Sioux and Chippewas, and were eager
to start hostilities. Furthermore, as he felt he could not always
be master of his men, he asked La Vérendrye to give him one
of his sons whom the Indians could obey as the French representative, and thus a certain amount of discipline could be maintained. La Vérendrye was nonplussed. He did not relish the
idea of entrusting his own flesh and blood to these savages, who
might—and probably would—go to war, for his son might well
be captured by the Sioux of the Prairies, sworn enemies of the
Crees and Monsonis. On the other hand, if he refused their
request they might label him a coward and shake off his yoke altogether. In this dilemma he consulted his colleagues who, somewhat to his surprise, urged him to comply with the Indian's

[3] Pierre must have been the son who headed the expedition. The Summary Journal (*ibid.*, p. 440), it is true, says the eldest son was the leader;
but, as we shall see, the eldest son had gone away with the Crees before
the party returned. As Pierre was sent down later to build the fort, it
was probably he who reconnoitered the site. Moreover, Jean-Baptiste
was dead when La Vérendrye wrote the Summary Journal; hence he
probably meant Pierre when he spoke of his eldest son.

demand. It would not be the first time, they said, that a French-man had joined an Indian war party. Then, in order to make the situation more palatable to him, they pointed out that since the young man would not be the commander of the party, he could not be held responsible for what might happen, a line of reasoning that may have seemed rather dubious to the anxious father. To do these advisers justice it must be said that several offered to accompany the young man, though the commander declined the offer on the ground that it might cause trouble in the future. At last, La Vérendrye, influenced by what he thought was best for French interests, decided to send Jean-Baptiste, a decision very much to the youth's liking; but before he left, his father gave him careful instructions in writing as to how he should speak in the councils, for he was anxious, in view of Beauharnois' policy, not to involve himself, either directly or by proxy, in any war of aggression.

This point being settled, the meeting adjourned until the fol-lowing day. Meanwhile, La Vérendrye took council with him-self as to the all-absorbing question of war. He now saw that the Indians had not altered their hostile intentions since the meeting at Fort St. Pierre; indeed, they seemed more deter-mined than ever to find some release for their warlike pro-pensities. Moreover, as he had already promised to raise no objections to hostilities against the Sioux of the Prairies, he de-cided to place the seal of his approval on an expedition against this tribe and, further, to permit Jean-Baptiste to join the under-taking in the capacity of a counselor who would have a voice in the deliberations without engaging in actual combat.

When the Indians assembled the next day, La Vérendrye was ready for them. Six hundred and sixty Cree and Monsoni war-riors, led by fourteen chiefs, were gathered within the court-yard, the Crees on one side, the Monsonis on the other. To open the meeting, La Vérendrye placed before them the gifts for the day: a fifty-pound barrel of gunpowder, one hundred pounds

of ball, four hundred gunflints, together with a collection of
fire-steels, ramrods, awls, and knives, and thirty fathoms of tobacco. Then putting his son beside him to act as interpreter he
said: "My children, see what I have prepared for the war; I
make you a present of it and you will distribute it amongst you
all, except the chiefs." He then tried to discourage the Indians
from thoughts of vengeance against the Chippewas and Sioux
by pointing out that in the last wars they had the advantage all
on their side and could scarcely claim themselves entitled to
revenge. He told them also that he was planning to go down to
Michilimackinac, perhaps even to Montreal, to get a fresh supply of merchandise, such as tobacco, guns, and kettles, which
he would exchange for the skins of martens and lynxes. Then
he presented Jean-Baptiste. "As you have obeyed the word of
our Father," he continued, "I entrust to you my eldest son who
is my dearest possession; consider him as another myself; do
nothing without consulting him, his words will be mine; and as
he is not so accustomed to fatigue as you, though he is equally
vigorous, I depend on you to take care of him on the journey."
The chiefs thanked the commander for this mark of confidence.
After a display of rivalry between the two tribes as to which
should have the privilege of having the young man with them,
it was finally decided that he should travel with the Crees.

This point settled, La Vérendrye sang a war song urging the
Indians to do their duty well; and to inspire them he gave a
graphic account of warfare in France where great armies, far
greater than any the savages could imagine, faced each other in
close formation in the open field. Then, casting aside his jacket,
he showed them the wounds he had received at Malplaquet.
It was a grand gesture, one that impressed the warriors, for
here was a man who had himself borne the brunt of battle, not
a mere fur trader who was deterred from condoning a war of
vengeance through fear of losing a profit.

Having thus impressed the Indians, La Vérendrye proceeded

to discuss the knotty problem of trade. He explained to them the benefits they would derive from the presence of the French among them, since they would be able to buy all they required throughout the year—a somewhat rash statement when we remember the several occasions when the French almost ran out of merchandise. For their part, the traders would purchase from the Indians bark, gum, and wattap [4] for the canoes, as well as provisions, which the Indians would otherwise be unable to sell during the summer season. La Vérendrye also took occasion to remind his allies of the credit extended them the previous year, a concession he had obtained from the traders with considerable difficulty. These debts must now be paid, or he would be obliged to reimburse his partners out of his own pocket. Then, to show them the advantages they would reap by confining their business dealings to the French, he reminded them that the English gave no credit and held them at arm's length. As to prices, he admitted that the French charged somewhat more than their competitors, but the French took what furs were offered them and did not, like their northern neighbors, reject those that did not suit them; and, further, French goods were decidedly superior to those obtainable at Hudson Bay. Matters being thus satisfactorily adjusted, the warriors took their leave on May 11, saying they wished to place their canoes at a fork of the Rainy River—presumably the Winter Warroad—by which the enemy were accustomed to pass, thus protecting their families. After this they would go to the prairies to join the Assiniboins. The campaign against the Sioux should take but two months; the army of Crees and Assiniboins would number eleven or twelve hundred men. [5]

Shortly after the departure of the Indians, Pierre arrived, accompanied by a chief and eighteen men, having completed the survey of the southern shore of Lake Winnipeg. He had been

[4] Roots of various trees used to sew the bark of the canoes.
[5] Journal of 1733–1734, *J. & L.*, pp. 178–186.

well received by the natives, so he said, but he had found it impossible to persuade them to visit Fort St. Charles, as they had learned somehow that the French were out of guns, kettles, and tobacco. He had also located, and now recommended, a suitable site for the fort, a place near the mouth of the Red River where there was "a fine wood of high timber, including a great deal of white oak." A two days' journey beyond this spot disclosed a mine yielding what was said to be silver, a sample of which he brought with him, as well as some salt he had found five or six leagues from the river.

The Cree chief who had come with Pierre thanked La Vérendrye in the name of his people for the promise of a trading post. He had also notified the neighboring Crees and Assiniboins of the French plan. Evidently it met with general approval, as it would bring the French with their merchandise into the very heart of the Indian country and spare the natives the long journey to the English post at York Factory which took thirty days (round trip) from southern Lake Winnipeg.[6] La Vérendrye asked him how the English felt about the presence of the French among the Crees. The chief answered that he had met the English factor the previous summer and on questioning him had learned that there was no ill feeling. The French, so the Englishman said, wanted their beaver skins fat while he wanted them dry; hence there should be no cause for rivalry. In dismissing the chief, La Vérendrye promised to establish the post within two months.

[6] Beauharnois to Maurepas, n.d., *ibid.*, p. 127.

VI

Obstacles to the Expedition

SATISFIED that the Indians, for the time being at least, would cause little trouble, La Vérendrye made arrangements for a journey to Montreal and Quebec, where he could discuss with the governor his achievements and his plans for the expedition to the Mantannes. He could not foresee at that time that trade difficulties, Indian unrest, and personal tragedy would postpone his expedition for another four years.

He placed Pierre in command of Fort St. Charles with ten men under him and started off on May 27, 1734. His first stop was Kaministikwia on June 16. Here he met a party of Frenchmen under René Cartier, a prominent trader he had known in Montreal, and to him he entrusted the work of founding the post on the Red River at the place selected by Pierre. This was evidently his first opportunity to keep his promise to the Indians, for his lieutenants were otherwise occupied. Jean-Baptiste had joined the Crees, Pierre was in charge of the important station

at Lake of the Woods, and La Jemeraye had not yet returned
from Quebec. François, the third son, was passed by at this
time, and for some unexplained reason he was never given the
important assignments delegated to his brothers; he seems to
have been subordinated even to Louis-Joseph, the youngest of
the family. René Cartier was, therefore, the one person available
who was responsible enough to be given the task. La Vérendrye
handed him a plan of the fort as he wished to have it built. Its
size was to be one square *arpent*, and its construction presumably
similar to that of the other posts. Cartier was also ordered to tell
the Indians that Pierre would visit Lake Winnipeg in August.

On reaching Michilimackinac, La Vérendrye met La Jemeraye
returning to the Northwest with orders from Governor Beauharnois. The commander gave him instructions to proceed to
Fort St. Charles, where he was to supersede Pierre and send
him to the Red River. There he would find the fort already built,
or, at any rate, nearly completed. Then, taking leave of his
nephew, he continued on his way to Montreal, arriving there on
August 16.[1]

The news which greeted La Vérendrye when he was shown
into the governor's presence at Quebec was not particularly encouraging. He was told point blank that the King was unwilling
to contribute anything to his enterprise; and he had also learned,
when at Montreal, that his business associates would advance
nothing more on credit, thus making it necessary for him to look
elsewhere for assistance. By dint of argument, however, supported by his own inextinguishable confidence in the favorable
outcome of his enterprise, he succeeded in persuading some
of the merchants to let him have additional supplies, even though
he still owed for what he had already borrowed. He also managed to impress Beauharnois with his ability by what he had
already accomplished. He told him how he had, by means of his
posts, deflected the flow of beaver from Hudson Bay into the

[1] Journal of 1733–1734, *J. & L.*, pp. 190–192.

hands of the French traders and how he had built a post on the Red River near Lake Winnipeg, only 150 leagues from the Mantannes, whither he expected to go the year after next, that is, in 1736. On this journey he proposed to take with him La Jemeraye, and one of his sons who had shown an aptitude for learning Indian dialects.

La Vérendrye's enthusiasm evidently had some effect on the governor, for he wrote Maurepas suggesting that help from the Crown would be welcome. The explorer's zeal, he believed, came solely from a desire to find the Western Sea and make his posts useful to the colony. The heavy expenses he had incurred thus far might have discouraged him if he had not hoped that the King would eventually render him some assistance. The high cost of transportation over the carries between Grand Portage and Rainy Lake was responsible for a large part of these expenses, and this cost had been cut down materially by improvements in the road. The route up the Pigeon River originally had forty-one portages; and now, by virtue of his efforts, they had been reduced to thirty-two. Furthermore, he had improved the trails over the portages in such a manner that the *voyageurs* could cover seven of them in a day without much effort. Thus, men who had received as much as 500 *livres* for covering the route now charged but 250 or 300 at the most.[2]

La Vérendrye turned over his journal for the period 1733 to 1734, together with a map, to Beauharnois and spent the winter as best he could, waiting impatiently for spring. He knew it would be a year before an answer to Beauharnois' communications could be received from the French Court and that whatever the government might do for him would be of no assistance for the journey he would begin in the spring of 1735.[3] As it

[2] Beauharnois to Maurepas, Oct. 8, 1734, *ibid.*, pp. 110–116.

[3] La Vérendrye drew up his yearly reports, or journals, in the summer. The journals of 1734–1735 and 1735–1736 have never come to light, and accounts of what happened in these years must be taken from other sources.

turned out he would have been no better off had communication been instantaneous, for Maurepas' answer, when it did come, merely expressed the King's approval of the explorer's achievements but was positive in stating that his Majesty refused to share in the expense.[4]

While La Vérendrye was engaged in his preparations for the coming expedition, there came to Canada a young man destined to play a brief though interesting part in the history of Fort St. Charles. Jean-Pierre Aulneau, for such was his name, was born on April 21, 1705, in the department of Vendée. He was one of five children, all of whom, save one, devoted themselves to the religious life. Pierre enrolled himself in the Society of Jesus, and filled with a desire to carry the Gospel to the Indians, joined a group of priests who were going to Canada in the charge of Bishop Pierre Bosquet. In this party was Father François Nau, to whose letters we owe some knowledge of Father Aulneau's missionary career in the Northwest. The party embarked at La Rochelle and arrived at Quebec on August 16, 1734.

At this time the community was agog with the news that La Vérendrye and his nephew had brought them of that peculiar people called the Mantannes, now magnified into a race of white men who might be Tartars or Japanese, living not far from the Western Sea. Father Nau, in speaking of Aulneau, wrote:

He may set out next spring [1735] for the discovery of the Western Sea, for the Court is set on having something more substantial on this subject than mere conjecture. The French who returned this year from the upper country have informed us that the savages told them that there were, 1,100 leagues from Quebec, white people who wore beards and were subjects of a king. These people built their houses in the French style and owned horses and other domestic animals. Would they not be Tartars or Japanese immigrants? The savages have spoken to them about the French, and they were pleased to learn that there were in Canada white, bearded people

[4] Maurepas to Beauharnois, April 12, 1735, *J. & L.*, pp. 195–197.

like themselves. "The French are apparently our brothers," they said, "and we would like to see them; do invite them to visit us." If this story is true, we have here a splendid opening for the Gospel. But one is apt to doubt the sincerity of the Canadians who brought back this tale, for there is no country in the world where there is so much lying as in Canada.[5]

On landing in Quebec, Father Aulneau learned that he had been detailed by his superior, Father Pierre de Lauzun, to establish a mission among these far-off people, an assignment he accepted with some misgivings. In a letter to Father Jacques Bonin he expressed surprise at his selection for the post, especially as he had not been warned beforehand, and he spoke with distaste of a mission that was to send him so far afield without even one white companion. Yet he accepted his cross as in the line of duty, and set about making his preparations. His plan, as he explained it to Father Bonin, was to go to Lake of the Woods, spend the winter there among the Crees and Assiniboins, then move on to the Mantannes. He was not too sanguine about his success in reaching these people, as the entire business, he thought, was founded on the none-too-reliable reports of the Indians.

If what they add about the region where the Ouachipouennes [Mantannes] dwell is true, I believe that they are not far from California, for if one is to believe them [the Indians] they are on the banks of a large river that rises and falls [with the tide] which goes to show that the sea is not far off. What is this river? That is something not easy to guess. I think, however, that it must be that great river shown by Father King [Kino], a German Jesuit, on the map he traced of the regions of America lying north of California. He calls it Rio Colorado or Del Norte.[6]

[5] Nau to Richard, Oct. 20, 1734, *R.A.Q.*, *1926–1927*, pp. 267–269; A. E. Jones, ed., *Aulneau Collection* (Montreal, 1893), pp. 21–27.

[6] Aulneau to Bonin, April 29, 1735, *R.A.Q.*, *1926–1927*, pp. 277–278; Jones, *op. cit.*, pp. 47–50. The river mentioned here is the Colorado, flowing into the head of the Gulf of California.

La Vérendrye was now making his final preparations for his return to the Northwest. In order to relieve him from the cares of trade, which so far had caused him heavy losses, Beauharnois gave him permission to farm out his posts to certain merchants for a period of three years, during which time he was to refrain from all trading and devote himself to the work of discovery. The governor also warned him not to loiter on the way or someone else would be found to take his place.[7] This arrangement ended for the time being the relations between La Vérendrye and the merchants, which doubtless relieved him of much anxiety, for the necessity of carrying on a fur trade in order to pay his expenses had always hampered him. And it was well that the change was made at this time, for Maurepas was beginning to suspect him of working secretly with the Canadian officials, all of whom, with the exception of the governor, regarded exploration, so the Minister thought, as being of secondary importance to the fur trade. In fact, Maurepas went so far as to say that the Western Sea would have been discovered long ago had not La Vérendrye's men been more interested in the "sea of beaver."[8]

In order to leave his affairs in good hands, La Vérendrye signed a document before a notary public on June 10, 1735, giving his wife power to collect from the government his salary as lieutenant, and also that of captain should he be promoted to that rank during his absence. She was also empowered to take charge of the supplies for Fort St. Charles, in consideration of which her husband agreed to make good any obligations incurred by her.[9] The business end of the undertaking now fell into the hands of a small group composed of two local merchants, Jean-Marie Nolan and Jean-Baptiste Legras, with whom La

[7] Beauharnois to Maurepas, Oct. 8, 1735, *J. & L.*, pp. 202–206.

[8] Nau to Bonin, Oct. 2, 1735, *R.A.Q., 1926–1927*, p. 286; Jones, *op. cit.*, pp. 55–67.

[9] "Procuration de Pierre Gaultier de la Vérendrye," *B.R.H.*, LVIII, 126.

Vérendrye's eldest son and La Jemeraye seem to have been associated.[10] The Sieur Nolan was a younger brother of Charles Nolan de Lamarque, one of Montreal's most distinguished merchants, who was said to have sent the most *voyageurs* to the west and to have sent them the farthest. The two brothers later followed La Vérendrye to the upper country, whence they accompanied him on his journey to the Mantannes in 1738.[11]

The Sieur Legras was a young merchant who had backed expeditions of this sort for several years, being at one time an assistant to Lamarque. He had just married the daughter of Pierre Gamelin Maugras, thus allying himself with a prominent merchant family. There were two other men who may have accompanied the expedition at this time, at least we shall meet them presently at Fort St. Charles: Daniel Legras, Jean-Baptiste's older half-brother, and René Bourassa, who is listed at this time as engaging men for the expedition. As for Nolan and Jean-Baptiste Legras, they now set to work with great vigor, signing up men for the service, some for Lake of the Woods and points west, others only for Michilimackinac.[12]

[10] *R.A.Q., 1949–1950,* p. 37, mentions a document that gives the names of these four men, although Jean-Baptiste and La Jemeraye were then in the Northwest.

[11] La Vérendrye in his narrative of this journey mentions the Sieur Nolan (Lamarque's brother) without giving his Christian name. *J. & L.,* p. 261n., says that it was Nicolas-Augustin, but quotes no authority. Tanguay, *op. cit.,* I, 453, tells us that one Jean-Baptiste Nolan married Marie-Anne Lamarque on January 26, 1688. There were fourteen children of this union, among whom were Charles and Jean-Marie. So far so good; but if we turn to Vol. VI, 155, we find a genealogy entirely different from that in Vol. I. Jean Noland is here mentioned as the one who married Marie-Anne Lamarque on January 26, 1688. This couple seems to have had but four children, among whom were Charles, the eldest, whose date of birth is given as November 25, 1694 (the same as in Vol. I), and Nicolas-Augustin. Jean-Marie's name is not given. But since we find in other records that Jean-Marie was the one interested in western fur trade we are inclined to assume that it was he who accompanied his brother, Charles de Lamarque.

[12] *R.A.Q., 1929–1930,* pp. 317–324.

La Vérendrye left Montreal on June 6, 1735, accompanied by his son, the Chevalier Louis-Joseph,[13] and by Father Aulneau, who replaced Father Mesaiger as chaplain. The appearance of this, the youngest of La Vérendrye's sons, presents us with something of a puzzle. From the moment he landed at Fort St. Charles he seems to have taken precedence over his older brother, François. It was to him that La Vérendrye, *père,* entrusted some of his more important activities, as, for example, the journey to the Rocky Mountains in 1742, in which François seems to have accompanied him in a somewhat subordinate position. It is impossible to say why this is so, but it may be assumed that Louis-Joseph was endowed with more native ability, and it is very likely that he was better educated, since he had remained in the East to pursue his studies; while François, on the other hand, may well have been a rather colorless fellow, unable to assume leadership. At any rate François had this satisfaction: he outlived all his brothers.

On leaving Montreal, La Vérendrye proceeded over the usual route and reached Fort St. Charles on September 6. On his arrival he found the place nearly destitute of provisions; nor was there any expectation of the annual crop of wild rice, for heavy rains had destroyed it. He did, however, receive some pleasant news, for La Jemeraye, during his uncle's absence, had been busy pushing the fur trade to the utmost of his ability. He was successful in collecting no less than six hundred packages of beaver, but owing to the shortage of manpower he could send only four hundred to Montreal. That same year, it so happened, a large supply of furs came down to Montreal from the post at Trempeleau, so that the entire receipts from the Far West amounted to 100,000 skins valued at 178,000 *livres.*[14]

It was now La Vérendrye's plan to send one of his sons to the fort on the Red River before the savages went into the

[13] See Appendix A for a discussion of the identity of the chevalier.
[14] Hocquart to Maurepas, Oct. 26, 1735, *Wisconsin Historical Collection,* XVII (1906), 230.

woods, but on second thought he sent La Jemeraye instead. The main purpose in sending a representative was to invite the Assiniboins to join the French in an expedition to the Mantannes which the commander had now decided to lead in person the following spring.[15]

During La Vérendrye's absence, La Jemeraye had received reports from Jean-Baptiste, giving a little additional information about the Mantannes which he had gleaned from the Assiniboins, though some of it merely confirmed what had been heard before. According to the new report the Mantannes resembled the French, having white skins and beards, with their hair dressed, not in Indian style, but plaited along the sides of the head. They also built their forts like the French, though they added drawbridges as a distinctive feature. There were seven villages in all, each with its own chief who in turn obeyed a head chief, ruler of the entire nation. These people lived on a river so wide that one could barely distinguish a man on the opposite bank. The river flowed, so the Assiniboins said, in a west-southwesterly direction, though how they could have given the direction with such precision without a compass is difficult to understand. It was probably a guess by the Frenchman who interpreted their story. Farther down the river, so ran the tale, there lived "other savages similar to these except that they use cloth for their clothing [instead of skins] and possess iron tools," which they obtained from the French at the mouth of the said river.[16] It was, nevertheless, a long journey to this nation; the route lying through seven tribes.

The story now begins to take shape, and we can readily see

[15] Beauharnois to Maurepas, Oct. 8, 1735, *J. & L.*, pp. 202–206.

[16] In the original French given in *J. & L.*, p. 200, the text reads: "qu'ils se servent d'étoffes pour leur vêtements et qu'ils ont des ferrements que les autres n'ont point, et qu'ils disent tenir des Français . . ." We are inclined to think that the word "tenir" is an abbreviated form of "obtenir" and that the translation should read: "that they use cloth for their clothing and possess iron tools of which the others are destitute, which [cloth and tools] they say they obtain from the French . . ."

the resemblance between La Jemeraye's account and the one given to La Vérendrye at the great council held on New Year's Day, 1734. It all boiled down to this: somewhere in the Far West a great river flowed in a southwesterly direction, presumably to the Western Sea. On its banks lived a people called the Mantannes, who resembled the French, or, perhaps, it is better to say that they did not seem at all like the Indians of the Northwest; and not far from this river's mouth dwelt a nation of European stock, probably French, possibly Spanish. Here, then, was enough in the way of definite information to justify action, and Jean-Baptiste decided to take the initiative. He began by giving the Assiniboins a collar of wampum to carry to the Mantannes in the name of Governor Beauharnois, inviting them, if they wished to meet the French, to come to a certain place designated by him.[17] This done, he sat down to await an answer before taking the next step.

La Vérendrye soon after his return to Lake of the Woods dispatched La Jemeraye to the fort Cartier had built on the Red River and had named Maurepas in honor of the Minister of Marine. The fort was not situated exactly at the mouth of the river, but some little distance inland. The Red River, three miles from the lake, is divided into three channels which flow through a low, marshy country. At the end of the three miles the river banks rise suddenly, forming a plateau, and on this plateau, on the west bank of the river, in the modern reservation of Peguis, about five miles north of the town of Selkirk, Fort Maurepas was built. No trace of it now remains, though there is a tradition that the French once had a post there.[18]

When La Jemeraye started on his journey to Fort Maurepas, the commander turned over to him the supplies he had brought

[17] La Jemeraye in his letter does not give the location of this place (*ibid.*, pp. 199–201).

[18] For full discussion of the site see N. M. Crouse, "The Location of Fort Maurepas," *Canadian Historical Review,* IX (1928), 206–222.

from the east, expecting to join him as soon as he received the additional goods ordered from Montreal. But here again La Vérendrye appears to have suffered the buffets of ill fortune, for the leader of the convoy, on reaching Kaministikwia, found the season too far advanced for further travel, and decided to remain there for the winter. Thus deprived of his provisions, La Vérendrye was unable to join his nephew at Fort Maurepas; and, what was still more distressing, the Indians, when they learned that the French could not supply them with merchandise, decided to take their furs to Hudson Bay.

The following spring (1736) La Vérendrye suffered a more serious setback. During the winter La Jemeraye had been stricken ill at Fort Maurepas, and as soon as he was able to move he started back to Lake of the Woods, hoping to reach St. Charles, where he could have better care. In this journey he was accompanied by two of his cousins, probably François and Louis-Joseph.

The route now taken by the party was a new one. Instead of returning by way of the Winnipeg River, they ascended the Red River to a small stream called the Roseau, which enters the Red about fifty miles south of the modern city of Winnipeg. The Roseau has its source near the southwest shore of Lake of the Woods; thus the traveler could reach the lake by a carry known as the Savanne Portage. On arriving at the mouth of the Roseau—Fourche des Roseaux, as La Vérendrye calls it—La Jemeraye took a turn for the worse, and was obliged to encamp there. Here he remained for several days hoping that a good rest would improve his condition; but unfortunately he was beyond recovery, and on May 10 he breathed his last. His cousins buried him on the spot and erected over his grave a wooden cross to mark the last resting place of the gallant explorer. This pious duty done, the brothers pushed on to Fort St. Charles by the Roseau, after caching their supplies at the Savanne Portage. They arrived at the fort on June 4. La Jemeraye

was the first of La Vérendrye's followers, of whom we have any
record, to be laid to rest in the wilderness about Lake of the
Woods, the region he had done so much toward discovering.
His death, coming as it did, proved a great blow to the commander, for La Jemeraye had been his right-hand man, the
one to whom he entrusted his more important undertakings.
Small wonder, then, that the journey to the Western Sea was
again postponed.

The situation was now a critical one for La Vérendrye. He
had lost his first lieutenant, and his supplies were almost exhausted. To push forward the work of discovery at this time
would have been impossible, so he was obliged to abandon certain plans he had made to build another fort just south of a
lake he called Lac des Prairies, the present Manitoba, or, perhaps, Winnipegosis. Yet, even before he received the news of
La Jemeraye's death, he had decided to call a meeting of his
colleagues to discuss the situation. The conference was held the
day before the La Vérendrye brothers arrived, and the commander, after listening attentively to the opinions of those
present, gave orders to send a party to Kaministikwia, perhaps
to Michilimackinac, to find out what had become of the now
long-overdue supplies and to hurry them forward to Fort St.
Charles.

This expedition, a mere routine affair as it seemed at the time,
was quickly organized. It consisted of twenty men under Jean-
Baptiste, recently returned from his excursion with the Crees.
Father Aulneau was also one of the party. Now that the expedition to the Mantannes was called off he had decided to
return to Montreal, though why he did not remain in order to
perfect himself in the Indian dialects and carry on his missionary
labors among the neighboring tribes is not clear. The men were
equally distributed in three canoes which carried a minimum
of supplies in order to attain a maximum of speed; but before

they left La Vérendrye saw to it that they were provided with ammunition and warned them to be on their guard, for he had received disturbing news of a band of Sioux who were combing the lake for Crees and might do the French some harm. These were the same Sioux who had attacked the Crees three years before. On this occasion, it will be recalled, the Crees in the heat of battle cried out to their enemies: "We are French Cree. Why are you killing us?" This caused the Sioux to realize that they had inadvertently attacked a tribe friendly to the French. Though the misunderstanding was patched up at the time, La Vérendrye was too well versed in Indian psychology not to suspect that the Sioux might well wish to avenge their dead even though they themselves had begun hostilities. Thus it was that he felt considerable alarm when he heard that the Sioux were in the neighborhood.[19]

The convoy left the fort on June 5 and headed for the Rainy River, leaving the commander in a rather apprehensive frame of mind. Three days later there arrived at St. Charles a fleet of canoes from Kaministikwia which had crossed the lake from the Rainy River over the same route as that followed by Jean-Baptiste and his party. As they grounded their boats on the shore La Vérendrye rushed to meet them, anxious to learn if they had met the outgoing contingent. To his dismay he was told that they had seen no one. The news struck him like a blow, for it was impossible for the two parties not to have seen each other, since their routes lay across the open expanse of the lake. But there was nothing to be done save wait and hope. Four days later three Monsonis appeared with a rather alarming report. It seems that René Bourassa had left Fort St. Charles with a small party in one canoe two days ahead of the main detachment.

[19] Beauharnois feared a war of vengeance and forbade La Vérendrye to send any Frenchmen on expeditions against the Sioux (Beauharnois to Maurepas, Oct. 14, 1736, *J. & L.*, p. 210).

The next day he was captured by a band of Sioux, robbed, and sent on his way, fortunately without being injured.[20] This meager account was presently supplemented by a letter written by Bourassa when he reached Fort St. Pierre, a letter which gave his version of the affair.[21]

According to Bourassa's story, he left Fort St. Charles on June 3 and spent the night on some island. Next morning, as he was about to embark, he was surrounded by thirty canoes containing ninety to one hundred Sioux who pounced on his men and plundered them; but they quickly released them when they learned from Bourassa that a detachment of Crees was encamped near the fort. They ordered the trader to wait for them while they went to finish off the Crees, promising to give him back his weapons; but he had the good sense to hurry on to the Rainy River as soon as they were out of sight. Governor Beauharnois, on the other hand, received a slightly different version of the affair. According to this account Bourassa was seized and tied to a stake when a slave of his, a Sioux woman, interceded for him. "My kinsmen," she said to the savages, "what are you going to do? I owe my life to this Frenchman; he has done me nothing but good; if you want to be avenged for the attack made on us, you have only to go farther on and you will find twenty-four Frenchmen, amongst whom is the son of their chief, the one who has slaughtered us." [22] It is difficult to accuse Bourassa of betraying his fellow countrymen, even if the account is true, since the information as to their whereabouts was given by the

[20] Beauharnois in his letter to Maurepas of Oct. 14, 1736, says that Bourassa had charge of Aulneau's canoe, but other accounts show this to have been impossible, as Aulneau traveled with the main party (*ibid.*, pp. 208–213).

[21] *Ibid.*, pp. 262–265. The other principal sources are: Jaunay to Mme. Aulneau, Sept. 28, 1739, *R.A.Q.*, *1926–1927*, pp. 305–306; Jones, *op. cit.*, p. 110; Report of La Vérendrye, *J. & L.*, pp. 217–222. See also L. J. Burpee, "The Lake of the Woods Tragedy," *Proceedings and Transactions of the Royal Society of Canada*, 2d ser., IX (1903), sec. 2, 15–28.

[22] Beauharnois to Maurepas, Oct. 14, 1736, *J. & L.*, pp. 208–213.

squaw; yet one can readily see why he omitted this detail in his report to La Vérendrye. At any rate nothing was ever done about the matter; Bourassa was never called to account. And now for the story of Jean-Baptiste and his men.

Jean-Baptiste left Fort St. Charles on June 5. That night the party encamped on an island (now called Massacre Island), a small, rocky hillock about three-quarters of a mile long by one-quarter wide, comprising some sixty-six acres, and situated off the northwestern point of Big Island, eighteen miles from St. Charles. Here they spent the night, resting peacefully from their labors with no thought of impending danger. Next morning, as they were preparing to shove off, they heard the dreaded warwhoop. A column of smoke they had lighted to prepare their breakfast had attracted a band of Sioux coming up from the Warroad River, who, landing unperceived on the other side of the island, now swooped down upon them. The Indians made no effort to take prisoners, not even for the pleasure of putting them to the torture according to time-honored custom, for the French at the first onslaught had managed to secure their arms and were gallantly returning blow for blow; but with such odds against them their cause was hopeless from the first, and after a short struggle all were either killed or drowned trying to escape. Such, presumably, are the main facts in the case (gleaned later from the Indians), the details of which must ever remain shrouded in mystery, since no Frenchman remained alive to tell the true story.

After the massacre the Indians proceeded to scalp the slain and sever the heads from the bodies, wrapping the heads in beaver skins in derisive reminder of the love the French had for this article of trade. This done, they turned their attention to Father Aulneau, who as a black robe was regarded with a certain amount of awe. He had not, of course, taken any part in the fighting but had remained a horrified spectator of the scene, doubtless on his knees imploring the mercy of Heaven for his fellow countrymen. His body was found in a kneeling position, an arrow in the side and a knife wound in the breast. Father du Jaunay, who informed Aulneau's mother of the death of her son, gives the following brief account from what he had been able to learn from hearsay:

In the first place, the majority of Indians implicated were adverse to putting him to death. In the second place, it was through sheer bravado that a crazy-brained Indian set at naught the consequences which held the others in awe. A third particular I have gathered is, that scarcely had the deed been perpetrated, than a deafening clap of thunder struck terror into the whole band. They fled from the spot, believing that Heaven was incensed at what they had done. Finally, that the portable chapel, and, namely, the chalice, which was plundered, had fallen into the hands of a widowed squaw who had several grown up sons, the pride and wealth of the tribe. In a remarkably short length of time, all, or nearly all of them perished in her sight. This she ascribed to the chalice, which her sons had given her; so she rid herself of it by throwing it into the river.

La Vérendrye for a time knew nothing of the tragedy, though he doubtless felt ill at ease. Then on the seventeenth came Daniel Legras and his party with two canoes of merchandise. He had remained at Kaministikwia since the previous autumn, but like Bourassa he could give no news of Jean-Baptiste. Realizing now that something was amiss, the commander wrote Governor Beauharnois telling him of his fears and dispatched Legras with the letter, giving him as escort a sergeant and eight men, at the same time ordering him to follow exactly the route taken by the lost party. Next day there arrived at the fort thirty Crees with a load of game. When they heard of the trouble they volunteered to join in the search; but no sooner had they launched their canoes than a strong wind arose which drove them back to the fort, where they traded their meat and provisions for merchandise and presently departed for home. A few days later the sergeant was back to report that he had found the bodies of the slain Canadians on Massacre Island. Most of them had been scalped, and the heads, severed from the bodies, placed on beaver skins. Jean-Baptiste's headless body lay prone, the back scored with knife cuts, a stake driven into the side, while the limbs and torso were decorated with leggings and ornaments of porcupine quills. As for Legras, he continued on to Montreal with the letter and, proceeding thence to Quebec, delivered it to the governor together with a verbatim account of the tragedy.

In attempting to explain this sudden attack, the authorities concluded that it was caused by the hatred engendered by the presence of Jean-Baptiste among the war party which had recently attacked the Sioux. True, the young man had left the band before the actual hostilities began and was therefore not responsible for the assault; but the savages were in no mood to weigh such nice distinctions and considered the French to blame for killing their men. Most of the Sioux concerned in the business were Prairie Sioux, though some of them were from the neighborhood of Chequamegon, where a friendly feeling for the French prevailed. Evidently they had been seduced by their allies and persuaded to join the expedition.

Exploration was now out of the question; it was in fact two years before La Vérendrye could recover from the blow and again take the field. His forces were disorganized; and the death of his eldest son, coming as it did just after that of his nephew, left him with only his younger sons, youths barely out of their 'teens, with whom to undertake the work of discovery. Nevertheless, he attacked the problem with his customary vigor. Being shorthanded in the midst of a country teeming with enemies, whose attacks might be expected at any moment, he decided to make his post strong enough to be defended by a small garrison. He does not tell us just what alterations were made, but he says that he had it "rebuilt and put in such a condition that four men could defend it against a hundred."

At this distressing moment, be it said to his credit, La Vérendrye had no thought of abandoning his cherished project or
even of going to Montreal to procure assistance; on the contrary,
after a brief outburst of rage against the Sioux, he set himself
to the task, now more difficult than ever, of maintaining peace
between the Sioux and his own Indians, while he took measures
to build up the fur trade at Maurepas in the hope of restoring
normal conditions before launching an expedition to the west.

Early in August there came four deputies from the Crees
and Monsonis with word that their chiefs would arrive in the
autumn to organize plans for a punitive expedition against the
Sioux.[23] The Indians were clever enough to see in this terrible
business an opportunity for rousing the French to a pitch of
anger that would lead them to approve a war. The temptation
to let loose the Crees on the Sioux was indeed a strong one for
La Vérendrye; in fact he even went so far as to write the governor that he was thinking seriously of leading such an expedition; but by the time the chiefs had arrived he had regained his
composure and managed to put them off with a word of thanks
for the interest they took in his bereavement, informing them at
the same time that he would first have to get the governor's
permission before joining them in such an enterprise. Nothing
daunted, the savages sent two more deputies a week later who
described graphically the grief felt by all the tribes at the death
of the man they had adopted as chief; even the women and children joined in the chorus of incessant wailing. And to them
La Vérendrye could do nothing but give the same reply.

Two weeks passed, then the savages struck again. This time
it was the Crees and Assiniboins at Fort Maurepas who sent a
delegation, twelve strong, to plead before the commander. They
were about to send a force to *pointe du bois fort,* a rendezvous
of the three nations, some little distance up the Red River, fifty

---

[23] The events from June 1736 to Feb. 1737 are taken principally from
La Vérendrye's Journal of 1736–1737, *ibid.,* pp. 213–243.

leagues from Fort St. Charles, a convenient place for getting
to the Sioux country.[24] They now felt confident that they could
embroil the French in their wars. After all one does not refuse
to avenge one's own flesh and blood. La Vérendrye knew this
perfectly well, and he realized the difficulty of refusing to lead
the savages and at the same time retaining their respect. In order to solve the problem—if it could be solved at all—he decided to call a council. Perhaps, in some way or other, he could
place the blame for a refusal on the governor's shoulders, pleading that he was under orders from the Great Father and could
take no action until he heard from him. At least it was worth a
try.

La Vérendrye opened the council on September 3. The rank-
ing chiefs present were La Colle of the Monsonis and La Mikouenne of the Crees. They opened the discussion by proposing
to send out a few small parties against the Sioux, just to see what
would happen. But the commander was ready for this move.
He said:

My children, I cannot allow you to go to war until I have received
word from your Father, which I will communicate to you. Besides
you know that we are short of powder and ball owing to our canoes
not having come through [returned], and how, in that case, can we
venture to go to war? But what I consider expedient is to send word
to the Monsonis of Lake Tecamamiouen [Rainy Lake] to form a
party and go to meet the French convoy and escort it, and to let me
have here fifty men to meet them likewise with one French canoe,
and that annually, so that we may not in future be exposed to the
aggressions of the Sioux.

As token he gave a collar to La Colle to be kept at Fort St. Pierre
and one to La Mikouenne to be kept at St. Charles.

[24] A rendezvous where there was a thick and heavy wood. A post may
have been built there (*ibid.*, p. 222n.). The word "fort" in this connection
means thick and heavy; it does not mean a fortified post as, for example,
Fort St. Charles.

With this arrangement La Vérendrye sought to appease the savages and insure the safety of the French, for he doubtless guessed what the governor's reply would be when he asked for permission to make war. All this was far from satisfying the Indians; they wanted punitive measures taken, not merely protection from future aggression. They looked upon the death of Jean-Baptiste as the one lever by which they could at last move the French to action. It was difficult, if not impossible, for them to understand the attitude of a man not eager to avenge his son, for this was contrary to the Indian's code of honor. La Vérendrye's excuse that he must first consult the Father was therefore accepted with reluctance for the time being, and the Indians sat down to wait for another opportunity to urge their request.[25]

On September 14 there came to the fort two canoeloads of Crees and Assiniboins from Fort Maurepas, for the purpose of obtaining supplies. La Vérendrye saw in this an opportunity to re-establish a representative at this post who could gain some measure of control over these tribes and prevent them from precipitating a conflict that might have serious consequences. He accordingly sent to Fort Maurepas his son, Louis-Joseph, accompanied by six men, with the orders he himself had received from the governor, orders commanding him to keep the Indians at peace; and he also told the chevalier to promise them assistance as soon as the canoes arrived from Montreal. Lastly, he ordered the young man to make up a party of his French followers and with an escort of forty or fifty Assiniboins visit the Mantannes, now believed to be some 150 leagues from Fort Maurepas. When, and if, he reached this nation he was to ask them to send envoys to Fort Maurepas to form an alliance with the French. He was also to apologize for the refusal of the garrison to entertain a Mantanne who had come to the fort at the time of La Jemeraye's illness and had been rather summarily

[25] Report of La Vérendrye, 1736–1737, *ibid.*, pp. 223–224.

ejected, due to an unfortunate misunderstanding. Louis-Joseph was then to inform the Crees and Assiniboins that La Vérendrye would be with them at Maurepas the coming January (1737) "at the time of the great moon," to make known the wishes of the Father.

After bidding farewell to his son, the commander busied himself with the task of collecting the bodies of Jean-Baptiste and Father Aulneau, together with the heads of the other victims, and giving them proper sepulture in the little chapel at Fort St. Charles. Shortly after this he received the alarming news from Louis-Joseph that the Crees and Assiniboins, eight hundred strong, had gone to a rendezvous at *pointe du bois fort*. They were, of course, preparing for a war against the Sioux, and they were determined to make La Vérendrye a party to the undertaking, or at least to obtain his approval. For this purpose they now sent a large delegation to Fort St. Charles. La Vérendrye watched their coming gloomily, and with a sigh of resignation he invited them to a conference, hoping to find some excuse for putting them off without incurring their ill-will, or, what was worse, their contempt. A Cree chief, delegated to speak for all, opened the pow-pow, saying:

My father, we have already sent you word many times that we were sick at heart and were incessantly weeping for the death of your son and the other Frenchmen; that we felt it more than if we had been killed ourselves; and that it is our purpose to take vengeance for the dead. We are here now to invite you to lead us. If you cannot walk we will carry you; we invite La Colle also and all the Crees and Monsoni.

Then coming down to the more practical cause of their grief, the savage pointed out that the massacre had caused the commander to put off the establishment of the post he had promised to erect at the northern end of Lake Winnipeg. In closing his speech, he asked La Vérendrye to let them adopt the chevalier as a chief in place of Jean-Baptiste.

It was the custom at these councils to allow a day to elapse before replying to a request, and La Vérendrye gladly took advantage of the precedent. The old excuse that he must await the Great Father's permission to make war had now become somewhat threadbare; but perhaps during the intermission he might think up something else. That night he held a consultation with La Colle and La Mikouenne, the result of which was embodied in a speech he made next day to the assembled braves. It was not an impressive piece of oratory; he really had nothing new to add to the hackneyed theme. But the situation was a desperate one; he must at all cost keep the peace, for on this depended the fate of all his expeditions. A blow struck against the Sioux might start a general conflagration that would make it impossible for him to travel through the western country.

When the chiefs assembled the following day, the commander took the floor. "Know, my children," he said, "that the French never undertake war without having consulted their Father and only do it by his order: you see therefore that, however angry I may be, my arms are tied." And that was that. Whether they liked it or not, La Vérendrye was going to stand pat on his responsibility to the governor. Then, in order to mollify his allies, he proceeded with a plea to postpone the war to a more propitious occasion, giving suitable arguments for doing so:

You know that there are Frenchmen dwelling with the Sioux. We must not therefore avenge French blood by shedding it anew. You could not control your young men, and, even if you should spare them [the French], could they escape from the Sioux who would take a second vengeance on them? Hence I conclude that we must defer this war to a more favorable time.

In replying for the chiefs, La Colle, who had been appointed spokesman, gave a dubious assent to La Vérendrye's proposal. His principal complaint was the failure of the French to keep his people supplied with merchandise. For two years they had lacked nothing and had cheerfully obeyed the Father's order not to trade with the English; but now the supply of goods was insufficient, and if they went again to Hudson Bay La Vérendrye would have no one to blame but himself. Then La Colle presented the commander with a collar, urging him to go to Quebec and see the Father, taking La Mikouenne's brother as a companion to speak for the three tribes. During his absence the Indians would see to it that the forts were well protected, and the following spring they would march against the Sioux before La Vérendrye's return, so that he would not be responsible for the trouble. Then one of the Crees took up the burden of the argument. He promised to go at once to *pointe du bois fort* and try to persuade the warriors assembled there to disperse, though he doubted the success of his mission. To all of this the commander apparently made no reply, and the meeting broke up at once.

Scarcely had the Crees left· when a party of some thirty Frenchmen arrived from Michilimackinac with the doleful tale that two traders, Bourassa and a man named Eustache, who headed a convoy destined for St. Charles, had stopped at the Vermilion River (with the merchandise, of course) where they intended to establish a trading post for the benefit of the Chippewas, a course of action bound to react to the detriment of the friendly Monsonis at Fort St. Pierre, since it would deprive them of their supplies. Nothing could have been more disloyal than such an action; it struck a blow at the very foundation of the trade system La Vérendrye had worked so laboriously to build up. The supplies in the charge of Bourassa and Eustache were just then badly needed to keep the savages living about the posts from going to Hudson Bay, and now this merchandise was to benefit their enemies the Chippewas. Was it possible that Bourassa did not care to face La Vérendrye after the part he had played, or rather his squaw had played, in the tragedy on Massacre Island? The commander at once sent orders forbidding the traders to winter anywhere except at Fort St. Pierre, but as the season was late Bourassa excused himself from complying. His reason was plausible enough, and La Vérendrye felt obliged to modify his orders by sending a clerk to instruct Bourassa to build a little post on the Vermilion as a protection during the winter months. This post was probably situated on Crane Lake, near Handeburg's Landing, where a line of piled stones, similar to the stone-wall footing at Fort St. Charles, has been recently found. Crane Lake is sometimes known as Little Vermilion, and through it the waters of the Vermilion are connected with the Pigeon River.[26] When the weather had moderated, Bourassa was to proceed to Fort St. Pierre, there to trade with the Monsonis. He was also to rebuild this post, as it had fallen into disrepair.

When the Crees left Fort St. Charles, La Vérendrye proceeded to put his house in order before going to Fort Maurepas. There was evidently some opposition, or perhaps better a lack of sympathy, on the part of those representing the trading interests when it came to the question of moving to Maurepas; for when La Vérendrye suggested sending two or three canoeloads of merchandise to that post, as he had promised his son Louis-Joseph, the clerks replied that they had no orders from their principals to this effect, and they even requested the recall of the men already there, as their services were needed at St. Charles. To this incipient mutiny the commander paid little attention but continued his preparations for the journey.

It was now past mid-October, almost the first of November, and the season was fast drawing to a close when La Vérendrye called the garrison together to announce his intention of going to Fort Maurepas. From the thirty-six men who comprised his command he selected a detail to remain as guard during his absence; the rest were to accompany him. He was particularly anx-

---

[26] Lee C. Bradford discovered remains of this fort which he believes is the one referred to by La Vérendrye (*Minnesota Archaeologist,* April 1947, p. 33)

ious to retain the Indians' good will, which could be best secured by furnishing them with enough for their wants. Bourassa had failed him, so he sent one of his sons to bring in the packages left at the Savanne Portage the previous spring when the brothers brought in the news of La Jemeraye's death; but the lad discovered, when he reached the cache, that twenty-six bundles had been stolen by the Indians, who had carried them off to Hudson Bay. Then, on November 4, the feast of St. Charles, as the men were holding a noisy celebration in honor of the occasion, La Vérendrye at last received the welcome news that La Colle was going in person to *pointe du bois fort* for a last attempt to prevent war.

On December 8 the commander held an inspection of his forces and ordered a detachment of ten men to go to Fort Maurepas and bring back news of Louis-Joseph. Pierre and François were to lead this contingent and were told to return promptly, as their father wished to leave as soon as possible, accompanied by his sons. The youths were to go by the Savanne Portage and the Red River, a course somewhat shorter than the Winnipeg route and more practical in winter when the ice had formed.

The new year (1737) opened auspiciously for the French. On January 2 five Indians arrived from *pointe du bois fort* bringing the welcome news that, thanks to La Colle's persuasive powers, the attack on the Sioux had been abandoned and the war party broken up. Nothing could have pleased La Vérendrye more. At last the threat of war was gone, leaving him free to begin his long trek to the Mantannes and the Great River of the West. With the tribes at peace he could now proceed with an easy mind to the discovery of the western plains. To make his joy still more complete a Cree came the same day from Fort Maurepas saying that the French were in the best of health and ready to receive him.

Preparations for the coming journey were now pushed forward in earnest. The event was a momentous one for the entire territory, and bands of Indians were soon on the move to assist the expedition or to be at the fort when the French chieftain arrived. On the last day of January a Cree, who had been kept in French pay since the previous autumn to act as guide, entered the gate of the fort with a following of forty-five men and women. Next day fifteen savages and their squaws were sent out to mark the campsites along the line of march, for it was evidently the explorer's intention to travel with all possible comforts. Word also came that the Crees and Assiniboins were gathering in large numbers at Fort Maurepas to await his arrival, while a large band of the same were encamped a day's journey from St. Charles, ready to form an escort. The commander summoned La Mikouenne and two other chiefs to a last conference. There he explained the reasons for his journey, chief among which was his desire to see their lands. He told them to leave the following day with their people and precede him to Fort Maurepas, there to prepare the natives for his coming.

St. Charles was now made secure, and a detail of twenty men under a sergeant left to guard it. Then taking with him Pierre, François, ten of the garrison, and eight savages with their wives, the explorer set out on February 8 for Maurepas. The weather was cold and clear, making the ground solid under foot, while the bright sunshine piercing the evergreen branches, lighted up the dazzling whiteness of the forest trail. As the party proceeded on its way over the Savanne Portage and along the Roseau River, lodges of friendly Crees came forth daily to wish the commander Godspeed. Pausing a moment at the mouth of the Roseau to kneel at the grave of his nephew, La Vérendrye then made his way down the Red River, accompanied by his French followers and his savage escort. The journey was more like the progress of a great personage coming to represent his sovereign in some distant province than the migration of a humble band of fur traders; indeed, La Vérendrye's skill in playing on the Indians' imagination was here used with telling effect.

When within two days' march of the fort, eighty Indians led by a Frenchman came to escort him to his destination with almost regal honors, and on February 25 he entered Fort Maurepas amid the enthusiastic acclamations of the native population. At last, La Vérendrye stood among his savage allies near the shores of Lake Winnipeg.

VII

The Journey to the Mantannes

LA VÉRENDRYE had three objects in going to Fort Maurepas: first, to obtain additional information about the geography
of the western country for the purpose of visiting the Mantannes; second, to thwart, if possible, any hostile moves against
the Sioux; and third, to discuss the establishment of additional
posts in the territory of the Crees and Assiniboins. While waiting
for the Indians to assemble at a council he had called for March
4, 1737, he applied himself to the first object. He began by making inquiries concerning the geographical features of Lake
Winnipeg, and of an adjacent body of water called the brother
of Lake Winnipeg (Winnipegosis), which was erroneously supposed to connect with it by a channel fifteen or twenty leagues
in length, flanked by wooded mountains. Then he persuaded
the chiefs to draw him a map of the western regions, which he
presently sent to Beauharnois who, in turn, forwarded it to the
Minister, attached to his letter of October 14, 1737. From this

map, and from the remarks the chiefs made in elucidating it, La Vérendrye learned that the river of the Mantannes did not run directly westward, but rather in a southwesterly direction to a sea which, he believed, was the Pacific Ocean, not the gulf-like Western Sea. This stream, as it turned out later, was actually the Missouri, which, during its meandering course, turns south-westward near the Mantanne settlement. He was also told that a nation of white men dwelt at the river's mouth, men who lived in towns and forts and were served by a black-robed clergy. The distance from Fort Maurepas to these people was said to be only 150 leagues.

As we scan La Vérendrye's commentaries on the map, we find him expressing for the first time an interest in the possibilities of using the Saskatchewan River as a route to the Far West. This river, he was told, rose in a lake situated in a height of land (possibly the Rocky Mountains), and from this height there flowed to the west-southwest another stream emptying into the Western Sea. The Cree brave who had drawn the map told him of having gone a five days' journey beyond the height of land "going down the river, which they call the River of the West," to a country of strange fruits and trees. Farther down, at a distance of three hundred leagues from the height, one came to a sea on whose shores white men lived in walled towns, though unlike the others previously mentioned, they had "no knowledge of fire-arms or prayer"—at least so the savage was told. La Vérendrye put this information away in his mind to be used in case the route through the Mantannes proved a blind lead. He did, however, send two families of Indians to the northern regions to procure specimens of iron, said to be found there, and to bring them to Fort Maurepas.

The council which opened on March 4 was well attended by the Crees and Assiniboins.[1] Owing to extreme cold the meet-

---

[1] For account of events up to Aug. 1737, see La Vérendrye's Journal of 1736–1737, *J. & L.*, pp. 249–262.

ings were held indoors. After the usual amenities and presents
had been exchanged, a Cree chief took the floor as the first
speaker. He reminded the commander of his promise to found
a post at the northern end of Lake Winnipeg near the source of
the Nelson River and not far from the mouth of the Saskatchewan, headquarters of the trade in beaver, marten, and lynx furs.
After him the Assiniboin spokesman made his address. He too
reminded La Vérendrye of a promise he had made to move Fort
Maurepas up the Red River to its junction with the Assiniboine,
a more convenient trading place for his tribe; [2] and in order
to show his appreciation he offered to help build the new post,
promising to found a village in its neighborhood where some
of his people would live permanently. All this was good, con-
structive planning, greatly to La Vérendrye's taste; but the
chiefs marred it all by announcing their intention to meet with
La Colle and La Mikouenne in a few weeks to form still another
war party against the Sioux.

The following day, when the chiefs were assembled for their
answer, the commander, who felt his position weak, since his
supply of merchandise was low, strove to regain their confidence
by a generous display of gifts and by impressing them with the
awful grandeur of his sovereign, King Louis; for he felt obliged
at all costs to prevent them from trading with the English. For
this purpose he drew a splendid word picture of the military
victories of his King in the War of the Polish Succession, then
raging in Europe; and he also spoke of the King's resources, his
mighty armies and his power, in a manner to make the British
king appear a monarch of secondary importance. He then transmitted the governor's orders to the chiefs, pointing out the favors shown them in the past by the Father, although his other
Indian children were legion, and assuring them that the Father
would never abandon his flock if they proved faithful to him.
And now coming down to more practical matters, he urged them

2 This is the first mention we have of such a promise.

to apply themselves diligently to the hunt, so that they might have enough beaver to satisfy the French and thus promote good understanding. In compliance with a request made by the Crees he detailed Louis-Joseph to remain at Fort Maurepas and lead them to St. Charles in the spring. At this point La Vérendrye asked the Assiniboins what their plans were for the summer, and on learning that they expected to visit the Mantannes, after a brief campaign against the Sioux, he gave them a present and a message from the governor to be delivered to this tribe. In this message Beauharnois expressed a wish to establish commercial relations with the Mantannes, and for this reason he invited them to come in the autumn to the mouth of the Assiniboine River where the French would presently erect a fort. They were to bring with them horses, Indian corn, beans, and iron, especially the iron which was of the color of the sun, and also such curiosities as "stones which shine in the dark." These curiosities La Vérendrye planned to have brought to Fort Maurepas, where Louis-Joseph would take charge of them and forward them to Michilimackinac, where they would be sent to Quebec for the governor's benefit.

As the meeting was about to break up, the Indians offered guides to La Vérendrye for a dash to the Mantanne settlements. The distance from Fort Maurepas to the Mantannes was reported to be, as we have said, 150 leagues. With the goal so near, the commander was eager to start, confident that he could reach it before the end of spring. But here, strange to say, he struck an unexpected snag, an obstacle difficult to explain: his own men were afraid to accompany him! To make matters worse, Pierre, whom he had ordered to start for the Mantannes the previous autumn, could not get the canoes he believed were necessary for the voyage. Thus the plans so carefully laid at the beginning of the year came to naught before the journey had even begun, and the explorer was once again obliged to admit defeat.

All this, of course, as we shall see, put him in a bad light with the officials at home. He tells us that his men were afraid, and perhaps they were; but this must have seemed to the governor a strange statement to make about experienced *coureurs* and *voyageurs* whose lives were spent in the wilderness among savages, in places far remote from civilization. These men were inured to hardship and danger, they had followed their leader farther westward than any white man, so far as we know, had ever gone before; yet they were afraid. Such an excuse did the explorer much harm in the eyes of the Minister and to a certain extent in those of the governor too. Nor can one blame them if they felt suspicious about the whole business. They had long been awaiting the day when their man would strike out for the Western Sea, and thus far had been met with nothing but postponements. And now, when at long last a favorable opportunity presented itself, only to be passed up for such a seemingly trivial reason, they must have been, to put it mildly, greatly discouraged. One cannot honestly blame them if they began to suspect that their agent was more interested in furs than in exploration. As for La Vérendrye, he felt ashamed to tell the chiefs the real reason for declining their offer, so he put them off by pleading the lateness of the season—though it was then early spring—and wound up by expressing his intention of returning to Fort St. Charles.

The conference now disbanded. In his farewell speech the Assiniboin chief thus addressed the commander: "My father take courage: you are going to see our Father at Montreal: be careful to assure him we are his veritable children and that we beg him not abandon us." Then turning to La Mikouenne's brother, who had been delegated to accompany La Vérendrye, he continued:

And you, my brother, you will have the happiness of seeing our Father: see that you acquaint him with our dispositions regarding him, and represent to him our needs, in order that he may give us

help by sending Frenchmen to us every year; and give close attention to all you shall see and hear so as to render us a faithful account of everything.

La Vérendrye left on March 11, taking the garrison with him, as
the clerks at St. Charles needed the services of the five men who
had spent the winter at Fort Maurepas with Louis-Joseph. The
party reached its destination on the thirtieth.

Toward the end of May a detachment of Crees arrived at St.
Charles with the doleful news that their fellow tribesmen at
Maurepas had died of smallpox, a disease brought there by the
savages who had gone to Hudson Bay. Needless to say, La
Vérendrye pointed to this as evidence of the punishment meted
out by an all-seeing Providence to those who had been faithless
to the French. A day or two later Louis-Joseph came to confirm
the news, adding that the Indians had thrown away their furs
under the impression that they were infectious. Fortunately, he
had some remedies with him, and was able to check the progress
of the disease in the lodges where he was living.

Failure even to start for the Mantanne country had caused
La Vérendrye to feel that he had better make his excuses to
the governor in person and justify himself, if possible, by a
frank explanation. He therefore made preparations to return
to Montreal. La Colle sent word that his daughter's death
would prevent him from joining the party, but he assured the
commander that the road would be kept open, as he was leading three hundred men against the Sioux; thus any repetition
of the massacre would be prevented.

On May 29 La Vérendrye had a final interview with the chiefs,
presenting them with powder and shot and urging them to
treat the French who remained at the fort in a friendly
manner. He also requested them to keep the road open to Lake
Superior, advising them at the same time to maintain peaceful
relations with his sons and to gather in the wild rice for the
large company he would bring with him from Michilimackinac

the following year. Five days later he held a review at which he formally turned over the command to Louis-Joseph; then selecting an escort of eleven men, including La Mikouenne's brother, he set forth on his journey to Montreal. On reaching Rainy Lake, he stopped at Fort St. Pierre to make some much-needed repairs—Bourassa had evidently paid no attention to his orders—then after a voyage of three weeks he reached Kaministikwia. Here he gave orders to send a goodly supply of merchandise to the upper country, and sixty leagues beyond the post he found the canoes carrying the wherewithal to fulfill these orders. It was a convoy organized at Montreal by the indefatigable Jean-Baptiste Legras, financial backer of more than one expedition.[3] At Michilimackinac, where he arrived on July 22, he found Charles de Lamarque, to whom he "imparted all necessary information respecting trade with the savages, advising him to go himself and re-establish the business of the company, which only became unprosperous through the fault of those who managed it." At the end of two weeks he left for Montreal.

From Montreal, La Vérendrye continued on to Quebec, where the governor was in residence. The welcome he received from that official was not what he had hoped for, though he may have expected it. Even that loyal friend was beginning to feel somewhat irritated by his failure to accomplish something definite. Six years had now elapsed since the explorer first started west, and he had gone no farther than Lake Winnipeg. Being in close touch with La Vérendrye—that is, in closer touch than the government at Versailles—and knowing something of his difficulties, both geographical and financial, Beauharnois sympathized with him, and the censure he meted out may have been inspired more by a desire to appease the government than to criticize his protégé, for he had just received word from Maurepas of the government's displeasure. In his letter the

[3] R.A.Q., 1929–1930, pp. 340–342.

Minister, after expressing perfunctory regrets over the disaster of the previous year, proceeded in this manner:

However that may be, all that has come to my knowledge as to the causes of that misadventure [i.e., the massacre] confirms the suspicion I have always entertained, and which I have not concealed from you, that the beaver trade had more to do than anything else with the Sieur de la Vérendrye's Western Sea expedition.[4]

The governor replied to Maurepas' strictures in a letter enclosing La Vérendrye's journal and map as evidence of the difficulties that had beset the explorer:

I blamed him, Monseigneur, severely for having left his post [wrote the governor], and let him know that that was not the right way to succeed in his enterprise . . . He brought with him a savage chief to speak to me in the name of three tribes (Monsoni, Cree, and Assiniboin), and to learn my intentions in regard to the attack made by the Sioux last year upon the French. My reply, Monseigneur, will be that I shall revenge myself in the first place, that I shall find a suitable occasion for doing so, and that meantime they were free to pursue the war that they had always been waging with them. I remember, Monseigneur, that you did me the honor to inform me that you thought that the views of the Sieur de la Vérendrye were to hunt for beaver, not to discover the Western Sea. Were it not for the blow which fell upon him and the debts which I know him to have incurred I might have a similar suspicion; but I know, Monseigneur, that he ran completely out of provisions and that he had no one to accompany him on the journey; besides he did not know whether any Frenchmen would be sent back to these posts; he thought that hired men might be sent to get the furs and bring back the goods. I warned him that if he came down [again] he should not return, and he promised me that next year he would go as far as 150 leagues [to] the country of the Ouachipouennes [Mantannes] who at present are called Koüathéattes, that he will reach them in the winter, and in the month of September, 1739. I shall

[4] Maurepas to Beauharnois, April 22, 1737, *J. & L.*, pp. 269–270.

receive an account of his journey. I told him that if he did not keep his word to me I would call him back.[5]

This threat, as we shall see, had a salutary effect in spurring La Vérendrye into action. On his next attempt his men seemed to have completely lost their fear of venturing beyond the Red River.

La Vérendrye sought to justify his conduct by writing personally to Maurepas. His letter is a plea, urging his misfortunes as the sole cause of his lack of success. He pointed out that he was handicapped in his work of exploration, not only by a shortage of manpower, due to the massacre, but by a paucity of goods which he needed for trading with any new tribes he might encounter. This latter situation arose from the necessity of first supplying Fort St. Charles with sufficient merchandise, and he had found the post almost destitute when he returned there. To make up for this he now promised to devote his energies to keeping the tribes at peace that he might have an "unimpeded route" to the west. He also assured the Minister that he was making no profit from the fur business; on the contrary, he had used up a considerable part of his own means in financing the undertaking. In closing his letter he reminded the Minister of the wounds he had received in his Majesty's service, and he requested, somewhat inopportunely, it is true, the command of a company—there being several vacancies at that moment—and the Cross of St. Louis.[6]

These letters and journals of the commander appear to have made little impression on the Minister of Marine, at least not enough to induce him to take a more lenient view of the case. He expressed surprise that so little progress had been made in the work of discovery since the explorer made his last report; and here, it must be admitted, he had a point. All that had occurred thus far had made him suspicious of La Vérendrye's

[5] Beauharnois to Maurepas, Oct. 17, 1737, *ibid.*, pp. 271–273.
[6] La Vérendrye to Maurepas, Oct. 1, 1737, *ibid.*, pp. 266–269.

zeal, and he bluntly attacked him for leaving his post instead of pushing on ahead. Then, dismissing this as water already over the dam, he expressed a rather dubious hope that the commander would soon be able to allay the suspicions, to which his conduct had given rise, by doing better in the future.[7]

There is no doubt that La Vérendrye at this time was in bad odor with the government at home. The governor sensed this; and though he stood loyally by his protégé he seems to have agreed in part with the opinion of the Ministry. He frankly told Maurepas that he was dissatisfied with the explorer's achievements up to date and berated him for not doing more. He even added that he could easily question his sincerity and believe the accusations charging him with being more interested in beaver than in discovery, were it not for the disaster which had overtaken his men and the continual shortage of supplies that dogged his footsteps. Then, in order to forestall further criticism, he pointed out that it might be difficult for the traders at Montreal to find men who would care to venture into the Northwest when they heard of the massacre at Lake of the Woods.

These reasons taken together [wrote the governor] seem to me to form a sufficient justification for not blaming him to the extent that I might have done, and in view of his promise to pursue the exploration with all the energy of which he was capable after his return to the fort, I accepted his excuses for the moment but gave him to understand not only that I would bring him back, but that he would lose my confidence entirely if he did not promptly accomplish what was expected of his zeal.[8]

This critical attitude toward La Vérendrye and his accomplishments, now current in government circles, was unfair to the explorer. Governor Beauharnois in his own mind may not have been so severe as his correspondence seems to indicate; he may have been trying to mollify the Minister by agreeing with

[7] Maurepas to Beauharnois, April 23, 1738, *ibid.*, pp. 275–278.
[8] Beauharnois to Maurepas Oct. 1, 1738, *ibid.*, pp. 279–289.

him to a certain extent and thus keep him from dropping the explorer altogether. It was, no doubt, impossible for Maurepas, or anyone else in France, to understand fully the tremendous obstacles that blocked the route to the Western Sea. All he could grasp was that La Vérendrye had as yet made no serious attempt to reach the Mantannes, though the Assiniboins had offered to lead him thither. He also failed to take into consideration the handicap imposed upon him by the government's refusal to underwrite the expedition, thus compelling him to finance himself by trade. This burden was indeed a heavy one, for it compelled him to devote much of his time to forming alliances with the Indians in order to draw them away from Hudson Bay. Such a work could not be accomplished in a few months once and for all; it was a problem that was constantly renewing itself; for when the Indians were drawn away from the English they had to be kept satisfied with their new trade relations by an abundant supply of merchandise. Whatever advantages La Vérendrye had derived from his previous visit to Montreal, such as farming out his posts, had been more than offset by the deaths of Jean-Baptiste and La Jemeraye and the loss of a large number of men, to say nothing of the constant shortage of supplies. The probable reason for the lack of sympathy from which he suffered at Maurepas' hands was due to the friction which had existed for years between the *coureurs* and the government, as is shown by the regulations, licenses, *congés,* and amnesties that were constantly being promulgated. The very fact that a man at the head of a large band of followers was penetrating into an unknown country rich in beaver was enough to make the officials suspect that something was afoot. La Vérendrye, in short, was being punished for the sins of his class.

The governor by this time had decided on the course to follow in dealing with the Sioux. As a man, he wished them punished; but as a statesman he realized that such action would lead to a prolonged war which might indeed put an end to French enterprise in the Northwest. He therefore impressed upon La Vérendrye the necessity of maintaining peace and ordered him to work toward a general reconciliation among the various tribes; and it was well that he did so, for shortly after the explorer's departure he received word from Fort St. Charles that eight hundred Assiniboins had gone in April (1738) to make war on the Sioux with the expectation of being joined by the Crees and Monsonis. Fortunately for the French, another epidemic of smallpox caused the warriors to suspend hostilities.[9]

La Vérendrye now made ready for his dash to the country of the Mantannes. With Beauharnois' threats still ringing in his ears, he realized that nothing must hinder him this time, as this might well be his last chance. One more failure and the governor would recall him. His principal immediate problem, he knew, was to maintain peace among the tribes. If he failed, there could be no journey to the Mantannes: he might even be obliged to abandon his posts. To avoid such a catastrophe, he determined to arrive at St. Charles with a generous supply of merchandise, enough to buy the loyalty of the Indians, at least for the time being. For this reason he now signed certain contracts, contracts destined to cause him no end of trouble later on. One was with his nephew, François-Marie Soumande de Lorme, for 6,693 *livres'* worth of goods to be paid for in August of the following year; another with a man named Louis d'Ailleboust, Sieur de Coulonges, for 2,787 *livres* of goods.[10] In recruiting his men he sought to forestall the trouble of the previous year, when the *voyageurs* had refused to follow him westward from Fort Maurepas, by enlisting men to go to Fort La Reine. This post had not yet been founded, but he expected to build it —and he presently did—far out in the Assiniboin lands.[11]

With these supplies loaded in his canoes, La Vérendrye left

[9] *Ibid.*   [10] Ordinance, June 12, 1739, *ibid.*, pp. 515–520.
[11] *R.A.Q., 1929–1930*, pp. 354–363.

Montreal on June 18, 1738 and, after an uneventful voyage, reached Michilimackinac, where he found the Sieur de Lamarque awaiting him.[12] This enterprising *voyageur* had carried out the commander's instructions, given him the previous year, to supply the western posts, and was now back at Michilimackinac for further orders. Pleased with the man's ability, La Vérendrye engaged him as lieutenant for the coming expedition to the Mantannes. For the present he was to remain at Michilimackinac to collect supplies, while the commander continued on his way to Lake of the Woods, where Lamarque was to rejoin him;[13] but circumstances were such that he did not see the *voyageur* again until he was well up the Assiniboine River. On July 20 he left the station for Lake Superior, his party of twenty-two men divided among six canoes. On reaching the lake, he went immediately to the Pays Plat (the Flat Country), a small region at the entrance to Nipigon Bay, so called because of the shallow water and low terrain of the neighborhood.[14] His reason for thus going out of his way was to investigate a report that the savages dwelling there had all gone to the Sioux country. If they had, it was a good indication that mischief was brewing.

On reaching the Pays Plat, the explorer found to his chagrin that the report was only too true; the place was deserted, save for a few old men and youths. Calling them together, he attempted to show them the disloyalty of their fellow tribesmen's action, so contrary to the promises of the previous year. Then he told them he was bringing a message from the governor bidding them all to remain at peace. To his intense surprise he was informed by the chief that the war parties were the work of a French trader named Paul Leriger de la Plante, known to the

[12] For the narrative of La Vérendrye's journey to the Mantannes see his Journal of 1738–1739, in *J. & L.*, pp. 290–361.

[13] Report of La Vérendrye, 1736–1737, *ibid.*, pp. 261–262; Journal of same, *ibid.*, pp. 297–298. The journal of 1737–1738 is missing.

[14] Henry, *op. cit.*, p. 232.

Indians as "the Canard," who by means of presents had seduced the warriors; only those now before him had been able to resist this man's blandishments, for they alone had respected their promise to the French commander. La Vérendrye thanked them for their loyalty and proceeded on his way to Kaministikwia. Here the caravan spent the night. Next day he departed after giving the local commander a copy of the governor's orders, which he was to hand Lamarque when the latter came to the post on his way to Lake of the Woods. This seems rather strange, for La Vérendrye had ample time at Michilimackinac to give Lamarque the governor's orders, but his journal merely tells us that he did so without giving any reason for his so doing or any explanation as to what these orders were.

Proceeding thence to Rainy Lake by way of the Grand Portage, La Vérendrye encamped near a tribe of Monsonis who lived in the neighborhood. These Indians were eager to learn the Father's will and to listen to a description of the civilized world as seen by La Mikouenne's brother. The commander therefore called the tribe together, made them a present in the governor's name, and read the message prepared for their instruction. The substance of this message, which was to be given to all nations friendly to the French, was general in tone, merely ordering them to keep peace among themselves and refrain from making war on their traditional enemies, so that the French would always find the road to the west open to them. Beauharnois expressed the kindliest feelings for the savages and pointed out the duty of obedience they owed him, thanks to their oath of allegiance. We have no record of what La Mikouenne's brother told his fellows. It was, no doubt, a verbose and flowery account of his impressions, for the chief in his reply showed considerable enthusiasm at the governor's attitude toward his people and agreed to carry the message to his fellow tribesmen.

The party proceeded on its way and reached Fort St. Charles on August 31. La Vérendrye immediately sent word to the chiefs living near by to meet him as soon as possible. They came in haste, his old friends La Colle and La Mikouenne and a third called Le Chenail. After the group had listened to the governor's instructions, La Mikouenne's brother—unfortunately we do not know his name—spoke of the governor's friendliness and loudly sang his praises; in fact, so great was his enthusiasm that La Vérendrye used him on every possible occasion as a sort of testimonial for Beauharnois. La Colle then brought up the subject of the massacre, ever a sore point with the Indians, for they believed with a persistence worthy of a better cause that it could be used as a telling argument to secure permission to make war on the Sioux. He wisely qualified his demands, however, by admitting that it was not for such as they to decide what should be done, for they were the Father's obedient children; but they did hope that sometime, somewhere, somehow, they would be permitted to exact vengeance. After this, La Mikouenne took the floor and asked La Vérendrye to tell the governor, when he should meet him again, how much he (La Mikouenne) appreciated the kindness shown his brother, and to assure him he would always be loyal to the French. Then, referring to the proposed journey to the Mantannes, he begged the commander not to abandon his people, but at least to leave one of his sons with them. In exchange for this favor La Mikouenne's brother and nephew would join the French party.

In order to please the savages, and also to take advantage of the opportunity of placing someone among them who would exert a restraining influence on their warlike propensities and to keep them from trading with the English, La Vérendrye detailed Pierre to remain at Fort St. Charles while he took François and Louis-Joseph with him. This done, he made his arrangements to depart; but, as he wished to give Lamarque time to join him, he put off leaving until September 11. On that day he gave up hope of seeing the trader and left for Fort Maurepas, which he reached on the twenty-second. This station had evidently been reoccupied since the smallpox epidemic, for he found there a garrison of fourteen men under one Louis d'Amours de Louvière. Here he paused but overnight, just long enough to publish the governor's orders, examine the military equipment, and select a detail from the garrison. This time no one exhibited any fear of venturing into the western country, a fact which makes one very suspicious of the excuse given the year before. From Fort Maurepas the party moved up the Red River to the mouth of the Assiniboine, where they found a detachment of Crees awaiting them with a supply of meat.

Encamping here, La Vérendrye gathered the savages into a conference, for he did not wish to proceed into the distant territory of the Assiniboins without making sure that neither they nor the Crees would rouse the terrible Sioux by launching an attack on them during his absence. He also took advantage of the occasion to accuse the Crees of trading with the English. In answering La Vérendrye, the chief stoutly maintained that neither he nor his people had any intention of harming the French and loudly branded as liars those who accused him of such treachery. But in regard to the Hudson Bay business he admitted guilt, pointing out, in palliation of the offense, that it had occurred only when the French had failed to supply his people with merchandise.

At this point La Mikouenne's brother stepped into the breach and smoothed matters over by telling of the friendly reception given him by Governor Beauharnois. So interesting was his story that the Cree chief was moved to express his thanks to La Vérendrye:

My father, we thank you for having spoken well in our behalf down there to our Father. We know today that he has pity on us in sending Frenchmen into our country to bring us the things we need. We will keep quiet as he desires, and let the Sioux do the same. Our

heart is still sore on account of your son, who was the first to come
and build a fort on our land; [15] we loved him deeply. I have already
been once at war to avenge him. I only destroyed ten cabins [of the
Sioux],[16] which is not enough to content us; but now our Father
orders us to keep quiet and we shall do so.

He then asked the French where they were planning to go and,
on being informed, told them that low water in the Assiniboine
would make it impossible for them to use their canoes. He described the Assiniboins of the West as a people of low intelligence—sectional bias, no doubt—who would have nothing to
offer the French, since they did not even know how to kill the
beaver. La Vérendrye did not bother to contradict; instead, he
explained carefully his plans to visit the strange white people
he had heard so much about, and also, as a minor issue, to bring
the western Assiniboins within the number of the Great Father's
children. The Indian dismissed the matter with a shrug of the
shoulders, hinting that the French would probably return with
empty canoes and expressing the hope that they would be able
to knock some sense into the heads of these backward aborigines.

La Vérendrye took leave of the Crees on September 26, leaving with them La Mikouenne's now celebrated brother, after
having obtained from this worthy the assurance that he would
do his best to prevent the Crees from trading with the English
and would rejoin the expedition in a few days. The Assiniboine
River, now explored by the French for the first time, proved
low in water and difficult to navigate. It is a wide, meandering
stream with a strong current, broken here and there by sand
bars. Magnificent trees line its banks, while the prairies extend
from it, flat and uninteresting, as far as the eye can see. La
Vérendrye found a shorter route for himself by marching overland, leaving what he calls the useless people to follow by river

[15] Evidently refers to Jean-Baptiste. It was Pierre, however, who laid
out the site for the fort and Cartier who built it.

[16] Just when this was done is not clear.

with the canoes, for the windings of the channel made the water route long and tedious. Presently he met detachments of the Assiniboins who had come to meet him, warned by wandering savages who had got wind of the expedition when they were at Fort Maurepas. On the evening of October 2, as he was preparing to turn in for the night, the Indians told him he could

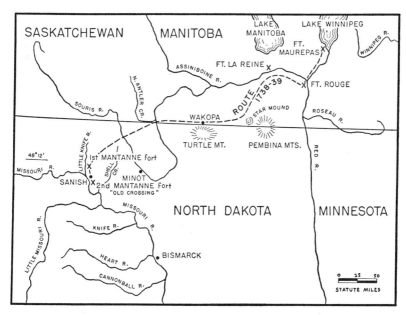

Pierre de la Vérendrye's route to the Mantannes, 1738–1739.

ascend the river no farther. He was then encamped at the portage to Lake Manitoba, where the modern town of Portage la Prairie now stands; and it was here the overland route to the Mantannes began. Since he could not continue his journey by water without injuring his canoes, and since there was neither gum nor roots at hand to repair them, he decided to halt and erect a post which would in time replace, so he believed, Fort St. Charles as his headquarters in the Northwest. This post he named La Reine. According to his rough calculations the site was about sixty leagues from the mouth of the Assiniboine by water, or thirty to forty as the crow flies. The place was well chosen, for the portage was the one used by the Assiniboins in going to Hudson Bay, and it was not far from the road to the Mantannes. A fort erected here would be well situated to serve Indians who would never go to Fort Maurepas.[17]

Work on Fort La Reine was begun and pushed forward with amazing speed, while La Vérendrye was busy establishing his position with the Indians. He gave them the usual assortment of presents: powder, ball, tobacco, axes, knives, and tools, articles they had never before possessed. All this was given them for nothing in return, except that they should obey the Great Father's orders, a condition they readily accepted and probably did not understand.

While thus engaged, the commander was cheered by the arrival of Lamarque and his brother, Jean-Marie Nolan, with a small party. He greeted the long-awaited trader warmly. Great was his joy, for now he was able to pursue his journey in full force. He inquired about the conditions at Fort St. Charles and Fort Maurepas, and Lamarque informed him that he had left eight men with two traders at the former, and had then hurried on to join his chief in the dash to the Mantannes. When passing by Fort Maurepas, he had paused long enough to bring De Louvière to the mouth of the Assiniboine, where he erected a fort on the southern bank of that stream, a post he called Fort Rouge. Thus was the promise made by La Vérendrye the previous year to the Assiniboins now fulfilled. At this point

---

[17] A. S. Morton, *A History of the Canadian West to 1870–71* (London, New York, 1939), says on page 190 that Fort La Reine was not originally built at Portage la Prairie but twenty miles east of this town on a spot two miles southeast of Poplar Point Station. A survey made for the Hudson's Bay Company in 1808 by Peter Fidler places it there, and Mr. Morton claims to have seen the remains of a post at this place in 1938. He believes that La Vérendrye moved the post from this place to Portage la Prairie a year after he founded it. There is no record, however, in his papers of any such change of site.

Lamarque offered to share the expenses of the coming expedition, but the commander would have none of it, saying that it was enough if he supplied a few men.

On October 16 the expedition was drawn up for review. A motley array of traders, soldiers, camp followers, and hunters, of Frenchmen and half-breeds, all trained to the call of arms and the ways of the forest, now made ready to start on the great quest for the mysterious people who dwelt on the banks of the still more mysterious River of the West. As they passed down the ranks, La Vérendrye and Lamarque selected the men best able to endure the rigors of the journey. Twenty men in all were taken from the group: ten from La Vérendrye's company and ten from Lamarque's followers. The commander also took with him his two sons, François and Louis-Joseph, while Lamarque was accompanied by his brother. A detachment of Indians was added to the force, making fifty-two persons in all. These men were generously equipped with powder, ball, tobacco, and miscellaneous articles. La Vérendrye took with him a leather bag, containing some valuables that later became a source of considerable trouble to him. This he entrusted to the wife of one of his guides, while his other personal effects were placed in charge of his servant and a native slave. Command of Fort La Reine during his absence was given to an intelligent sergeant named Alexis Sejourné, more popularly known as Sanschagrin, who was to hold the place with ten hired men and two soldiers. Two days later the expedition set out for the country of the Mantannes.

The work of exploration was from now on a succession of tedious marches over the prairies, of which La Vérendrye gives but a bare outline. The season by this time was well advanced beyond the enervating heat of mid-summer, but the monotonous humdrum of the march, a march lengthened by the whims of the Indian guide, who led the party on long detours, proved a severe trial to the explorer, anxious as he was to reach the River of the West.

Three days after leaving Fort La Reine, the travelers came
upon a village of Assiniboins numbering forty cabins. Their
chief asked the French to spend a day with him that he might
have the pleasure of a friendly visit. The request was granted
as a matter of course; after all, it was part of La Vérendrye's
program to make as many friends as possible among the savages. And so the two chieftains spent the day exchanging amenities, the Frenchman using his persuasive powers to enroll the
savage band under the aegis of the Great Father, telling their
leader he must now obey the mandates of the French governor
and presenting him with a few trinkets to cement the alliance.
For his part the chief promised to furnish the expedition with
fresh provisions when they were required.

That day the travelers reached Star Mound, a part of the Pembina Mountains near Snowflake, Manitoba, which La Vérendrye
refers to as the first mountain, distant about twenty-six leagues
from La Reine. Thus far he had been following an old trail used
by Indians going from the south to York Factory on Hudson
Bay. The course, according to La Vérendrye's compass, was
south by west.[18] From there to his second mountain was twenty-
four leagues, the course, west by north, bringing him to a butte
on the northern edge of Turtle Mountain.[19] La Vérendrye tells
us little of what happened during the first thirty days of the
march. It was, no doubt, a tiresome experience, and the tempers
of the explorers were not improved by the actions of the guide,
who led them on a zigzag course, so that they covered three or
four leagues for every two they made in a direct line. Nothing
La Vérendrye could say had any effect on the fellow. He halted
when there was no reason for it, marched when it suited him,
and subjected his employer to all sorts of conditions and delays,

[18] See Appendix B.
[19] We are following the route mapped out by Orin G. Libby in his
introduction to H. E. Haxo's "The Journal of La Vérendrye, 1738–39,"
North Dakota Historical Quarterly, VIII (1940–1941), 229–241.

while the latter fumed and fretted, unable to do anything about it.

On one occasion, after a brief excursion of his own, the guide returned bringing eight men from a village he had discovered some distance off. These men were sent by their chiefs to escort the French to the village encampment. The chiefs extended a hearty invitation to La Vérendrye and his men to visit them, saying they would gladly accompany him to the' Mantannes, as hostile Sioux were prowling about the neighborhood, making an escort desirable. There was nothing to do but accept the invitation with as good grace as possible, though it meant going some twenty leagues out of the way. The party proceeded in a general westerly direction and arrived at the place on November 18, where they were given a warm welcome. There is no information in La Vérendrye's narrative that gives us the site of this village, but it may have been at the junction of North Antler Creek and the Souris River where the remains of an earth-lodge village have been found.[20]

On reaching the settlement, La Vérendrye and his sons, together with the Nolan brothers, were ushered into the chief's wigwam, where everything was done for their comfort. Next day the French commander called the leaders to a meeting in the cabin assigned to him; and after the usual formalities received the Indians into the number of the governor's children, promising never to abandon them and proclaiming the Father's policy of maintaining peace among the nations. To seal the pact the Indians placed their hands on the commander's head, taking the governor as their Father and the French as their brothers. All this was accompanied with a loud wailing and weeping, which was supposed to indicate the importance they attached

[20] Libby, who is the only one to hazard a guess as to where this village might have been, places it at the junction of the North Antler with the Assiniboine, but this must be an error as the North Antler flows into the Souris (*ibid.*, p. 232).

to the business. When the ceremony was over the chief addressed La Vérendrye:

We thank you, my Father, for having taken the trouble to come to us. We are all going to accompany you to the Mantannes, and then conduct you back to your fort. We sent four men to notify them and those, who have just arrived, report that the Mantannes are greatly delighted at your coming amongst them and will come to meet you. We have sent four other young men to bring them to the spot we have marked out for them. We shall go there by easy marches, hunting by the way, in order to have fat when we arrive there to eat with their grain, which they always eat plain, having for the most part neither meat nor fat.

La Vérendrye was now beginning to grow impatient. It was already mid-November and there was little time to lose; yet so much had been lost by the shilly-shallying of the guide that the commander decided to pass the winter with the Mantannes instead of pushing on to the mysterious Western Sea or to wherever the River of the West might lead him. On the twentieth, therefore, the entire party, that is the French and the Assiniboins, set forth to cover the seventeen leagues separating them from the rendezvous. While on the march, the savages whetted the Frenchmen's curiosity by assuring them that the tribe they were about to visit were white men like themselves.

As the company trudged along, La Vérendrye and Lamarque walked side by side commenting on the disciplined way in which the Assiniboins conducted their march. The Indians were divided into three columns: the warriors forming the vanguard and rear guard, while the third group, comprising the old and physically incapacitated, marched in the middle division. If the skirmishers in front discovered a herd of buffalo, they raised a cry which was taken up by the rear guard, and presently the able-bodied braves dashed out to surround the animals and shoot them down. In this manner they killed their game, and each man took his share of the meat without stopping the march.[21] When the day's work was ended, the van marked out the encampment, to which the squaws at once repaired. There they proceeded to dress the meat and prepare the wigwams for the coming night.

The march was a leisurely one, too leisurely to suit the eager explorers, for it took them eight days to reach the Mantanne rendezvous from the Assiniboin village, a distance of only seventeen leagues. In the evening thirty Mantanne braves appeared, accompanied by the four Assiniboins who had been sent on ahead to arrange the meeting. La Vérendrye received the chief in his tent, and the two leaders, after greeting each other in the customary manner, exchanged gifts. Great was the explorer's surprise, not to say chagrin, when he saw the Mantannes to be, not white men like himself, but redskins like the Assiniboins, "being naked except for a garment of buffalo skin carelessly worn without any breechcloth." Where were the white men whose presence in this settlement had been so earnestly vouched for by the Indians, even by the Assiniboins now escorting the French to the Mantanne villages? Could this story have been a deliberate falsehood fabricated by the savages in order to lure the French far into their country, or were they honestly confused as to what was wanted of them when they concocted this strange tale? The more La Vérendrye pondered over the problem the stranger did it seem, until he finally dismissed it from his mind as one of those things one must expect in dealing with Indians; and he resolved never again to accept their stories without a large grain of salt.

The Mantanne chief now addressed the French leaders in the Assiniboin dialect, telling of the joy he felt at being able to welcome them, and expressing an ardent desire to be taken under the Father's wing—he had evidently been well coached —saying he wished to deal with the French and not with the English. He further invited the French to stay at his fort, the

[21] See Haxo's translation, *ibid.*, p. 254 and note.

nearest and the smallest of the Mantanne villages, but one well
supplied with food. The other forts, six in number, all belonged
to his nation, so he said, and were situated on the bank of a
great river, his being the only one on the prairie. To all this
La Vérendrye answered that he had come a long way to make
an alliance of friendship with the Mantannes and would hold
parley with them as soon as he reached the fort.

Meanwhile, the wily Indian had been sizing up the number
of Assiniboins accompanying the French, for it was an old Mantanne custom to feed gratis all who came to them, selling only
the food which their visitors took away and did not consume on
the spot. This Assiniboin army, he quickly realized, was large
enough to make a considerable inroad on his stores. He therefore resorted to a trick to rid himself of so many unwelcome
guests and keep with him only the French and a small number
of their savage companions. The Assiniboins, from what it
seems, were, despite their robust appearance, rather afraid of
the warlike Sioux; and so the Mantanne, in welcoming his
guests, told them they could not have arrived at a better time,
as he was expecting an attack by these savages, and was greatly
pleased to have so valiant a nation to fight by his side in the
coming hostilities. But the scheme missed fire, for when La
Vérendrye, who was not averse to seizing such a good excuse
for exacting the vengeance he had so long desired, expressed
pleasure at the prospect, the Assiniboins were shamed into remaining with him. The keynote speech was made, while the Assiniboins were wavering, by one of their chiefs, who said:

Don't think that our Father is a coward; I know him better than
you do; I have been with him ever since he left his fort, and don't
you imagine that the Sioux are able to frighten him or any of his
men. What will he think of us? He has lengthened his journey in
order to join us, in accordance with our request, we undertaking to
accompany him to the Mantannes and then conduct him back to his
fort. He would be there [with the Mantannes] today if he had not

listened to us, and you would think of abandoning him and letting him go alone. That shall never be. If you are afraid of the Sioux let us leave our village here till we return, and let the men who are fit to march follow our Father.

This harangue carried the day, to the great disgust of the Mantanne leader.

It was now decided to speed up the rate of travel. A few men were left behind to protect the squaws, and the entire male contingent of six hundred souls, with a few women who were known as good walkers, started for the village of their prospective hosts. They broke camp on the last day of November, and three days later reached a spot seven leagues from the fort, where they pitched camp for the night. La Vérendrye does not tell us how much ground they covered during these three days, but it was probably five leagues a day. These fifteen leagues, added to the seventeen already covered and the seven still to go to the fort, would make the distance from the Assiniboin village to the first Mantanne fort about forty leagues all told. While preparing to turn in, La Vérendrye was informed that an Assiniboin had taken the bag from his slave, under pretense of relieving him of his burden, and had run off with it. The bag happened to contain a box which held his papers and other valuables, particularly certain things he had brought as presents for his hosts. Runners were immediately dispatched after the thief with orders to bring him or his loot to the Mantanne village where the commander could claim it. The fellow was quickly overtaken and compelled to disgorge; but the runners did not dare return to the Mantannes through fear of the Sioux, so they took the bag to their village with the intention of restoring it to its owner when he should pass that way on his return journey.

Next day, after an early start, the French arrived toward noon at a small river where a group of Mantannes, who had come to meet them, stood around a fire cooking their midday meal. It

was the advance guard or welcoming committee. After a brief
rest La Vérendrye ordered his company to fall in for the last
stage of the journey, a distance of a league and a half. He wished
on this, the final march, to make something in the way of a
military display and enter the Mantanne village in a manner
calculated to impress the natives with the importance of the
sovereign he represented. Jean-Marie Nolan was placed in front
of the detachment with one of the commander's sons at his
side, bearing aloft a flag on which were painted the arms of
France. Behind him the French soldiers and hunters were drawn
up in marching column, while La Vérendrye himself was carried on the shoulders of willing braves. When they arrived
within four *arpents* of the village the procession halted. The
commander gave the word to Louis-Joseph, who drew up his
men in line with the flag four paces in front of the main body,
while such of the Assiniboins as had muskets were placed in
a similar formation. La Vérendrye then took his place at the
head of his troops, but scarcely had he done so when a delegation issued from the village and came forward to greet him,
bringing with them, to his great astonishment, a pipe and two
collars he had sent them four or five years before. La Vérendrye
raised his hand and a salute of three volleys rang out over the
prairie. The order to march was now given; the men shouldered
their guns; and thus in a strictly military formation, with drums
beating and colors gaily flying, Pierre de la Vérendrye and his
followers marched triumphantly into the long-sought village
of the Mantannes on December 3, 1738, at four o'clock in the
afternoon.

Before continuing our narrative, we shall pause here in order
to give the reader an indication of the route taken by the French,
and the approximate location of the Mantanne fort, or fortified
village, if one prefers the term, at which they had just arrived.
Up to the time the explorers came to Fort La Reine, it is a simple
matter to trace their itinerary accurately, for they followed the

course of rivers easy enough to identify. From then on, however, when they left the waterways to strike out overland, the
route becomes uncertain, for the distances La Vérendrye gives
were estimated, not measured, and the compass courses are approximate at best. Several scholars have made elaborate and
painstaking analyses of the explorer's data in the hope of being
able to trace the route; but as they do not agree in their conclusions, and as a full estimate of the merits of each theory
would involve us in a too lengthy discussion, we shall content
ourselves with outlining the probable route followed by the
French on this their first journey to the Mantannes.[22] And this
involves, of course, locating the Mantanne settlements.

On leaving Fort La Reine, La Vérendrye proceeded, as we
have seen, south by west to Star Mound, then west by north to
his "second mountain," some projection of Turtle Mountain on
its northern side. Here he was obliged to leave the direct route
in order to humor his guide who took him to the Assiniboin
village, which was probably situated at the mouth of North
Antler Creek. He does not tell us what course he steered from
there to the Mantanne fort, but we get a hint of the general
direction from his statement that the course from La Reine to
the Mantannes was west-southwest, and, from the "second
mountain," southwest by west. The distance from La Reine
he estimated at 120 leagues. In point of time his meanderings
cost him a whole month; according to his report he spent forty-
six days on a journey he could have made in sixteen or twenty
at the most. We shall see farther on that the latitude of the
Mantanne fort was computed at 48° 12′ N., while La Vérendrye
placed it at about a league and a half from a small stream. Putting these two facts together we can safely conclude that it
was somewhere near the upper waters of either the Little Knife
River or Shell Creek, not far from the forty-eighth parallel and
about twenty miles from the modern town of Sanish.

[22] For full discussion of the route see Appendix C.

Who were the Mantanne Indians? It was for a long time the custom to identify them with the Mandans, a tribe living about one hundred miles southeast of Old Crossing, the place where, as we shall see, La Vérendrye's party first saw the Missouri River. This assumption was a natural one, owing to the similarity of the names—in fact, it is the same name differently spelled— yet a careful study of the explorer's itinerary and of the characteristics shown by the various tribes has led some scholars to believe that La Vérendrye's Mantannes were probably the tribe known variously as the Hidatsas, Gros Ventres, or Minnetarees. The question then naturally arises as to why the French were led to the Hidatsas when they were looking for the Mandans. To this there is no satisfactory answer. We may suggest, however, that the Mantannes, about whom the French had heard so much, were indeed the Mandans, but that the guide and the Assiniboins had no exact knowledge of where these people lived and had led the explorers, *faute de mieux*, to the Hidatsas. After all, the French were looking for a tribe living on the River of the West, i.e., the Missouri, and the Hidatsas filled the bill. We should also bear in mind the difficulties the French had in understanding these western Indians (witness the misinformation given them about the Mantannes being white men like themselves) in order to realize what opportunity there was for error.[23]

On entering the fort, La Vérendrye and his French followers were led to the chief's residence, a vast, commodious house built to hold large gatherings of people. A crowd of Indians, Mantannes as well as Assiniboins, surged into the building on the heels of the white men, until all available space in the reception hall was filled with a mass of curious savages, crowding and pushing each other in their efforts to get a glimpse of the newcomers. So great was the confusion that La Vérendrye was

[23] See Appendix D for a discussion of the probable identity of the Mantannes.

obliged to request the Indians to leave and give his men an opportunity to deposit their baggage in a place of safety. They withdrew promptly; but in doing so an enterprising brave carried off a package containing some presents the commander had brought to distribute among his savage hosts at the coming ceremony of welcome. The loss put him in an embarrassing position, especially as he had many valuables in the box, including 300 *livres* in cash, and he had already lost a bag containing some much-needed articles. To do him justice the chief was quite as much annoyed at this breach of hospitality as his visitors, and he immediately gave orders for a thorough search, with the result, as is usual in such cases, that the culprit could not be found.

The day after his arrival La Vérendrye addressed the Mantanne and Assiniboin chiefs. He first gave them a small amount of powder and ball, apologizing for the paucity of the gift—a somewhat unnecessary gesture since a Mantanne had already stolen some of the presents. This done, he informed his hosts of his intention of making a prolonged stay in order to undertake a thorough survey of the country. The Mantannes received this announcement with joy, and assured him they had ample provisions for the maintenance of his party. At this point the Assiniboin chieftain said that since he had brought the French thus far in safety it was time for him to depart with his people, but that he would come back to escort them home whenever they wished to leave. Unfortunately, he could not resist the temptation of paying his respects to the Mantannes for the way in which they had allowed the commander to be robbed; and he volunteered, if La Vérendrye wished it, to conduct a search which he prophesied would bring results. This was too much for the Mantannes. A chief quickly jumped to his feet with a retort:

Neither I nor my people have any part in the accusations you are making: I do not answer for the others; I feel sore enough about it.

I have made all inquiry in my power with the aid of my young men, and I have nothing to reproach myself with. Who knows that it was not an Assiniboin? There were men of both tribes in the crowd; you cannot answer for anything yourself.

At this point La Vérendrye thought it wise to intervene. He placed his hands on the heads of the Mantanne chiefs, formally enrolling them as children of the Great Father. This was received with shouts of joy, and further trouble was avoided. The meeting closed when La Vérendrye detailed four of his Canadians to return to Fort La Reine, and asked the Assiniboins to escort them thither.

The Assiniboins, however, were not yet quite ready to go, despite the statement made by their chief, though they had purchased all they could in the way of painted ox-robes, deerskins, ornamented furs and feathers, peltry and wrought girdles. They wished to enjoy the hospitality of the Mantannes for a while longer. Their hosts, it may be imagined, held very different views. They were willing, it is true, to entertain the northern Indians for a while as customers, since they (the Mantannes) were excellent craftsmen and had much to sell; and, furthermore, they had developed the practical as well as the artistic side of their trade and could cheat their guests out of all they possessed. But when they had milked these customers dry and saw their own provisions getting low, they realized quickly enough that something must be done to get rid of such unwelcome visitors. In casting about for a solution of the problem, they hit upon the idea of spreading the report that the Sioux were marching on them. The ruse succeeded this time, for the Assiniboins felt that they had done their duty when they had delivered the French to the Mantannes. Thus it was that on the morning of December 6 they decamped in great haste, fearing lest the road home should be blocked by these bold warriors; but before departing, their chief had the foresight to present La Vérendrye with five men to act as guides when the French should return to La Reine. This offer was most opportune, as the commander's only interpreter decided to follow the retreating Assiniboins, attracted by a young squaw who refused to remain with him among the Mantannes. The loss was a serious blow to the French. The man was a Cree who spoke the Assiniboin tongue, and as several Mantannes spoke that language and Louis-Joseph spoke Cree, conversation could, after a fashion, be relayed back and forth.

La Vérendrye had expected to acquire a thorough knowledge of the country and its inhabitants through the services of this interpreter and had therefore been in no hurry to make inquiries; and now the opportunity was gone. He did, however, in some manner or other, manage to extract a little information from his hosts. He learned, for instance, that on the banks of the famous River of the West there were five Mantanne settlements, each one larger than the one where he was staying. The nearest of these was a day's journey away. A day's march from the farthest were to be found the Panaux and Pananis tribes, allies of the Mantannes for a long time, but now at war with them. If the Panaux were really the Mandans, then the Pananis were probably the Arikaras, living near the modern city of Pierre, South Dakota.[24]

It was the people beyond the Pananis that really excited La Vérendrye's interest. He was told that the river farther down became so wide that one could not see across it, and that its waters were not drinkable. This, he believed, must be the sea or some other body of salt water. Here dwelt people who worked in iron, and, as La Vérendrye wisely observed, iron among Indians means any sort of metal. At any rate, these men were white and wore armor, in all probability a corselet and helmet, that made them impervious to arrows. They were armed with lances, sabers, and bright iron bucklers. They lived in houses built of stone. All this seemed to indicate the Spaniards on the

[24] *J. & L.*, p. 335n.

Gulf of Mexico or the French in Louisiana. It was a long distance to this country, so the Mantannes said; it took an entire summer to go there and back, even if the men traveled alone, unencumbered by squaws, children, and other impedimenta. At present they could not go there as the road was blocked by the Panaux. All this, though interesting enough as far as it went, gave La Vérendrye no clearer picture of the strange white people or any better indication of their whereabouts than he had gathered at Lake of the Woods. It was all very vague.

Having obtained all the information he could from his hosts, La Vérendrye determined to learn by proxy something of the great river he hoped would be found to hold a westerly course. He therefore sent Nolan, Louis-Joseph, and six Frenchmen, accompanied by Mantanne guides, to the nearest fort on the banks of the river. They left on December 6,[25] the same day the Assiniboins started off, with orders to stay overnight, if they were well received, and learn what they could of the great river, particularly its lower course. The journey was a short one, only a day's march to the river, and they were to return the following day.

After they had left, La Vérendrye and Lamarque improved their time by making a complete survey of the village. This, they found, consisted of 130 cabins. Its streets and squares, which all resembled each other, were unusually clean; its ramparts wide and level; while the entire place was surrounded by a palisade built on cross pieces mortised into posts fifteen feet apart. It stood on a hill in the open prairie, and was encircled for purposes of defense by a ditch fifteen feet deep and from fifteen to eighteen wide. To gain access to the fort one had to use a stair which could be removed in time of danger. The explorers did not consider these fortifications to be of typically Indian construction, judging from what they had seen of similar posts farther north; and the belief that they had discovered a

[25] The French text (*ibid.*, p. 338) says they left on the sixth, not six days after the departure of the Assiniboins, as the translation indicates.

different race of aborigines was strengthened by the appearance of the savages, whose complexion seemed to be a mixture of black and white instead of the usual color of the redskins. The men were for the most part big, strong, good-looking fellows with excellent features and affable dispositions. They went abroad naked save for a buffalo robe thrown carelessly around the body. Many women adopted this informal costume, adding to it a loin cloth to serve as girdle, over which some wore a sort of petticoat and some a jacket of soft buckskin. These people worked with great diligence; their huts, large and well kept, were separated into apartments by partitions. Nothing was left lying about the dwellings; personal property was stored in large bags attached to posts. The fort had many cellars used for the storage of grain, foods, fats, dressed robes, and bear skins, with which the settlement was well supplied; for these articles were used in the country as a medium of exchange. The Indians manu-factured all kinds of wicker work, an art in which they were highly skilled. They were also very hospitable, and as evidence of their hospitality, for they were valiant trenchermen, they brought La Vérendrye every day more than twenty dishes, to the great joy of Lamarque, who, less abstemious than his com-mander, never missed any feast given in honor of the French.

The party under Louis-Joseph had, meanwhile, journeyed to the fort on the banks of the great river. This fort, or village, was as large again as the one where La Vérendrye was staying, and was built on the same general plan, as indeed were all the Man-tanne settlements, so that, as the commander put it, "when you see one you see them all." Louis-Joseph, who had been in-structed to obtain all possible information about the river, now stationed himself on a high bank, from which point of vantage he could see downstream for a short distance, and taking a com-pass found that the river flowed southwest by south. To com-plicate matters, he was given to understand, by means of the Indian sign language, that farther down it swung to southwest

by west.[26] The place where he took his bearing was at Old Crossing, where the river takes a sharp turn to the southwest. Here
there are high bluffs that prevent the observer from seeing
farther down the river to where it swings back to its normal
southeasterly course.

Since Louis-Joseph and Nolan spent but one night in the
village, they had no time to make exhaustive investigations of
local topography, and they returned to La Vérendrye with news
that they had found a westward-flowing river. After all, what
could this river be other than the River of the West which the
French had heard so much about for so many years? This opinion was reinforced by the Indians' statement that lower down
along its banks were people like the French who made cloth
and engaged in warfare. So far everything seemed to dovetail
into the first account of the great river given by the Crees at
Fort St. Charles. Louis-Joseph and Nolan were back at the first
Mantanne village on the afternoon of the seventh.[27]

When La Vérendrye first came to the Mantanne village, he
planned to winter there in order to study the neighboring territory, and then, when spring came, to push on to the Western
Sea, if the distance was not too great and conditions were
favorable. But now the desertion of the interpreter and the loss
of the bag and box containing the presents, without which it
would be difficult to persuade the Indians to help them, caused
the French to change their plans and decide on an immediate
return to Fort La Reine. For this there were several reasons.
For one, the season was too far advanced for any more excur-

[26] Not that the Indians gave any such explicit compass bearing, but
La Vérendrye means that the savages said that it took a more westerly
direction.

[27] There seems to be some question about the day of their return. In
the *J. & L.* text the figure is given as "4," but Mr. Haxo has corrected it
to "7," and Mr. Burpee has accepted the correction. See L. J. Burpee,
"La Vérendrye's 1738-9 Journal," *Canadian Historical Review,* XXIII
(1942), 407.

sions that year. Then, they had no interpreter, nor was there any possibility of obtaining one; and to make matters worse they had barely enough gunpowder to last them through the winter, while in the spring there would be floods that would cause serious delays. There was also a shortage of goods wherewith to buy the services of guides, and without pay the savage would not move. All these reasons, it seemed, far outweighed the one argument against leaving, namely, that they were now entering the worst season of the year.

Having reached this decision, La Vérendrye determined to leave among the Mantannes two Frenchmen who would devote themselves to studying the local dialect and thus relieve the explorer from the need of relying on native interpreters. One of these men was to be left at the first village, as La Vérendrye called the one he had entered so triumphantly, the other in the village nearest to it. Lamarque offered his ablest follower, a fellow who, *mirabile dictu,* could read and write, while La Vérendrye nominated his own personal servant, described as a God-fearing man with an aptitude for languages. The commander promised to send for them sometime during the coming summer.

Preparations were now made for leaving at the earliest possible moment. The five Assiniboins who had accompanied the party from Fort La Reine were summoned. They were told by means of signs to start the next day with two Frenchmen and go to the Assiniboin village, the one the French had visited on the way down, and warn the inhabitants of the commander's coming, for he would follow in four days.

On December 8 the advance party set forth. Before they left, the Mantanne chief presented La Vérendrye and Lamarque with a supply of flour and expressed his regrets at their departure. La Vérendrye, in order to keep his good will—for he intended to return in the future—presented him with a few trifles, and gave him a flag and a lead plate to be kept as tokens of the annexation of the Mantanne territory to the Crown of France. This plate was, no doubt, similar to the one buried by the chevalier four years later at the mouth of the Bad River. It was given to the Mantannes to be treasured by them and handed down from father to son in the family of the chief.

The arrangements for leaving had been hurried forward with such rapidity that the French were ready to start before the day set for their leaving. Unfortunately, on the night of December 8, La Vérendrye became violently ill and was confined to his bed for three days. At the end of this time, though by no means well, he had so far recovered as to be able to travel. He accordingly took leave of the two Frenchmen who were to remain behind, giving them enough supplies to hire a guide, if they should find it necessary to return to Fort La Reine before Lamarque sent for them. The commander impressed upon them the importance of learning the Mantanne language in order to find out all they could about the strange white men who lived far down the river. They were to inquire particularly what sort of metal these people used, whether there were any mines in the neighborhood, what tribes lived farther up the river, and whether there was a height of land in the upper reaches of the stream.

On the thirteenth La Vérendrye and his companions set forth. The Mantannes' grief over their departure was great, and one chief led an escort to accompany his guests over the first league and a half of the road. When the two men parted, the commander dismissed the brave with a promise not to forget him, but to return in the near future, while the chief on his part volunteered to take care of the two Frenchmen left in the village and to lodge them in his own house. With such assurances of mutual esteem the explorer and the chieftain bade each other farewell.

The French headed straight for the Assiniboin village, where they arrived on the twenty-fourth, excessive cold having compelled them to travel slowly. Here La Vérendrye found his box untouched. He at once took the Assiniboins to task for the lies they had told him about the Mantannes being white people like himself. The savages denied having intentionally deceived him, saying that they had in mind a nation living farther down the river; and in this they were probably speaking truthfully. There is no reason to suppose that they had any object in deceiving the French, for they knew well enough that they would be found out as soon as La Vérendrye reached the Mantanne village. The entire business seems to have been the result of a misunderstanding due to linguistic difficulties.

At this point, one Assiniboin stepped forward and boasted of having killed one of these white men who was clad in iron and rode on horseback. Being asked what he had taken from the body as proof of his statement he said:

As I was about to cut off his head I saw some men on horseback who were intercepting my retreat, and I had much difficulty in escaping. I couldn't bring anything with me; I threw away everything I had even to my blanket, and ran away naked. What I tell you is true, and next spring I can get others who were with me to tell you the same. They are not here now, but you shall see them. What I have told you I repeat; you can't see the other side of the river; the water is salt; it is a mountainous country, with wide spaces between the mountains, consisting of fine land; a vast quantity of buffalo large and heavy, some white, others of different colors, many deer and roebuck. I have seen their cornfields; you don't see any women in them. I am telling you this frankly, and you will learn more about it by and by.

And with this La Vérendrye had to be satisfied.

After a rest of three days the French continued their journey, and on January 9, 1739, reached the hill they called the "first mountain." Here they remained for some time, as the commander was still quite ill; in fact, his condition became such as to induce Lamarque to hasten to Fort La Reine for assistance.

La Vérendrye, however, was able to follow him shortly afterward and met the party sent out to aid him when within thirty-
five leagues of the fort. On February 10 he reached La Reine in
a state of complete exhaustion.

VIII

Farthest West

THE illness from which La Vérendrye was suffering, though severe, was not too serious, and a fortnight's rest put him again on his feet. During his convalescence he learned from Lamarque that the garrison at Fort Maurepas was short of provisions, so he at once dispatched him—for he had volunteered to go—with orders to take charge of the post and see what could be done. Lamarque left on March 16, 1739, and wrote La Vérendrye a month later that the food situation there was little better than at Fort La Reine, for there were only a few Indians to bring in provisions. "Here we are," he said, "on the sixteenth of April, and we have not yet seen anybody. God knows what there is in store for us."

The situation at La Reine was also fast becoming alarming, for the forty-two persons gathered there were almost destitute of food. By chance a party of Indians came to the post, and La Vérendrye managed to persuade them to supply his wants

by organizing a moose hunt in the neighborhood. It also occurred to him that now was the opportunity to fulfill the request
so earnestly put forward by the Crees for a post on the northern
shores of Lake Winnipeg. Such an undertaking would relieve
Fort La Reine of a certain number of men, who could sustain
themselves by hunting and fishing in more abundant regions
while looking for a suitable site. Louis-Joseph was accordingly
dispatched on April 16 for this purpose.[1] He was given instructions to examine the various rivers flowing into the lake, especially the Saskatchewan, whither La Vérendrye proposed to
go himself at a later time, and to look diligently for the iron-
ore deposits the Indians said would be found there. He was also
to use his influence, whenever possible, to keep the Indians
from going to Hudson Bay and to urge them to wait for the
French traders who would soon be along with sufficient merchandise. Meanwhile, Lamarque at Fort Maurepas appears to
have been no more successful in his search for provisions than
his superior at Fort La Reine. After a brief stay at this post he
went to Lake Winnipeg in the hope of finding some Indians
who would help him, a move La Vérendrye considered prema-
ture, as he thought the savages might arrive at Maurepas at any
time.

The events of the next three years may well be said to form
the darkest period of La Vérendrye's career. For the present,
his trade with the Indians, which he had so laboriously built

[1] The original French text reads: *pour aler faire la decouverte du fort
du lac 8nipigon,* which we believe should be translated: "to go and make
the discovery [of a site for] the fort on Lake Winnipeg," a project La
Vérendrye long had in mind. The translation given in *J. & L.* (p. 357)
reads: "to go and explore the region near the fort on Lake Winnipeg";
and a footnote states that this refers to Fort Maurepas near the mouth
of the Winnipeg River, although this fort was situated on the Red River.
Moreover, in the Summary Journal (*ibid.,* p. 447) La Vérendrye plainly
says that he sent his son on this occasion to look for a suitable site on
Lake of the Prairies.

up, appeared on the verge of disintegrating, unless other posts could be erected farther north; and even this would be labor wasted if he had no merchandise to give the savages in exchange for their furs. Despite all his efforts to please the Indians, they still lacked confidence in his ability to deliver the goods, with the result that he soon received the unpleasant intelligence that the Assiniboins were building canoes on Lake Manitoba, just north of La Reine, for an excursion to Hudson Bay. To counteract this, he sent his sergeant, Sanschagrin, to bring the savages to the fort, where he might be able to dissuade them from their purpose. While awaiting the return of Sanschagrin, matters went from bad to worse. On May 10 the Sieur Nolan gave up in despair and asked permission to leave. La Vérendrye did his best to get him to stay, holding out hope of early relief, but when he saw him determined to quit he reluctantly let him go. Perhaps in his heart the commander knew the futility of attempting to hold the fort. A few Assiniboins arrived on the day of Nolan's departure with the welcome news that a large village was following them. The village presently came, did their trading, and promptly disappeared.

La Vérendrye now saw the uselessness of keeping his people any longer at La Reine. They had collected what furs they could, and there was little likelihood of any Indians coming there to trade, at least for the present. He himself would remain with a small detachment while the rest would carry the furs to Montreal. He would follow later. On the twenty-eighth a convoy set forth. Its leader—we do not know his name—took with him a letter to Governor Beauharnois, in which La Vérendrye expressed the hope that the following year he would be able to give an account of further discoveries and of interesting activities at the various posts. He also reported with much satisfaction the determination of his men to make some really worth-while discovery and gave an enthusiastic description of the good feeling toward the French that existed among the several Indian nations.[2] And with this he settled down to await the return of Louis-Joseph and the arrival of the two men from the Mantannes before setting out for Montreal. These two men, as it turned out, did not come until the end of September, when it was too late to undertake such a long journey.[3]

On September 29 the men appeared, led by an Assiniboin guide. They had done their work well, keeping eyes and ears open for anything they could learn about the mysterious white people; but the sum total of what they had gleaned added little to what was already known. Every year in the month of June, they said, there came to the Mantanne village a host of Indians, mounted on horses, who wished to trade their goods for grain, goods consisting chiefly of skins trimmed with feathers and porcupine quills. The previous spring some two hundred families had arrived and encamped on the farther bank of the Missouri. They were not all of the same tribe; they were rather a group of tribes, and comprised one contingent whose members claimed to come from the land of the setting sun, where there were white men living in forts built of brick and stone. These savages, on hearing of the presence of Frenchmen among the Mantannes, had expressed a desire to see them, and asked the Mantannes to bring them to their encampment. The French, of course, were as eager to see the Indians as the Indians were to see them; and so, crossing the river, they betook themselves to the hut of the chief, who was said to speak the white people's language. This language, whatever it was, was a strange one to the Frenchmen, tolerable proof that it was probably Spanish. In the course of the conversation, held in the Mantanne dialect, the chief told them, among other things, that the white people would be happy to see the French and would receive them in friendly fashion should they ever decide to pay

[2] Beauharnois to Maurepas, Oct. 6, 1739, *ibid.*, p. 364.
[3] Journal of 1738–1739, *ibid.*, pp. 356–360.

a visit. He also offered to act as guide. It was a long journey, he admitted, especially as it was necessary to make a long detour to avoid the Snakes,[4] a powerful nation which generally lived in fortified settlements or roamed about the countryside, spelling danger to defenseless travelers. They were brave—there was no question about this—and for this quality they were feared by their neighbors. They were also enemies of the white people. But the chief claimed that he could by-pass them by taking a circuitous route; and, as he had horses, he could get the French to their destination and back before cold weather set in. The offer, though a tempting one, was declined with thanks, for the Frenchmen felt they should get the commander's permission before venturing so far afield.

Once this point was settled, the explorers turned to the main purpose of their visit and asked for a description of the white people. The chief was willing to oblige, and he gave such a profusion of detail that his listeners were convinced that he spoke from personal observation. These people, he said, were white —of this he was certain—and the men wore beards like the French. They prayed from books to the Master of Life in houses built for that purpose. The chief himself seems to have been a Christian, since he often spoke the names of Jesus and Mary, and he showed the Frenchmen a cross suspended from his neck which had been placed there at his birth. The dwellings, he went on to say, were of brick with vegetable gardens on their roofs. The bedrooms were equipped with beds raised well above the floor and covered with fine cloths, while a large torch placed in the courtyard served to light the apartments in lieu of candles and tapers. For protection against possible attack the towns

[4] Snakes: a name applied to various tribes of Shoshonean stock, particularly those of eastern Oregon (F. W. Hodge, *Handbook of American Indians North of Mexico* [Washington, 1907–1910], II, 606). Charles DeLand identifies them with the Kiowas ("The Vérendrye Explorations and Discoveries," *South Dakota Historical Collections*, VII [1914] 269).

were surrounded by walls flanked by ditches filled with water and crossed by drawbridges. The garrisons were well supplied with cannons, guns, hatchets, and knives. As evidence of their craftsmanship the chief showed his guests a cotton shirt he had obtained from them embroidered along the edges with silk and colored wool. The Frenchmen would have gladly bought some of these articles, but unfortunately they had already used up all their goods trading with the Mantannes. The women of this nation, the chief went on to say, were of light complexion and fairly handsome, wearing their hair in coils and displaying earrings of brilliant stones and bracelets of some yellow metal. From the gestures he made the French concluded that the women played the harpsichord or base viol, perhaps both. The men, when on the warpath against the Snakes, which was fairly often, dressed in cuirasses of iron mesh and marched in column formation, not in the careless manner of the Indians. The towns of this mysterious people were near a lake, or similar body, whose nonpotable waters rose and fell like the tides. The country about the towns was mountainous, and from what the Indians said it was inhabited by a race of bearded black men who worked in iron. Before reaching this country one must pass through the land where these blacks dwelt. Who they were no one seemed to know.[5]

Here we have a fulsome account of the strange white nation of the Far West (or Far South), bits of information put together in pell-mell fashion in La Vérendrye's journal, that seem to agree in general with what the French had heard many times before. It told little that was new, but it served to revive the explorer's faith in the Assiniboins, a faith badly shaken by their false description of the Mantannes. Here was a stranger, a chief of a migrant tribe, who vouched for the existence of the white people. They must, then, exist; and to find them would be to find the Western Sea. At least La Vérendrye thought so.

[5] Journal of La Vérendrye, n.d., *J. & L.*, pp. 366–373.

The party which La Vérendrye had sent down to Montreal
on May 28 had meanwhile run into difficulties when they
reached Michilimackinac. The reader will recall the contract
entered into by the explorer and his nephew-in-law, François
de Lorme (see page 131), for 6,693 *livres'* worth of goods to be
supplied him for the recent journey. This debt fell due in August 1739. La Vérendrye, before leaving Montreal, had promised to send down one thousand pounds of beaver and a canoe-
load of peltries when he reached the upper country; and this
promise he had fulfilled. But he also gave orders that part of this
consignment should be sold for the benefit of his earlier creditors
and to meet certain bills he was drawing on De Lorme. Nephew
De Lorme carried out these instructions in the belief that the
creditors mentioned by his uncle were the only ones, and that
he himself would be paid in full during the coming year, that
is in 1739; since by paying off these creditors he would then
have first lien on any furs sent down. He soon learned to his
surprise, however, that the explorer had without his knowledge
made another contract with Louis d'Ailleboust for 2,787 *livres,*
which debt, contrary to general practice, was to be paid at
Michilimackinac. This arrangement, De Lorme feared, would
make D'Ailleboust a preferred creditor, as D'Ailleboust would
thus be able to obtain payment for the sum owed him before the
goods could reach De Lorme at Montreal. To protect his interests, De Lorme decided to go to law. His first step was to appear before the governor, who thereupon summoned D'Ailleboust before him to hear his side of the story. According to De
Lorme's version of the interview, the governor told the two men
to proceed in the usual manner, while D'Ailleboust stoutly maintained that a settlement had been effected in Beauharnois' presence, though what the settlement was does not appear in the
record. At any rate, De Lorme proceeded in the usual manner
and took the case to Intendant Hocquart, asking for authority to
seize the peltries at his own risk when they arrived at Michili-

mackinac and to have them brought to Montreal, where government officials could hold them until the case had been adjudicated. The intendant sided with De Lorme, issued an order on June 12, 1739, appointing arbitrators to examine the contending parties, and on the report of these functionaries he granted De Lorme's petition. Our old friend, René Bourassa, was appointed bailiff to effect the seizure at Michilimackinac.

Governor Beauharnois now stepped in and denounced De Lorme for having carried the case to Hocquart after he himself had settled it. Hocquart replied by blaming D'Ailleboust and La Vérendrye for the way in which they had conducted their business; then, in order to justify his position, he pointed out that it was the custom in such cases to bring to Montreal the furs necessary to pay those who had furnished the supplies, and it was for this reason that he had ordered Bourassa to seize the goods. But the governor, feeling his authority infringed, ordered the commanding officer at Michilimackinac to hold the consignment there instead of sending it to Montreal. Later, he caused De Lorme to be paid in full by La Vérendrye. The governor's course was afterward approved by Maurepas, not so much because it rendered justice in this particular case, but because the Minister frowned upon the idea—as did also Beauharnois—of extending the judicial power of the intendant into the western country. In truth, this seems to have been the cause of the trouble between the governor and intendant rather than the merits of De Lorme's complaint.[6]

When La Vérendrye's furs, valued at 4,000 *livres*, were seized at Michilimackinac from the traders in whose care they had been placed, they in their despair pointed out the danger to the explorer and his men, out at Fort La Reine, to be thus deprived of the means of obtaining necessary supplies in exchange for their furs. Though unable to countermand the orders he had received, the commander of Michilimackinac secured for the

[6] For documents covering the case see *ibid.*, pp. 515–530.

party a small supply of goods for which he made them pay a handsome price, and with this they returned to Fort La Reine, arriving there on October 20.[7]

This transaction does not, it is true, place La Vérendrye in a very favorable light; indeed, Hocquart in his report to Maurepas accuses both him and D'Ailleboust of tricky dealing.[8] Putting the best construction possible on the business, one can urge that La Vérendrye was facing a very difficult problem in trying to obtain goods and that as an explorer he had been continually hampered by lack of financial support from the home government, a situation that forced him to devote much of his time to the fur trade in order to carry on his discoveries. For this reason he was obliged to borrow money wherever he could, and his creditors were in a position to dictate terms. Doubtless in this case he chose the easiest way out of his difficulties without stopping to reckon with the legal aspects of the question, if indeed he fully understood them. Without wishing to be severe, one can say that La Vérendrye was guilty of a practice not in keeping with the business ethics of the day, and he let his eagerness to reach the Mantannes get the better of his sober judgment.

This unfortunate business, when reported to Maurepas, did the explorer no good in quarters where he was not particularly popular; in short, it seemed to justify the suspicions which the officials already had of his lack of singleness of purpose. They saw in it only a confirmation of their belief that he was more interested in feathering his own nest than in pushing forward the work of discovery. Fortunately, Maurepas had received La Vérendrye's journal by this time, and the news that he had at last reached the Mantannes caused the Minister to modify his opinion somewhat and regard the explorer in a more favorable light. He even admitted to Beauharnois that La Vérendrye appeared to have made progress and would probably make further dis-

[7] Summary Journal, *ibid.*, p. 449.
[8] Hocquart to Maurepas, Sept. 27, 1741, *ibid.*, p. 525.

coveries. He also applauded the idea of leaving two men with
the Mantannes to learn their language, as this would enable the
French to move more rapidly through the western country and
with greater ease.[9]

La Vérendrye at Fort La Reine now felt unable to continue
his work. The supplies brought him by his agents, supplies purchased at Michilimackinac at fancy prices, were insufficient for
his needs; with them he could barely provide for the men under
him; and, of course, his trade with the Indians was seriously
curtailed. In Montreal one of his backers, Ignace Gamelin, secured at this time a permit from the governor to send him five
canoes of merchandise, manned by thirty-two men, which would
have helped the situation to some extent; but of this, of course,
he could have had no knowledge.[10]

Late in the spring of 1740 La Vérendrye left Fort La Reine
in the hope of securing from Governor Beauharnois the means
for financing another expedition to the Mantannes. It was his
last hope; the only thing he could do; if he failed in this it would
put an end to his dream of discovering the Western Sea. Leaving
Louis-Joseph as commander during his absence, he started for
Michilimackinac, arriving there on July 16. Here he collected
supplies and sent them to the chevalier. He also sent a special
message to Pierre, who by this time had left St. Charles to join
his brothers at La Reine, telling him to go in the autumn to the
Mantannes, taking with him two Frenchmen, one of whom
should be an interpreter, and, after securing guides from this
nation, make an earnest attempt to discover the Western Sea.[11]

Pressing forward, La Vérendrye reached Montreal on August
25, to learn that his wife had passed away in that city on September 25 of the previous year and now lay buried in the church
of Notre Dame. From Montreal he descended the river to Que-

[9] Maurepas to Beauharnois, May 2, 1740, *ibid.*, pp. 373–374.
[10] *R.A.Q., 1922–1923*, p. 200.
[11] Summary Journal, *J. & L.*, p. 450.

bec, where he presented the governor with a personal account of his recent voyage. The governor received him cordially and lodged him in his own house for the winter. The commander complained bitterly, and with considerable justice, of the treatment he was receiving from the French Court, a treatment he blamed on 'the envy and jealousy of certain persons in Canada. He pointed to his 40,000 *livres* of debt as evidence of the complete absence of commercial motives in his efforts to' find the Western Sea. He complained later:

People do not know me; money has never been my object; I have sacrificed myself and my sons for the service of His Majesty and the good of the colony; what advantages shall result from my toils the future may tell. . . . In all my misfortunes I have the consolation of seeing that the General [governor] enters into my views, recognizes the uprightness of my intentions, and continues to do me justice in spite of the opposition of certain parties.[12]

On June 26, 1741, La Vérendrye left Montreal for his final journey to the Northwest. During his stay in that town he again entered into a financial transaction that was to cause him trouble later on. In October of the previous year he had signed an agreement with Lamarque and a group of associates to deliver sixty-five packs of beaver to them, or their agents, at Michilimackinac, in return for supplies furnished him for his coming expedition. Pierre Gamelin Maugras, one of La Jemeraye's relatives, appears to have been his principal backer, as he signed up a large number of men for the journey.[13] Of these beaver packs, thirty-three were to be paid the following year and thirty-two the year after. Jean-Baptiste Legras and his associates also claimed to have left some merchandise at Fort St. Charles for which La Vérendrye still owed them. A year later (that is, in 1742), when the explorer had managed to send a consignment of furs to Michilimackinac, his creditors filed a complaint with the governor stating that they had received only nine packs

[12] *Ibid.*, pp. 451–452.   [13] *R.A.Q., 1929–1930*, pp. 396–408.

so far and requesting that he issue orders for full payment. This he did; and he also gave a permit to Legras to go to the western posts and recover his merchandise, if La Vérendrye had not sent down enough furs to pay for it. When our old friend, Jarret de Verchères, now commander at Michilimackinac, received notice of the governor's order, he looked into the situation and found that La Vérendrye had sufficient furs there to quiet his creditors. Fifty-six packages were therefore handed over to Lamarque and twenty-four to Legras in payment of their claims.[14]

La Vérendrye was now in his fifty-sixth year, past his physical prime, if one may judge him by most men, yet able and eager to undertake a journey fraught with hardships. His life in the wilderness now stood him in good stead; he was inured to cold, fatigue, long marches, inadequate food, and all the privations of pioneer life. He now probably thought that this was his last chance to attain the object to which he had devoted himself for the past ten years; and thus it was that he promised the governor not to return until he had penetrated the most distant places he could reach. Beauharnois was confident that his friend would do his utmost, even though he may not have been sanguine of the result; but he felt bound to warn him that he would not be sent to the Northwest again and that his sons would be recalled from their posts, if he should return without permission.[15] The governor was still full of faith in La Vérendrye's ability and integrity, and he requested Maurepas at this time to give him the command of the military company, recently vacated by Louis-Philippe Denys de la Ronde when he took over the post at Chequamegon,[16] as a mark of appreciation for his services. On this journey the explorer took with him

[14] Order of Beauharnois, June 22, 1742, Archives des colonies, C¹¹A-74, 162–165; Beauharnois to Maurepas, Oct. 12, 1742, *J. & L.*, pp. 382–389.

[15] Beauharnois to Maurepas, Sept. 25, 1741, Archives des colonies, C¹¹A-75, 278–284.

[16] Beauharnois to Maurepas, May 12, 1741, *J. & L.*, pp. 376–377.

a Jesuit father named Claude Godefroy Coquart, who had recently come to Canada to preach the Faith to the most distant nations. He left Montreal with La Vérendrye, but on reaching Michilimackinac the explorer received orders to leave the missionary at this post, for there seem to have been certain petty jealousies at work to prevent him from fulfilling his ambition. Coquart later managed to get to Kaministikwia, where he gathered information that throws some light on the situation in the Northwest.

After saying farewell to Father Coquart, La Vérendrye continued on his way by the usual route. At Rainy Lake he found the savages singing their war songs in preparation for an attack on the Sioux. At Lake of the Woods it was the same. There the Monsonis and Crees told him that arrangements had been made for all the tribes to meet at a rendezvous in the prairies the following December to organize an expedition against the ancient enemy. They did not think, so they said, that he would object, since they were to avenge French blood and that of their own leaders, slain by the Sioux—all this despite La Vérendrye's repeated attempts, made over a period of years, to impress upon them the governor's absolute prohibition of punitive expeditions. It seemed almost hopeless to make the Indians understand the French attitude; or, perhaps, they understood it well enough but were determined to have revenge at any cost. When La Vérendrye heard of this plan, he expressed surprise, though, knowing the Indian's mentality, he may not have been so surprised as he pretended to be. He explained to them again, as he had done many times before, that since he had long ago pardoned the Sioux for the murder of his son, it was not necessary for others to rekindle the quarrel, particularly as a state of war would block the road against the French. He reminded them also that a son of one of their chieftains was held as a slave by the Sioux and that a French trader, one Paul Marin de la Margue, who had been active in the regions south of Lake

Superior for several years, was now working for his release. An act of war would, therefore, be likely to thwart his efforts.[17]

All this was without avail. Scarcely had the commander turned his back than La Colle led a party of two hundred men, most of them Crees and Assiniboins, against the Sioux of the Prairies and routed them in a four days' battle, killing seventy men besides women and.children and capturing such a large number of slaves that they made a line four *arpents* long. In this contest the Cree-Assiniboin army lost only six men. Father Coquart reported later that La Vérendrye had done all he could to prevent the catastrophe, but his presents had made no impression on La Colle. To make matters worse, the Indians, their appetite whetted by this successful skirmish, were planning more trouble. The following spring another attack was to be launched, despite Father Coquart's protests. The scheme was to let the Chippewas live peacefully with the Sioux during the winter, in order to lull them into security, then the Crees, Monsonis, and Assiniboins around Rainy Lake were to fall upon them and destroy them.[18]

This situation caused La Vérendrye to alter his plans. With the savages of the Northwest on the verge of war against the Sioux, the French ran the risk of being attacked as they wandered about the plains, and their posts might also be destroyed. Such a calamity might well put an end to French enterprise in this region for some time to come. For this reason La Vérendrye now decided to remain at Fort La Reine to handle the situation, since he was the one best qualified to keep the Indians from each other's throats, and to send his sons to search for the Western Sea on their own initiative. Knowing the interest the government had in the trading posts, he felt that no matter what his personal inclinations might be his first duty was to save them from destruction. After all, it would make little difference to

[17] Beauharnois to Maurepas, Oct. 12, 1742, *ibid.*, pp. 382–389.
[18] *Ibid.*

the government whether he went in person or by proxy, if only the Western Sea were discovered.

Continuing on his journey, La Vérendrye reached Fort La Reine on October 13. Here he learned to his chagrin that Pierre had returned from the Mantannes without having made any important discovery, a failure the young man blamed on the impossibility of finding a suitable guide. He had hoped to secure a member of the tribe that had visited the strange white people. For two months he awaited their arrival at the Mantanne village, then when they did not come he went with his two French companions to a place not far from certain Spanish forts, probably near the Gulf of Mexico, where he had been driven back by hostile Indians.[19] On his return to Fort La Reine he brought with him a coverlet of embroidered cotton and some porcelain beads, said to have come from the strange white people, which he gave to his father, who sent them to Beauharnois, who in turn forwarded them to Maurepas.[20]

As the season was now well advanced, La Vérendrye decided to wait until spring before launching what was to be his last expedition. Meanwhile, he sent Pierre to build a post on Lac des Prairies, as it was necessary to do something to hold the wavering Crees. This post, as recent investigations have shown, was not built on Lake Manitoba, as Lac des Prairies is now called, but on a small lake west of it called Lake Dauphin. Here on the northwestern shore, a mile or two from the mouth of the Valley River, on a little peninsula, Pierre built the post called Fort Dauphin; and at a spot one hundred yards from the shore traces of its ruins have been found. He was also commissioned to build a post near the mouth of the Saskatchewan River, and it was probably at this time that he constructed the first Fort Bourbon there. The second Fort Bourbon will be described later. The Saskatchewan flows into Cedar Lake. Near its mouth

[19] Memorandum of Pierre de la Vérendrye, *ibid.*, p. 496.
[20] Beauharnois to Maurepas, Oct. 12, 1742, *ibid.*, pp. 382–389.

lies a small group of islands, and on one of these, Fort Island,
Pierre erected Fort Bourbon. Cedar Lake is situated a short distance west of northern Lake Winnipeg; and the Saskatchewan,
after leaving the former, flows into the latter, thus connecting
the two bodies of water.[21]

Arrangements were now made for the dash to the Western
Sea. The party was to be a small one consisting of Louis-Joseph,
who seems to have been the leader, François, and two experienced *voyageurs*, Édouard La Londette and Jean-Baptiste
Amiotte, who had served in the *pays d'en haut* for some three
years.[22] What must have been La Vérendrye's disappointment
when at the last moment, just as the dream of a lifetime was
about to be realized, he found himself obliged to stand aside,
while others went forth on the great quest! But there was nothing he could do, save face the situation philosophically; and this
he did, taking what consolation he could from the fact that it
was his own sons who were going to reap whatever glory the
discovery would bring them.

The brothers left Fort La Reine on April 29, 1742, and after
an uneventful journey reached the Mantannes on the nineteenth
of the following month. This is all the chevalier, Louis-Joseph,
chronicler of the expedition, tells us.[23] After three weeks of
travel he gave no details of what took place during the journey.
It was probably a rather monotonous march over a now well-
known trail, and Louis-Joseph, no doubt, felt it better to save
his comments for the new territory he was about to enter. It
is interesting to note that the time taken to cover this stage of
the journey, namely twenty days, is what La Vérendrye, four
years before, had said would be the maximum time needed to

[21] Summary Journal, *ibid.*, p. 454. See also Appendix G for the location of these forts.

[22] See Appendix A for the identity of these men.

[23] Journal of the expedition of the Chevalier de la Vérendrye and
one of his brothers to reach the Western Sea, addressed to M. le Marquis
de Beauharnois, 1742–1743, *J. & L.*, pp. 406–432.

cover what he estimated was the 120 leagues separating the first
Mantanne village from Fort La Reine. It also gives the key to
the rate of travel at which the brothers were proceeding. It
was probably the maximum rate, too (six leagues a day), as it

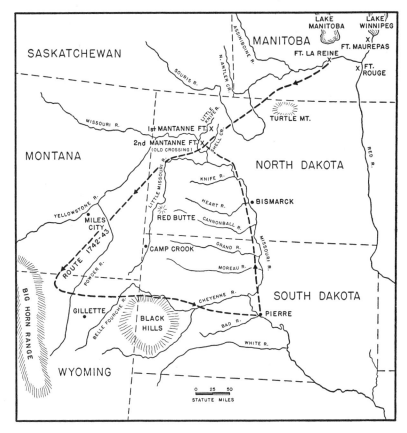

Louis-Joseph de la Vérendrye's route to the West, 1742–1743.

is doubtful if they traveled as rapidly later on, when they were
accompanied by bands of Indians who were seldom pressed for
time.

Now that they had reached the Mantanne village, one would
expect, after reading La Vérendrye's account of the first journey

there, that his sons would seek the Western Sea by descending
the Missouri River, for the French commander closed his narrative by proclaiming his discovery of the River of the West.
Yet, strange to say, Louis-Joseph makes no mention of the
stream; he takes his party overland in a westerly direction as
though no river of any consequence ran through the neighborhood. Pierre, on his recent visit, had probably learned the true
direction of the Missouri, and had told his father that it would
be of no service in finding the Western Sea or the Pacific Ocean.
At any rate, it disappears entirely from the family's calculations.
Later, when La Vérendrye's sons again took up the work of
discovery, they directed their steps to the Saskatchewan as the
one river offering a solution of their problem.

At the Mantanne village—the one near Old Crossing—the
brothers learned that the Horse Indians, who were expected at
any moment, were the ones from whom they should obtain
guides. These savages, like most tribes mentioned by the
chevalier, are difficult to identify, especially as horses were
used by more than one prairie nation. Francis Parkman, who
knew the Indians of the western plains from personal observation, calls them the Cheyennes, and his opinion may well be
accepted.[24]

During the tedious period of waiting, the chevalier and his
brother improved their time by familiarizing themselves with
their hosts' dialect and by gaining what information they could
about western geography. As the season wore on and the Horse
Indians failed to put in an appearance, Louis-Joseph decided
to seek them out. For this purpose he secured the services of
two Mantannes to lead him across the unknown prairies.

The party left the Mantanne village on July 23 and, crossing
the Missouri, set out in a west-southwesterly direction, a course
which the chevalier thought was not a particularly appropriate
one for reaching the Western Sea; yet he was bound to follow
the guides. For twenty days they plodded along over the rolling

[24] Parkman, *op. cit.*, II, 43.

prairies, under the burning midsummer sun, unprotected by the friendly shade of trees, for trees in this region grew only along the banks of rivers and in secluded spots. Food was plentiful; herds of buffalo roamed the plains, offering excellent game for the French muskets. At night camp was quickly pitched, and the weary travelers lay down after a hearty supper to snatch a few hours' sleep, while one of the party kept watch to guard his companions against the wolves whose howls could be heard in the distance. At sunrise they rose for an early start, anxious to get under way before the sun's rays became too intense, for they wished to cover as much ground as possible before the heat compelled them to take a midday siesta. Their course led them to the badlands area of North Dakota, where the chevalier noticed the beautiful coloring of the earth, which in these regions forms such a contrast to the otherwise barren scenery. In some places it was azure blue, in others vermilion, green, black, or ochre, while the broken nature of the soil gave the country the weird appearance of desolation. "Had I foreseen at the time that I should not travel over this territory again," wrote Louis-Joseph, impressed by the polychrome beauty of the land, "I should have taken specimens of each kind. I could not load myself with them then, knowing I had a very long road to travel."

On August 2 they reached a hill called the Mountain of the Horse Indians. Here the guides refused to go any farther, so the French erected a small cabin wherein to live while awaiting the possible arrival of any savages who might be willing to act as guides. Watchfires were lighted every night to attract the attention of wandering Indians, while Louis-Joseph sent a man, or went himself, each day to scan the prairies from the neighboring hill. Toward the middle of September—on the fourteenth, to be exact—a pillar of smoke was seen in the distance to the south-southwest. The chevalier immediately sent a messenger and the remaining Mantanne—the other had returned home a few days before—to see what tribe was encamped so near them. They found a friendly nation, which Louis-Joseph called the Beaux Hommes, probably a tribe of Crows whose members are noted for their handsome appearance. Neither the Frenchman nor the Mantanne understood the dialect spoken by these men, but they managed to make them understand that their companions were encamped near by. The chief sent the two men back with guides to bring the French to his camp. Feeling that his work was done, the Mantanne brave expressed a desire to return to his village, for he felt uneasy in the presence of this strange tribe. Louis-Joseph was willing to let him go, now that he could obtain other guides, so he dismissed the savage with a liberal reward.

The French spent three weeks with their new-found friends, experiencing all the delays incident to life with a savage tribe. The chief was amiable enough, entertaining him with his rude hospitality in return for the curious experience of having these white strangers as guests in his wigwam. At last, after a long wait, the chevalier succeeded in making known to the chief that he wanted guides to lead him to the Horse Indians. The chief proved obliging; he supplied the Frenchmen with a guide to lead the party to the nearest village—he did not know where the Horse Indians were—and sent them forth with his blessing. On October 9 they left the Beaux Hommes and set out in a southwesterly direction; after a march of two days they came to a tribe of the Little Foxes (a branch of the Cheyennes),[25] who appeared very pleased to see the white men. The chevalier informed them that he was looking for the Horse Indians to lead him to the sea, and the entire tribe turned out to accompany him.

By now Louis-Joseph had come to the conclusion that if he should be successful in his quest he would merely discover a sea already known, such as the Pacific or the Gulf of California, for the general direction he had taken since leaving the Man-

---

[25] A soldier society existed among the Cheyennes known as the Fox soldiers or Little Fox men..

tannes would hardly lead him to the mythical Western Sea, said to be due west of Lake Superior. This conclusion was something of a disappointment to him; but he consoled himself with the reflection that, should he find it, he would have spanned the continent and settled the vexing question of the Western Sea by showing that it was merely another name for the Pacific Ocean. This in itself should satisfy the anxious Minister at home.

After a two days' march with the Little Foxes, the explorers came to another large village of this tribe which presently joined them. On the fifteenth they met a band of Pioyas (possibly Kiowas) whom they asked to lead them "to some tribe that was on the road to the sea." Two days later they were joined by another group, and then, on the nineteenth, they at last reached their goal, a settlement of the Horse Indians. They evidently did not arrive at a propitious time, as the Indians were making the welkin ring with doleful lamentations, weeping and howling lugubriously, for their village had just been sacked and destroyed by those terrors of the plains, the Snakes, a tribe identified by some authorities as the Comanches.[26] These Snakes, so their enemies said, did not make war according to accepted customs, which may be another way of saying that they were more efficient. They carried on their depredations continually from spring to autumn, instead of resting on their laurels after a successful raid, in accordance with prairie etiquette. They were a numerous nation, and woe betide those who crossed their path, for they were the friends of none. The year before they had destroyed seventeen villages, killing the men and aged women and selling the young squaws as slaves to people living along the seaboard, exchanging them for merchandise and horses.

After expressing his condolences for their misfortunes, Louis-Joseph inquired if they knew aught of the people living by the sea. Somewhat to his disappointment they answered that no

[26] John W. Smurr, "A New La Vérendrye Theory," *Pacific Northwest Quarterly*, XLIII (1952), 51–64.

member of their tribe had ever been there, as the road was blocked by the Snakes; but if the French made a circuit to avoid this savage nation they would presently meet with tribes who trafficked with these mysterious whites. They also told him of a nation which did not fear the Snakes; it was called the Bows (Gens de l'Arc), possibly a branch of the Cheyennes, though there is considerable difference of opinion as to who they were.[27] These Indians, Louis-Joseph concluded, might perhaps be the very ones from whom he could obtain some definite information about the object of his quest, as they were said to be friends of the tribes who traded with the white men on the coast. At any rate, he would attempt to visit them; and so by means of judicious presents he persuaded the Horse Indians to lead him to them.

The French now headed in a southwesterly direction, and on November 18 arrived at a village of Indians known as the Gens de la Belle Rivière, probably a stray band of Arikaras. They informed the chevalier that the Bows were not far off, and joining forces with the French they all marched together for three days until they came to a Bow encampment. It was a rather large encampment, and the tribe had a goodly number of horses, donkeys, and mules, which they used for transportation and hunting. Just now they were about to undertake a punitive expedition against the Snakes.

Up to this time the French had met with the usual Indian hospitality, but the Bow chief's enthusiasm far exceeded any thing they had yet experienced. Here, then, was an opportunity not to be missed. The chevalier promptly cultivated the man's friendship and soon learned the Bow dialect, at least enough to make himself understood and to understand what was being said to him. Thanks to this achievement he was soon able to inquire if the Bows knew the white people of the Far West, and if so would the chief conduct the French to them. The chief

[27] *J. & L.*, p. 413n.

told his guests at great length all he knew about these strange people. His information, however, shed but little light on the subject, as all his knowledge was merely hearsay, similar to that of the other savages Louis-Joseph had previously questioned. The chief told him:

We know them through what has been told us by prisoners of the Gens du Serpent [Snakes], amongst whom we shall shortly arrive. Don't be surprised if you see so many villages assembled with us. Word has been sent in all directions for them to join us. You are hearing war shouts every day; it is not without intention; we are going to march in the direction of the high mountains [Rocky Mountains] which are near the sea to find the Gens du Serpent. Do not be afraid to come with us, you have nothing to fear, and you will be able to see the sea that you are in search of. The French who are on the coast are numerous; they have a large number of slaves whom they settle on their lands in each tribe; they have separate apartments; they marry them to one another and do not oppress them, so that they like being with them and do not seek to run away. They breed a great many horses and other animals which they use in tilling the land. They have many chiefs for the soldiers and have some also for prayer.

The chief then uttered some words in the white people's language which the chevalier recognized at once as being Spanish. This identification was confirmed when the chief spoke of a massacre of Spaniards who had come to the Missouri on a military expedition, a massacre which, so we learn from other sources, took place in 1720. The Spaniards had become alarmed at French encroachments in the lower Missouri Valley and, collecting a force of 200 men, had marched from New Mexico with a band of Comanches for the purpose of destroying the settlers. Fortunately, the war party was discovered by a detachment of Pawnees, allies of the French, who attacked them with such vigor that they nearly annihilated the little army.[28]

[28] Such is the account given by Parkman, *op. cit.*, II, 14. A Spanish version of the incident, found in J. B. Dunbar, "Massacre of the Villazur

The whites of the sea, then, were Spaniards living, not on the shores of the Pacific, nor on the Gulf of California, still less on a putative Western Sea, but in settlements near the Gulf of Mexico; and the direction to be taken to reach them was a southerly, not a westerly, one. The chevalier was quick enough to realize this; at least he saw that he was being directed to a sea already known. Yet, despite his disappointment, he expressed a wish to visit this body of water if it were feasible.

The march with the Bows was therefore continued, sometimes southwest, sometimes northwest, the party being continually increased by the arrival of new bands. On January 1, 1743, they found themselves within sight of a chain of mountains, probably the Big Horn range in Wyoming. The entire force now consisted of over two thousand warriors, who with their families made up a formidable host. During the evenings the French gathered before the chief's wigwam, around a great fire, where the squaws were cooking the evening meal, and plied the Indian leader with questions. Then, after a rude repast, the warriors seated themselves in a circle and indulged in peculations about the coming conflict with the Snakes, while ie squaws claimed what was left of the meat, snatching bits f food here and there which they carried away to devour or 1are with the numerous dogs that made up the tribe's principal .vestock. When the men had retired and the women had ceased .heir lamentations over the dead, killed in the recent struggle with the Snakes, these animals would raise a mournful chorus of howls that resounded over the prairies like a dismal chant.

It was on one of these nights, when the men had gathered

Expedition by the Pawnees on the Platte in 1720," *Collections of the Kansas State Historical Society*, XI (1909–1910), 397–423, tells us that the affair took place in August, 1720, and that the Indian allies were Apaches. There were only forty mounted Spanish soldiers in the party.

around the campfire, that the chief approached the French and begged them to join him in the coming attack on the traditional enemy. Louis-Joseph at first declined, on the ground that he had come to bring peace, not to encourage war; and, moreover, he had no desire to involve himself in any unnecessary trouble. Pained at this neutral attitude, the chief expostulated for some time, urging the French to come as spectators without exposing themselves to danger, for, as he pointed out, the Snakes were enemies of the French as well as foes of his people. After a brief discussion the chevalier decided to humor his hosts: first, because there was no decent alternative; secondly, because he wished to see the ocean he had been told lay just beyond the mountains. When this decision was announced to the assembled braves, the chief proceeded to explain the plan of campaign, the measures they would take to protect their families during their absence, and the methods to be used in approaching the enemy. Louis-Joseph then made an address, translated by the chief, in which he told the assembled host that the Great Chief had given him orders to secure peace if possible; but realizing now that the Bows were justifiably angered he (Louis-Joseph) would bow to their wishes and accompany them, if only to help with his advice.

When everything was ready, the entire force—men, women, and children—set forth and marched until January 8, when a more or less permanent camp was pitched. Here the baggage was left with the noncombatants. Louis-Joseph detailed François to guard their supplies, while he pressed on with the warriors, taking La Londette and Amiotte with him. Progress became more difficult when the band approached enemy territory, for it was then necessary to observe caution; and it was the twelfth of the month before they reached the Snake encampment at the foot of the mountains. The dash from the baggage camp had taken them three days. Here the main body paused and sent forward scouts to reconnoiter. To everyone's surprise these men presently returned with the news that the Snakes had broken camp and disappeared. The Bows were amazed, and their amazement quickly turned to dismay when someone suggested that the Snakes might have got wind of the coming attack and gone around their enemies to fall upon the baggage camp during the latters' absence. This rumor completely broke down the party's morale. Panic ensued; and soon the Indians were in full flight toward their camp, each one for himself.

On the retreat, the chief took charge of the chevalier and his two French companions. As they pressed hurriedly forward, Louis-Joseph at the chief's side discussing the situation, they suddenly noticed that the two Frenchmen who were following them a short distance behind had disappeared. Fearful that they might have met with some mishap, Louis-Joseph started back in search of them, while the chief hastened forward to halt the main body, traveling some distance ahead. But demoralization had set in, and none was willing to stop in enemy territory to look for missing strangers. The chevalier, fortunately, had no trouble in finding his companions, who had ensconced themselves on a small oasis where they were feeding their horses, totally unconscious of the trouble they were causing their leader. He was not long in bringing the laggards to their senses and ordered them to mount; but as he did so he noticed a group of fifteen Indians coming stealthily forward, their bodies protected by their shields. One was ahead, and the French, allowing him to come within gunshot range, let loose a volley that broke the attack before it had a chance to get under way; for, as the chevalier remarked, the musket is a weapon greatly respected by these people, who soon learned the folly of testing their shields against gunpowder. That night the trio started back to camp. The ground was hard and dry, a condition which prevented them from detecting the hoofprints of their allies' horses; but good luck was with them, and steering by a general sense of direction they were able to reach the camp on the fourteenth or fifteenth, this being the second day of the retreat.[29]

The Bow chief, meanwhile, had been searching high and low for the missing Frenchmen, spreading his warriors out over the plains to prevent them from wandering off into unknown territory. The day after the French returned, a heavy storm broke, covering the prairie with a mantle of snow; and the chief, feeling that his friends must have lost their way and perished, returned to the camp five days later. Great was his joy when he found his allies safely housed in his wigwam.

The return journey began on January 20, to the great distress of the chevalier, who felt himself robbed of the opportunity of ascending the Rocky Mountains and at last getting a glimpse of the sea beyond them. The Bows and French proceeded in a southeasterly direction. On March 1 the chevalier announced his intention of leaving his savage friends and joining a tribe of Little Cherries or Arikaras who were encamped some distance away, though how he learned about these people he does not tell us. He sent forward one of his men with a guide to sound out the Little Cherries' chief about his proposed visit, and when they returned ten days later with a pressing invitation, Louis-Joseph decided to accept at once.

The Bow chief, as might be expected, was grieved to lose his white guests, and the French felt real sorrow at leaving him, for never in all their wanderings had they met an Indian who had shown such interest in their welfare or treated them with more disinterested hospitality. In order to console him the chevalier promised to return someday if the tribe would settle on the banks of a little nearby stream and undertake to raise grain, a proposition to which the chief agreed, if the Frenchman, for his part, would rejoin him the following spring, as soon as he

[29] There is some confusion in the narrative about the length of time taken by this excursion, and the dates are not clear. For full explanation see Appendix E.

had seen his father at Fort La Reine. Whether the chief kept
his part of the bargain we have no means of knowing, for Louis-
Joseph never returned. Taking leave of the Bows, the French
joined the Little Cherries on March 15. Louis-Joseph found
them encamped at a two days' journey from their fort on the
Missouri at the mouth of the Bad River; they reached the fort
after a leisurely march of four days. They were received by the
garrison with great demonstrations of joy.

Louis-Joseph found among the Little Cherries an Indian who
had been brought up by the Spaniards and who spoke their language as though it was his mother tongue. This man told of his
having been baptized, and he still remembered the prayers the
priests had taught him. Asked how long it would take the
French to reach the Spanish settlements, he said it would take
a twenty days' journey on horseback, but the road was dangerous as it led through the Snake country. These Spaniards, he told
the chevalier, worked in iron and bought buffalo hides and
slaves, giving the savages horses and merchandise in exchange,
but under no circumstances would they let them have guns.
This account confirmed what the chevalier had suspected when
he talked with the Bows, namely, that the long-sought Europeans were Spaniards, not Frenchmen, as the other Indians
had hinted, and that the Western Sea he had heard so much
about was actually the Gulf of Mexico. The Indian also spoke
of a Frenchman who had lived for several years at a place situated a three days' journey from the Arikaras. Louis-Joseph
would have gone to see this man if his horses had been in
good condition, but as they were exhausted by the recent
gruelling marches, he contented himself with inviting the man
to visit him, promising to wait until the end of March. The
presence of a French settler in this locality was already known
to the authorities in Louisiana. Governor Jean-Baptiste Lemoyne de Bienville, in a letter written to Maurepas in 1734,
spoke of a fellow Frenchman who had lived for some time

among the Pawnees on the Missouri, and had even been as far as the Arikara villages—the first Frenchman to visit this tribe —where he had found deposits of silver.[30]

Louis-Joseph was as good as his word; he waited until April 1 before preparing to return home. As he wished to leave in the Arikara territory a token of his visit which would give his sovereign a claim to the immense territory he had traversed, he buried on a hill, situated 1,500 feet northwest of the junction of the Bad and Missouri Rivers, a lead tablet, prepared for him by his father. Here it lay hidden until the year 1913, when it was discovered by chance. On one side was the Latin inscription: *Anno XXVI Regni Ludovici XV Prorege Illustrissimo Domino Domino Marchione de Beauharnois MDCCXXXXI Petrus Gaultier de Laverendrie Posuit.* On the reverse, the chevalier, or one of his men, scratched the names of the party. It was a bungling job at best; thus it is impossible to decipher some of the words to everyone's complete satisfaction. In general, it has been interpreted to read: *Pose par le chevalyet de Lav [La Vérendrye] to jo [to St] Louy la Londette Amiotte [or A. Miotte] le 30 de mars 1743.* Since Louis-Joseph was the chevalier, François' name is not included, a strange omission, as the names of the two hired men are clearly limned. Perhaps François was not present on this occasion; he may have been otherwise occupied in the Indian village; at any rate one can hardly believe that Louis-Joseph would have intentionally snubbed his older brother.[31]

Having buried the tablet and erected a cairn over it, the chevalier told the Indians—who knew nothing of the plate— that the monument was to commemorate the visit of the French to their country. He also tells us at this point that his wish to

[30] Margry, *op. cit.*, VI, 455.

[31] Reproductions of the inscriptions are given in Doane Robinson, "La Vérendrye's Farthest West," *Proceedings of the State Historical Society of Wisconsin*, 1913, pp. 146–150. For full discussion see Appendix A.

take an observation for latitude, in order to fix the site of the village, was frustrated because his astrolabe had been out of order since the beginning of the journey. This accounts for the lack of any definite information as to the locations of the various places he mentions in his narrative.

Lead tablet buried by Louis-Joseph de la Vérendrye at the mouth of the Bad River.

As the French settler from down the river had not put in an appearance by April 1, the brothers decided to start for home. The guides engaged for the journey were anxious to get started, and the horses were now rested and in good condition. Louis-Joseph accordingly took leave of the chief the following day, telling him to urge the Frenchman, should he come, to follow the party to the Mantanne village, whither they were going. He also assured him that he would care for the guides and see that no harm befell them, for the Arikaras were then at war with the Mantannes. After an uneventful journey of forty-six days—at least it must have been uneventful since no details are given in the narrative—the French reached the Mantanne village (second village of 1738) without having met anyone save a tribe of Sioux near whom they chanced to encamp. Here they expected to rest for a fortnight or a week; but when they learned of the presence of some Assiniboins at Fort La Butte (probably the first Mantanne village of 1738) who were about to go to Fort La Reine, they hurriedly left their hosts and, pressing forward, reached La Butte the following day, only to find the Assiniboins had just left.[32] Traveling under forced marches they soon overtook the tribe and covered the rest of the distance with them. Little of interest occurred on this the last stage of the homeward journey. A brush with the Sioux, who mistook the party for a group composed wholly of Assiniboins, but fled when they found Frenchmen among them, proved to be the only diversion from the monotony of travel. On July 2, after an absence of fifteen months, they marched into Fort La Reine where La Vérendrye, *père*, welcomed them.[33]

Here ends the journey of the Chevalier de la Vérendrye. He had failed to reach his goal, the Western Sea and the white people living on its shores, but he had gained the distinction of being the first white man, as far as we know, to gaze upon the lofty Rocky Mountains, a fact which does not seem to have impressed him at all. His narrative, like the journals of his fa-

[32] It has been suggested that Fort La Butte was the modern Dogden Butte in North Dakota. Unfortunately this is situated about 100 miles from the Mantanne village at Old Crossing. As the chevalier says he left the Mantannes on one day and reached La Butte the next, La Butte cannot have been Dogden Butte. We are inclined to follow O. G. Libby in his belief that the Mantanne village reached by the chevalier after forty-six days was the second village of 1738, and Fort La Butte the first. The distance between the two was only a day's march, as we know from the elder La Vérendrye's narrative. "Some Vérendrye Enigmas," *Mississippi Valley Historical Review*, III (1916–1917), 143–160.

[33] For full discussion of the route see Appendix F.

ther, is that of a man little accustomed to making precise observations and committing them to paper. It was not written
during the journey—of that we may be certain—but was com-
piled from memory shortly afterward in the form of a report
to Governor Beauharnois; at least, such is the impression one
gains from reading it. From the data given, we get the idea
that the explorers started from the Mantanne village and headed
in a southwesterly direction, wandering for miles over the prairies, stopping from time to time to visit and travel with various
Indian tribes which the narrator designates by names different
from those of today, until they came to a lofty range of mountains. Here, to Louis-Joseph's chagrin, as he himself admits,
they were forced to turn back when the Bow Indians became
panicky. Then came the return journey, the details of which
are even more meager than those of the outward march, and
the itinerary is as difficult to trace. In order to identify even
approximately the route followed by the brothers it is necessary
to use considerable imagination in interpreting the information
before us; and the various scholars who have studied the record
have come to different conclusions.

IX

The Last Years

THE Chevalier de la Vérendrye's expedition had been, considering its ultimate object, very much of a failure. The French had advanced across the prairies to a mountain barrier, beyond which, so they were told, lay the sea; but they had been unable to reach this ocean, or even come in sight of it, and thus could not verify by personal observation the whereabouts of those mysterious white people whose existence had intrigued them for so many years. Only when they met the Bow Indians did they learn that these people were probably Spaniards. This, of course, was something; and it had its effect on the elder La Vérendrye's future plans. It showed him that a journey to the white people would take him to the Gulf of Mexico, or, perhaps, to some place in California; at any rate he would discover no Western Sea by going there. Thus, we hear nothing more of the Mantannes when we find him making plans for his next voyage.

From now on we see him looking for a more northerly route—
one by the Saskatchewan River.

La Vérendrye was now in poor health, loaded with debts, and
discouraged. He had been obliged, during the absence of his
sons, to abandon Forts Maurepas and Dauphin because of lack
of supplies; and the Indians, offended by these tactics, were now
carrying their furs to Hudson Bay. Gamelin Maugras, who had
helped him with his recent expedition, did, it is true, obtain
permission from the governor to send out six canoes, manned
by forty-six men, to relieve the western posts; but these supplies,
if they ever did reach La Vérendrye do not appear to have
helped him very much.[1] We are not surprised therefore to learn
that he wrote Beauharnois at this time asking to be relieved of
his command because of poor health, his resignation to take
effect in 1744.[2]

This request was not altogether unexpected, nor was it likely
to disappoint the home government, for Maurepas, though he
admitted that La Vérendrye's reports showed promise, had
politely hinted to the governor some time before this that it
would be advisable to associate with the explorer some officer
of merit, as he was undoubtedly in need of assistance. "An arrangement of this kind," wrote the Minister, "is all the more
suitable on account of the importance of training in the colony
officers who, by their conduct and through the knowledge they
may acquire of the habits of the tribes with whom the Sieur
de la Vérendrye has established relations, may later render
service in governing them." [3] The officer of merit suggested by
the Minister was one Jacques Pierre Daneaux, Sieur de Muy,
a man in the prime of life, who had held a post on the St. Joseph
River in the Illinois country; yet in the end the choice was left

[1] R.A.Q., 1922–1923, p. 205.
[2] Beauharnois and Hocquart to Maurepas, Oct. 29, 1743, J. & L., p.
396.
[3] Maurepas to Beauharnois and Hocquart, April 17, 1742, ibid., p. 390.

to the governor. Maurepas also hinted that it might be well to employ another man in place of one of La Vérendrye's sons, for these young men should not, he felt, be left permanently at such distant posts. Yet here again he left the decision to Beauharnois. Then, in order to provide for the Sieur de Muy, he had the effrontery to suggest that in addition to the supplies furnished him he should receive an annual salary of 3,000 *livres* to be paid by La Vérendrye himself. And this sum was to be extracted from a man whose debts at this time totaled over 50,000 *livres!* [4]

The governor and the intendant in their reply voiced objections to the plan by pointing out its impracticability, since the organization of posts in the Northwest had not yet been completed; in fact, the abandonment of the posts, as mentioned above, showed, in their opinion, a serious state of affairs. They also pointed out that the only hope La Vérendrye had of extinguishing his great debt lay in the profits of the present year's business, a rather slender possibility. For this reason the two officials decided not to press him for the 3,000 *livres* assessed on his posts by the government. For the same reason Beauharnois deemed it inadvisable to saddle him with an assistant's salary. He had tendered his resignation to go into effect the following year, and then it would be time enough to choose his successor. [5]

Maurepas was now at the end of his patience. To Beauharnois' representations he replied that the chevalier's expedition would probably produce no better results than La Vérendrye's previous excursion—he had not yet received Louis-Joseph's journal—and that it was now high time to carry out the King's wishes in regard to the posts, and not be influenced by the explorer's business affairs or by his abandonment of Maurepas and Dauphin. He closed his letter with a peremptory order: "It

[4] Beauharnois and Hocquart to Maurepas, Oct. 29, 1743, *ibid.,* p. 397.
[5] *Ibid.,* pp. 393–398.

is His Majesty's intention. Kindly take the necessary steps in the matter." [6]

La Vérendrye resigned in 1744 and came down to Quebec. He was accompanied by Father Coquart, who had managed to reach Fort La Reine the previous autumn, just after the chevalier's return from the West.[7] His return must have been something of a relief to the governor, who was now in a position to carry out the King's orders in regard to the western posts without resorting to the disagreeable task of imposing an unnecessary financial burden on his old friend. It was no longer a question of naming a lieutenant, such as De Muy, but of selecting a commander for the entire northwest territory. He finally chose a man of considerable experience named Nicolas-Joseph de Noyelles, Sieur de Fleurimont, who had married a niece of La Vérendrye. De Noyelles was a man of mature years. He had been appointed commander at Detroit in 1720 and had held that position for two years. He had also made a campaign against the Foxes. On the whole his achievements in the West fitted him well for his new position; and his appointment was particularly pleasing to La Vérendrye's family, as he had a high opinion of his predecessor's ability and at once associated the explorer's sons with him in his enterprises. He was expected to keep peace among the savages, at the same time encouraging them to make trouble for the English, for which services he would receive a salary of 3,000 *livres* a year to be paid by the people furnishing him with merchandise.[8]

La Vérendrye now attempted to justify himself with the authorities at home. During the autumn of 1744 he sent Maurepas his Summary Journal giving the gist of his achievements

[6] Maurepas to Beauharnois and Hocquart, March 30, 1744, *ibid.*, pp. 398–400.

[7] L. A. Prud'homme, "Pierre Gaultier de Varennes," *Proceedings and Transactions of the Royal Society of Canada*, 2d ser., XI (1905), 51–52.

[8] Beauharnois and Hocquart to Maurepas, Oct. 21, 1744, *J. & L.*, pp. 400–401.

since 1731, accompanied by a letter laying the blame for the
governor's misunderstanding of his conduct on the slanders cir-
culated about him; and to these slanders he attributed his failure to receive the promotion to which he felt his services and
seniority entitled him. He also specifically pointed out the fal-
lacy of the accusation leveled against him of enriching himself,
for this had always been the principal charge he had had to
combat:

Money, Monseigneur, was moreover always a secondary consideration with me, and although I am poorer today than I was before I
began my explorations, I should consider myself completely com-
pensated if the care and attention I have devoted to the business
had merited me the favor of Your Highness, as I hope they yet may,
if you will grant some reward to nine wounds I have on my body,
thirty-nine years of service in France and in this colony, and to the
difficulties and fatigues that I have endured during the last thirteen
years in order to create establishments which I have made in places
where no person before myself had ever penetrated, which will
effect a considerable augmentation in the trade of the colony, even
if no one fully succeeds in discovering the Western Sea, and for
which I did not involve His Majesty in any expense.[9]

At the same time the governor backed up his protégé by a
letter to Maurepas enclosing the chevalier's journal as evidence
of what he had accomplished. He also urged the Minister to
show some mark of appreciation for a man who had given so
much of his life to the King's service, and, whatever his short-
comings may have been in finding the Western Sea, had at least
erected posts in hitherto unpenetrated regions, thus securing
for Canada the fur trade that once went to the English. His
poverty, continued the governor, was *prima facie* evidence that
he had not enriched himself, for as matters now stood he would
have, after twelve years' labor, only 4,000 *livres* left when he

[9] La Vérendrye to Maurepas, Oct. 31, 1744, *ibid.*, pp. 432–435.

had paid all his debts. In suggesting a suitable reward, Beauharnois exclaimed:

In reality, Monseigneur, six years of service in France, thirty-two in
this colony without reproach—at least I am not aware of any—nine
wounds on the body, were reasons which made it impossible for me
to hesitate in proposing him to you to fill one of the vacant com-
panies, and if I have had reason to hope, Monseigneur, that you were
persuaded that I would admit to my lists the names of such officers
only as were capable of service and deserving of your kindness, it
was particularly in connection with the favorable attention I relied
on your giving to the case of Sieur de la Vérendrye.[10]

Maurepas does not appear to have received these requests
with any degree of enthusiasm, and his reply to the governor
was far from gracious. After examining the report of the last
journey, he concluded that no actual attempt had been made to
find a route to the Western Sea; the explorers, he thought, had
not even taken the trouble to go in the right direction. Yet,
since La Vérendrye had now been relieved by De Noyelles, he
considered the incident closed, and informed the governor that
the King had decided to grant the explorer a captaincy.[11] In the
year 1745 the military company originally allotted to Claude
de Beauharnois, a nephew of the governor, was placed under
La Vérendrye's command; but the same reasons which deterred
the King from granting him a commission the previous year·
were advanced by the Minister as good and sufficient for refusing him seniority over those preferred the year before. "The
reason," said Maurepas, with amazing indifference to the actual facts, "is that, having for several years been solely occupied with his own affairs, he has done nothing for the service;
all those journeyings of his ending in nothing but trade with the
savage tribes whose settlements he frequented." [12] If this was

[10] Beauharnois to Maurepas, Oct. 27, 1744, *ibid.*, pp. 402–406.
[11] Maurepas to Beauharnois, April 26, 1745, *ibid.*, pp. 458–459.
[12] Maurepas to Beauharnois, May 12, 1745, *ibid.*, pp. 459–461.

so, one is inclined to wonder why La Vérendrye received the captaincy as a reward. Perhaps Maurepas granted it to appease the governor. At any rate, the Minister's reasoning is difficult to follow.

Turning now to the Northwest, we find the situation no better than in La Vérendrye's time. Pierre, who had been commissioned to build Fort Dauphin in 1741, returned to Fort La Reine, and four years later followed his father to Montreal, leaving the post on the Assiniboine in the charge of the younger brothers.[13] The Sieur de Noyelles, as soon as he became commander, saw the obstacles standing in the way of a discovery of the Western Sea and quickly reached the same conclusion as his predecessor. Like him, he found difficulty in securing guides, and without guides exploration was impossible; even with them it was none too easy, for the savages had a habit of leading their employers to and fro according to their whims, instead of conducting them directly to the places they desired to reach. Then, too, he found a deplorable lack of tranquility among the Indians of the Northwest.[14] All this led to his asking the governor to relieve him of his post, a request the latter was not slow in granting. This corroboration of La Vérendrye's experiences by De Noyelles was, of course, eagerly seized upon by the governor as a justification of the confidence he had reposed in the explorer, and he had no hesitation in reappointing him when De Noyelles resigned his command.

It was with a feeling of grim satisfaction, then, that the governor wrote the Minister in October 1746, telling him of his intention of reinstating La Vérendrye, at the same time politely pointing out that De Noyelles had done nothing in the way of

[13] Memorandum of the services of Pierre Gaultier de la Vérendrye the elder, etc., *ibid.*, pp. 496–497. From internal evidence we know that it was written by Pierre, the son, and that he calls himself the elder as he wrote it after his father's death.

[14] Beauharnois and Hocquart to Beauharnois, Archives des colonies, C^{11}A-85, 95.

exploration during the two years of his incumbency, despite
the memoirs and instructions that had been sent him.[15] La
Vérendrye for his part showed his appreciation for the opportunity thus placed before him (after he had considered himself
virtually shelved) by writing Maurepas a letter thanking him
for the captaincy and expressing confidence in his own ability
to handle the situation, since he knew the territory from long
experience and since his sons were still in the Northwest keeping
in close touch with its affairs. "The knowledge I have of that
region," he wrote, "joined to that which my sons have acquired
(of whom two are in this post today) will enable me to make
further discoveries of a still more satisfactory character; at least
it will not be my fault if I do not." [16]

In order to show his good will Beauharnois issued a permit
on May 18, 1747, authorizing La Vérendrye to take four canoes
with six men each to the western posts, carrying all the necessary
supplies. The *voyageurs* thus engaged were prohibited from
trading with the Indians at any other post; and each was to
bring back his own gun to show that he had not exchanged it in
the forbidden traffic. The penalty was three months in jail. All
were to be back in the time specified by their contracts or be
declared *coureurs de bois*.[17] It was Beauharnois' parting gift to
the explorer; in a few months he was back in France.

An important change now took place in the administration
of affairs. The Marquis de Beauharnois, who for the past twenty-
four years had governed Canada with skill and consciousness,
brought his administration to a close in September 1747. He was
now past the age of three score and ten, and it was deemed advisable to replace him by a younger man. The following year
Gilles Hocquart closed his Canadian career; his place was taken
by François Bigot. A year later the Comte de Maurepas was

[15] Beauharnois to Maurepas, Oct. 15, 1746, *J. & L.*, pp. 461–462.

[16] La Vérendrye to Maurepas, Nov. 1, 1746, *ibid.*, pp. 463–464.

[17] *R.A.Q., 1922–1923*, p. 229.

dismissed from office, and was succeeded by Antoine-Louis, Comte de Jouy-Rouillé. Thus La Vérendrye was obliged to deal with an entirely different trio of officials from the ones whose administrations had spanned his career in the Northwest.

The person appointed as successor to Beauharnois was Jacques-Pierre de Taffanel, Marquis de la Jonquière, a man of rather grasping disposition who showed but little consideration for the La Vérendrye family. Maurepas in a letter gave a *resumé* of the situation and sketched a plan for him to pursue. He explained how the Sieur de la Vérendrye, who had been attempting to discover the Western Sea, had established several trading posts in the upper country, but satisfied with the trade he found there had taken little interest in pushing forward the work of discovery. Governor Beauharnois had had him replaced by another who proved even less efficient, hence La Vérendrye had been again selected as commander of the Northwest. For this reason the Minister now ordered La Jonquière, as soon as he arrived in Canada, to seize all maps and journals pertaining in any way to the subject so as to get a thorough knowledge of it and be able to guide the work accordingly. He was also to advise La Vérendrye that if the King was not better satisfied with his work than in the past he would be deprived of all command in the colony.[18]

Fortunately for La Vérendrye, La Jonquière did not get to Canada immediately. The vessel on which he embarked was captured by the English, who held him in captivity for two years. His place was filled temporarily by Rolland Michel Barrin, Marquis de la Galissonnière, who arrived in Quebec in September 1747. The new governor at once took up the matter of La Vérendrye's explorations, and it was not long before he reached the same conclusion as Governor Beauharnois. Writing to Maurepas five weeks after his arrival, he remarked somewhat tartly:

[18] Maurepas to La Jonquière, March 6, 1747, *J. & L.*, pp. 465–467.

I hardly thought of replying [to your letter] on the subject of the discovery of the Western Sea, being still insufficiently informed regarding it. I would only say that it appears to me that what has been reported to you with reference to the Sieur de la Vérendrye having bestowed more pains on his own interests than on the exploration is entirely false, and moreover that any officers who may be employed on that task will be under the necessity of giving a part of their attention to commerce as long as the King shall not furnish them with other means of subsistence. The system may not be good, but it is a poor way to encourage them to reproach them with any slight profits they may make, or to delay their promotion under this pretext, as the Sieur de la Vérendrye says has been done in his case. These explorations cause heavy expense and expose a man to greater fatigue and greater danger than regular wars.[19]

Then, like Beauharnois, La Galissonnière granted La Vérendrye permission in June 1748 to send four canoes manned by six men each to the western posts, under the same conditions as Beauharnois had stipulated.[20] It is interesting to note that at this time the explorer purchased a Negro slave named Robert for the sum of 400 *livres*. Indian slaves are not infrequently met with in the records of that time, but the sale of a colored man was something quite unusual.[21]

Maurepas, to do him justice, appreciated the necessity of explorers engaging in trade when on an expedition of discovery, as this was the only way such undertakings could be financed if the government refused to advance the money; but he was convinced that La Vérendrye had abused his position and had directed his steps to places where trade was abundant rather than to the Western Sea. It must be admitted that his point of view was not without foundation, if we bear in mind the difficulties under which he labored in getting at the true state of affairs regarding an unknown region situated so far away. La

[19] La Galissonnière to Maurepas, Oct. 23, 1747, *ibid.*, pp. 468–469.
[20] *R.A.Q.*, 1922–1923, p. 233.   [21] *Ibid.*, 1921–1922, p. 115.

Vérendrye had gone into the Northwest in 1731, and for seven years had occupied himself with founding posts and making trade agreements with the Indians. Then, in 1738, he at last attempted to solve the riddle by visiting the Mantannes. This journey proved of little value, and there was another delay, this time of four years. Then La Vérendrye sent his sons in search of the sea, and they, after wandering about the country for fifteen months, came back no wiser than before. Neither the Minister nor his colleagues appreciated the immense distance across the continent, nor did they realize that the Western Sea their agent was seeking was purely a myth. The reports La Vérendrye had gathered from the Indians assured them of the approximate nearness of this sea, and these the Ministry was contented to accept at face value. The explorer did, to be sure, list the difficulties he had had to encounter, but even these did not seem valid excuses for such constant delay in covering what was believed to be a comparatively short distance. The authorities, considering their lack of exact information, were not entirely unreasonable in their demands. What they wanted was action, not excuses; deeds, not words.

And besides all this there were doubts—valid ones in the minds of the officials—that La Vérendrye really cared to make the attempt. As an example of what they considered as a failure to grasp an opportunity we may cite the incident at Fort Maurepas when La Vérendrye excused himself from going to the Mantannes because his men were afraid. The continual financial strain under which the explorer labored should have exonerated him from the charge of selfishness; yet this point so frequently stressed in the letters sent by him and the governor to the Minister seems to have made little impression. Perhaps it was not fully believed. There were also mean and jealous persons in Canada ready to discredit the explorer, as the chevalier points out in a letter to Count Rouillé:

Envy, as it exists in this country, is no half envy; its principle is to calumniate furiously in the hope that if even one-half of what is said finds favor it will be enough to injure; and in point of fact my father, thus opposed, has more than once been obliged to his sorrow to turn back and make us turn back owing to lack of help and protection.[22]

The complaints made by the La Vérendryes of unfair treatment, due to slander, have in them a strong element of truth, for judging by the letters on the subject Maurepas and his colleagues must have lent a ready and sympathetic ear to any malevolent criticisms brought against the explorer. Prejudices of this nature, once firmly lodged in the mind, are difficult to eradicate; and although Maurepas toward the end of his administration came to regard La Vérendrye in a more favorable light, after De Noyelles had failed, he appears to have been actuated more by the belief that the explorer was the least objectionable of a rather poor assortment, than by any regard for the man himself. The Minister did show some appreciation for his work by recommending his sons, Pierre and Louis-Joseph, for junior ensigncies when vacancies should occur.

Governor la Galissonnière was now superseded by La Jonquière, who had been released by the English in time to reach Quebec in September 1749. Count Rouillé had replaced Maurepas the preceding April. La Vérendrye's affairs seem to have been uppermost in the new minister's mind, for a few days after assuming office he wrote La Jonquière that while the accusations against the explorer appeared borne out by his own journals, De Noyelles was even more inefficient; hence the suggestion to entrust the former once more with the task of exploration had met with the grudging approval of His Majesty.[23] Thus the incoming governor found a new minister with whom he had to deal, fortunately one who, though he had inherited to a large extent his predecessor's prejudices, was, at least, open to

[22] Chevalier to Rouillé, Sept. 30, 1750, *J. & L.*, pp. 503–504.
[23] Rouillé to La Jonquière, May 4, 1749, *ibid.*, pp. 472–475.

reason. And now, going back somewhat in the chronological sequence of our narrative, we shall say a few words about the activities of La Vérendrye's sons.

Pierre came to Montreal in 1745. Shortly after his arrival he was sent to join an expedition against Saratoga, for the war with the English colonies, known as King George's War, was then raging. On returning from this venture, he was sent back to the same general locality, there to spend the winter. May of the following year saw him in Acadia taking part in the attack on Prince Edward Island, after which he returned to Montreal. It was during the month of June 1747 that a mixed band of Dutch, English, and Iroquois, numbering over one hundred warriors, moved down the St. Lawrence to launch a surprise attack on Montreal. The alarm was given and two hundred men were hurriedly gathered together to repel the invaders; and among the officers was Pierre. The enemy were quickly routed in a brief campaign of a few days, a campaign in which Pierre seems to have distinguished himself, for on his return Governor Beauharnois rewarded him by making him a *cadet à l'aiguilette*.

Two months later, on August 13, the elder La Vérendrye and De Noyelles arrived at Montreal with disquieting news from Michilimackinac. De Noyelles brought with him a letter from his son, Charles-Joseph, acting-commander at this post, informing the governor that the Indians were again on the rampage and giving him some unpleasant details of their activities.[24] For the time being, the younger De Noyelles said, he would detain all canoes destined for the West until further orders, unless the situation cleared in the meanwhile. The governor acted

[24] It was probably La Vérendrye, senior, who came down from Michilimackinac, for the "Journal of Occurences, 1746–1747," in J. R. Brodhead, ed., *Documents Relative to the Colonial History of the State of New York* (Albany, 1858), X, 119, in referring to De Noyelles' companion, calls him the Sieur de la Vérendrye, while in mentioning the sons always refers to them as the Chevalier de la Vérendrye, or La Vérendrye, junior.

promptly. He at once sent Pierre with letters to the commander telling him what steps were being taken for his relief.[25]

Pierre was ready to go—perhaps this was why the governor selected him—as he had spent the month of July recruiting men for a western trading voyage that would enable him to revisit the northern posts.[26] On reaching Michilimackinac, he was detained by De Noyelles on the ground that the Indians were still active. Here he tarried awhile, then, becoming restive, broke away, and in due time reached the northern posts, which he found deserted by the savages. Yet he was not discouraged, and by a series of speeches in which he stressed the power of the Father at Quebec, and by a judicious distribution of presents, managed to lure them back to their old loyalties. It is impossible to give a detailed account of his activities during the next three years, but we may be sure that he did not return to Montreal.

The following year (1748) Pierre was back in Michilimackinac, having left his brother François in charge of the posts. At Michilimackinac he received orders from La Galissonnière, who enclosed therewith an ensign's commission. These orders evidently sent him west again, for he tells us that he returned to Fort La Reine, which he found in ruins, and to Fort Maurepas, which had been burned by the Indians. These posts he repaired as best he could, an undertaking that left his purse sadly depleted. This done, he returned again to Michilimackinac.[27]

The career of Louis-Joseph during this period offers some interesting details—only poor François is omitted; he vanishes into obscurity, probably occupied in the northern posts. In the summer of 1747 Louis-Joseph appeared at Michilimackinac, where he met Pierre on his way to the northern posts.[28] Leaving

[25] *Ibid.*, p. 120.   [26] *R.A.Q., 1930–1931*, pp. 362–365.
[27] This account of Pierre's activities is taken from his narrative in *J. & L.*, pp. 495–502.
[28] "Journal of Occurences, 1746–1747," *op. cit.*, X, 129. After this meeting the "Journal of Occurences, 1747–1748," *ibid.*, pp. 137, 149, 154, 167, mentions the name of La Vérendrye four times: thrice as La

his brother, he proceeded to Montreal, where he found himself under the orders of the newly arrived La Galissonnière. His first assignment was the command of a minuscule detachment consisting of a dozen men, including five Crees he had brought with him. With these he left Montreal on February 16, 1748, to attack the Mohawks. He appears to have been successful in a small way, for he returned late in March with two scalps as evidence of his prowess. What this raid accomplished is not recorded. During the spring of that year he went to Michilimackinac, whence he made his way to the western posts.

It was probably on this voyage that Louis-Joseph ascended the Saskatchewan River, the first white man to penetrate into this territory. We know that he left Montreal in June, 1748, and an entry in the baptismal records of Michilimackinac of April 6, 1750, tells us of an Indian slave "given to this mission last year [1749] out of gratitude by M. le Chevalier de la Vérendrye on his return from the extreme west," [29] proof that he was back from his journey the year after he left Montreal. Assuming, then, that it was in the latter part of 1749 rather than in the earlier part that he arrived in Michilimackinac from the west, he had ample time to ascend the Saskatchewan for a good distance. There are, unfortunately, no details of this important journey. From the meager data available we are able to give a brief sketch of his achievements. Eventually he reached Fort La Reine and from there proceeded to Fort Dauphin, which had suffered from neglect, and this he repaired. His next step was to erect a post at the mouth of the Rivière aux Biches (Red Deer River) where it empties into Lake Winnipegosis. He called it Fort Bourbon. By this time, we are safe to assume, Fort Bourbon on Cedar Lake had been abandoned.[30] This done, he

Vérendrye, junior, and once as the chevalier. Evidently these all refer to Louis-Joseph since we know from Pierre's own memorandum that he (Pierre) was in the Northwest. The Occurences deal only with a La Vérendrye who was in the East.

[29] Quoted in *J. & L.*, p. 499n.   [30] See Appendix G.

proceeded up the Saskatchewan as far as the fork where its northern and southern branches meet, a spot used as a meeting place
by the Crees. Here he is said to have built a small station called
Fort Poskoyac, and here he attended a Cree gathering and
gleaned some information about reaching a great lake beyond
the mountains, a lake whose waters were salt. It was by this
route that La Vérendrye, senior, intended to make a drive for
the Western Sea when he made his plans for his last journey,
a journey destined never to take place. Later on the chevalier
directed his steps to the post at Chequamegon, where he took
part in local activities for the next few years.[31] Louis-Joseph
was twice married: his first wife was Marie-Amable Testard de
Montigny, whom he wedded in 1755; his second, Louise-
Antoinette Mezière de l'Epervanche, was married to him three
years later. He met his death in the wreck of the *Auguste* in
1761. Pierre was employed by the governor on minor commis-
sions with Indian affairs, and in 1752 he was in charge of a
garrison at Beauséjour. He died in Quebec in September 1755.
As for François, he lived to a good old age and died in 1794.

The above account is submitted to the reader with some misgivings, for the obtainable data are very meager and subject to
different interpretations. In some cases no dates are given to
important events, so that it is difficult to decide just when they
occurred. In others, one cannot be absolutely certain which of
the brothers is being mentioned; the author, or authors, of the
documents do not seem to differentiate between the chevalier
and his older brother, sometimes using the term "younger" in
referring to either one; and, to make matters worse, in no case
do they refer to these men by their Christian names. All this,
of course, makes for confusion, and we can only sum up the
situation, and our own interpretation of the facts, by saying:
caveat lector.

[31] Grace L. Nute, "Marin versus La Vérendrye," *Minnesota History*,
XXXII (1951), 226–238.

During the winter of 1749 La Vérendrye, while laying plans for another expedition, enjoyed himself immensely, entertaining and being entertained by the fashionable society of Montreal. He even dined the governor at his house. We find evidence, too, that despite his years—he was then sixty-four—he was pursuing a comely widow—object, matrimony. This rather amusing incident is recorded by Mme. Claude-Michel Bégon. And it is particularly amusing as La Vérendrye had a rival. Mme. Bégon in her gossipy letters tells us that she had learned the reason for Bermen de la Martinière's sudden appearance in the town. He had his eye on the widow of a well-known merchant prince, one Pierre de Lestage, who had been engaged in the fur trade for many years. This was the lady who was being pursued by La Vérendrye. "It is the funniest thing in the world," wrote Mme. Bégon, "to see the grimace La Vérendrye makes at La Martinière." At this point the explorer's brother, Jacques-René, ably assisted by his wife, took a hand in the game, and sought to help their brother by paying court to Mme. de Lestage in his behalf. La Vérendrye, so Mme. Bégon tells us, thought that he had but to speak and the matter would be settled. It was settled, when he spoke, but not in the way he had expected. Mme. de Lestage declared that she wanted a husband who would amuse her and not be her master, a decision that seems to have eliminated both contestants. So the whole affair ended in a draw.[32]

In laying plans for the coming journey, La Vérendrye selected the Saskatchewan route. In a letter to the Minister, written September 17, 1749, he said:

My zeal accompanied by gratitude impels me to leave here next spring honored with the orders of the Marquis de la Jonquière, our general, to continue the establishment of posts and the exploration of the West, which for several years have been interrupted. I have delivered to the Marquis de la Jonquière the map and memorandum

[32] *R.A.Q., 1934–1935*, pp. 37, 42.

showing the route I am to follow for the present. . . . I shall keep
a very exact journal of my travels from my first advance into the
interior to the farthest I and my sons may reach. I am not able to
leave Montreal till the month of May next [1750], which is the time
when navigation opens for the upper country. I mean to make all
possible diligence so that I may be able to winter at Fort Bourbon
on the lower course of the Rivière aux Biches, the last one I have
established.[33]

A more detailed outline of the itinerary is to be found in a report, dated April 1750, accompanied by a map, which tells us
that the Sieurs de la Vérendrye—Louis-Joseph and probably
François were to join their father—intended "to go early in
December 1750 to Fort Bourbon," by which is meant that this
was the time set for their arrival at the fort. Then as soon as
navigation opened—sometime in the following spring—they
would ascend the Saskatchewan to the height of land and there
build a fort for the convenience of the Crees. The winter would
be spent at this post, and when spring came an attempt would
be made to find the great salt-water lake or sea. All this would
take time, and La Vérendrye warned the governor not to expect a complete report before the third year, though he would
attempt to write him as often as possible.[34]

Thus did the explorer in planning his expedition abandon
the old Mantanne route for the northern trail blazed by the
chevalier when he ascended the Saskatchewan to the fork. The
reason for this is not hard to understand. La Vérendrye by now
knew for certain that the so-called River of the West was no
other than the Missouri, which flows southeasterly to the Mississippi. Pierre found this out when he journeyed south from
the Mantannes to the Spanish fort in 1741; at any rate a map
showing La Vérendrye's discoveries, dated 1750, traces the
river with the inscription: "River of the West or River of the

[33] La Vérendrye to Rouillé, Sept. 17, 1749, J. & L., pp. 477–478.
[34] Report, April 1750, ibid., pp. 489–492.

Mantannes believed to be the Missouri." [35] This knowledge had been his for some time; he had known about it when the chevalier, on his long expedition to the Rocky Mountains, had struck out over the prairies instead of following the river. But it was not this alone that decided him to take the northern route. The journey over the plains, as Louis-Joseph had learned, was a hard one, with its intense heat in midsummer, and the difficulties, linguistic and other, one had to face in dealing with different and sometimes hostile tribes. The northern route, on the contrary, offered much better facilities. It would be far easier to transport supplies by river than on the backs of horses and men over a hot, dusty plain; and since the explorers would have only their old friends the Crees to deal with, at least until they reached the mountains, they would have no trouble in finding guides.

La Vérendrye now believed that his trials at the hands of the French authorities were over and that he had at last succeeded in convincing them that he alone was the man best fitted to discover the Western Sea, even if he had not convinced them entirely of his disinterestedness. Though no longer in the prime of life, his body racked by hardships, and his confidence shaken by the injustices done him, he once more made preparations to accomplish the object for which he had labored so long. But the privations he had suffered had by now undermined his health and sapped his vitality. He spent the summer of 1749 busily engaged in making preparations for an early start the following spring, collecting supplies, hiring men, and doing the thousand and one things necessary for success. In the midst of his labors he was stricken ill. Of the nature and details of this illness we know nothing. We can surmise, however, that it was sudden and of brief duration, for we are told that on December 5 he expired in Montreal between nine and ten o'clock in the evening.

[35] A copy is given in *ibid.*, opposite p. 488.

Strange to say, the passing of this distinguished man, whose activities during the past twenty years had received the government's close attention and had been the subject of so much high-level correspondence, seems to have attracted but little notice from his contemporaries. A brief statement appears in a letter of La Jonquière to the Minister saying that M. de la Vérendrye had died, and the writer proceeds to explain that the work of discovery in the Northwest will be continued by Legardeur de Saint-Pierre. There is neither eulogy nor criticism of the man or his work; he was gone and someone else had been retained to take his place. Two days after his death La Vérendrye was buried in Ste. Anne's chapel in the church of Notre Dame.

Pierre de la Vérendrye left considerable property in the shape of personal belongings. Shortly after his death a committee, charged with the appraisal of the same, went over all his effects with a fine-tooth comb. The committee worked indefatigably for several days, stopping only for meals and sleep, and made a report in which is listed every article in detail, with a full description and an estimated value. Nothing was overlooked. From the inventory we gather that the owner must have given considerable attention to his personal appearance—perhaps some of these articles were bought during his abortive courtship of Mme. de Lestage—for the list is replete with items covering clothing and adornment, including a silver watch and chain valued at eighty *livres*. There is a striking contrast between this inventory and the humble estate left by his father.[36]

To appraise the character of La Vérendrye in the light of his achievements is no easy task for one who is not acquainted by personal experience with the sort of obstacles he had to face. No one can blame him, of course, for not finding the Western Sea, since none existed, nor even for his failure to reach the Pacific Ocean, as this was clearly more than one could reasonably ex-

[36] *R.A.Q., 1949–1950*, pp. 51–67.

pect; but the armchair critic might well accuse him of unnecessary dilatoriness in reaching the Mantannes, and in truth such
a charge cannot be lightly brushed aside. The principal difficulty lay, as we have repeatedly pointed out, in the time La
Vérendrye was obliged to devote to the fur trade. The government had refused to finance his expeditions, regarding them as
something to be carried out at the explorer's expense, and this
expense he could only meet by establishing trade with the Indians. His enterprises therefore became primarily commercial
ones, with discovery relegated to the background, until he could
meet the obligations he had incurred in fitting out his ventures.
Then, when he was relieved of the fur business, which was
farmed out to certain interests, traders were established at his
posts who in all probability did their utmost to promote trade
at the expense of exploration. The reader will remember in this
connection how the traders at Fort St. Charles demanded the
recall of their clerks from Fort Maurepas. Yet La Vérendrye cannot be held wholly blameless for his failure to push through
with more speed, for when he returned to Montreal in 1737
even his staunch supporter, Governor Beauharnois, lost patience
with him and threatened drastic measures if he did not push
forward the work of discovery with more energy. Spurred on
by this warning, he had no difficulty in reaching the Mantannes
the following year.

Though La Vérendrye can be safely exonerated from the
accusation of trying to enrich himself by the fur trade, it was
unquestionably the fur trade that took up most of his time while
in the Northwest. Whatever may have been his own interest in
exploration, or whatever may have been the governor's wishes
in regard to discovery, the influential merchants of Canada undoubtedly hoped to reap profits from a more extensive commerce with the Indians, and were not inclined to aid him save
for this purpose. Misunderstood by his government in France
and envied by the merchants of Canada who regarded his op-

portunities in the Northwest with a jealous eye, La Vérendrye was handicapped from the start; and though he did not display the energy and resourcefulness of a La Salle, he deserves a high place in the estimation of posterity for his courage and perseverance in the face of unusual obstacles.

Appendix A

THE identity of the Chevalier de la Vérendrye has in the past been a matter of considerable controversy, though recent scholars are fairly well agreed that Louis-Joseph was the one who bore that title.

At first, some authorities cast their votes for Pierre; but this opinion is no longer held; thus François and Louis-Joseph are left as contenders for the distinction. Those who favor François point to the custom, then prevalent, of giving the title to the second son, who in this instance was Pierre. After Jean-Baptiste's death Pierre became the eldest son, and the title would naturally devolve on François.[1] For our purpose, however, the question as to whether Pierre ever bore the title is somewhat academic, for the first time La Vérendrye mentions the chevalier

---

[1] DeLand, in "The Vérendrye Explorations and Discoveries," *op. cit.*, pp. 128–129. DeLand here states that this theory is also held by Benjamin Sulté. Doane Robinson also agrees with it (*ibid.*, p. 129n.).

is after Jean-Baptiste's death, and there is ample evidence that
the father then applied it to either François or Louis-Joseph.
For instance, the chevalier led the expedition to the Rocky
Mountains with one of his brothers, and we know that Pierre
was not one of the party.

Whatever may be the validity of François' claims, as set forth
by his advocates, they seem to us rather negative and much less
convincing than those advanced for Louis-Joseph. The pro-
ponents of the latter bring forth a document, dated July 15,
1750, wherein La Vérendrye's three sons are listed as Pierre,
Sieur de Beaumois (Boumois, La Vérendrye's old title), François, Sieur du Tremblay, and Louis-Joseph, Chevalier de la
Vérendrye. They also present several documents listing those
who perished in the wreck of the *Auguste* in 1761, and these describe Louis-Joseph as the chevalier.[2]

A. H. de Tremaudan, one of François' champions, counters
this by saying that documents of this nature are not always
correct, especially if they are drawn up in the absence of the
persons whom they mention (as was the case in the document
of 1750) or after their death (as was the case in the documents
listing the victims of the *Auguste* disaster). This may be so,
but it is not really proof, and we must not take it as such. It
is a possibility, not a fact. M. de Tremaudan then goes on to
say that Saint-Luc de la Corne, in his account of this unfortunate event, speaks of Louis-Joseph as a lieutenant, not as a
chevalier. As further evidence De Tremaudan cites the official
record of the chevalier's marriage to Mlle. de l'Epervanche, in
which his name is given without the title, though the same title
is given to two men who acted as witnesses.[3]

All this is perhaps true; yet what does it prove? We are asked

[2] P. G. Roy, "Communication," *Le Canada français*, 2d ser., III (1918–
1920), 294–295.

[3] A. H. de Trémaudan, "Who Was the Chevalier de la Vérendrye?"
Canadian Historical Review, I (1920), 246–254.

to discard the documents giving Louis-Joseph the title because they were drawn either in his absence or after his death, and to accept at face value documents in which his name is given without the title. This last raises a question: Is the omission of a man's title in certain records proof that he did not hold it? In our opinion it is no proof at all, especially when it is offset by other records giving the title.

But we have also some excellent positive evidence in favor of Louis-Joseph as the proper candidate. In the year 1752 he was active in making preparations for a journey to Chequamegon. There are ten documents extant, ranging from February to June of that year, showing that he was enlisting recruits for this voyage. We find the score as follows: he is mentioned as M. de la Vérendrye once; as Joseph de la Vérendrye, four times; as Joseph Chevalier de la Vérendrye, twice; as Chevalier de la Vérendrye, three times.[4] All these entries evidently refer to the same man—Louis-Joseph the chevalier.

To sum up: There are a number of documents giving the title to Louis-Joseph, while not a single one, so far as we know, has been discovered which specifically gives it to François. This, in our opinion, should clinch the matter, for *all* these documents cannot be wrong. And now let us turn to the evidence given by the lead plate, buried by Louis-Joseph at the mouth of the Bad River in 1743 and discovered in 1913.

When François and Louis-Joseph started out on their journey to the Rocky Mountains in 1742, their father gave them a lead plate to be deposited at some place selected by them to commemorate the presence of the French in the newly discovered territory. On its obverse side it bore a Latin inscription, carefully engraved by a skilled craftsman, to wit: *Anno XXVI Regni Ludovici XV Prorege Illustrissimo Domino Domino Marchione de Beauharnois MDCCXXXXI Petrus Gaultier de Laverendrie Posuit.* When the chevalier, leader and chronicler

[4] *R.A.Q., 1930–1931,* pp. 425, 440, 443, 448.

of the expedition, came to bury it, he decided to note the names of those present and the date on the reverse side. Unfortunately he had no engraving tools at hand, nor was there anyone in the party capable of doing a decent job with any tool. An inscription was therefore scratched on the lead with the point of a knife that has puzzled those who have tried to decipher it. Of two things we may be certain: the engraver abbreviated whenever he could and marred his work with several scratches. It reads: *Pose par le chevalyet de Lav to jo [to St] Louy la Londette Amiotte le 30 de mars 1743.*

Now, there were in the party four Frenchmen: François, Louis-Joseph, and the two *voyageurs* named La Londette and Amiotte. From the inscription one would surmise that La Londette's first name was Louis, and some scholars have thought that Amiotte should read A. Miotte, thus giving a first name and a first initial to the two *voyageurs*. If we turn to the *Rapport de l'archiviste de la province de Quebec pour 1929–1930* and glance at page 370 we find that on May 4, 1739, Louis Gatineau et Compagnie engaged two men, Édouard Lalonde and Jean-Baptiste Amiot, to go to the *pays d'en haut*. Making due allowance for the variants in spelling, so often found in colonial French-Canadian names, it is not unreasonable to suppose that these two men were those who followed the chevalier's fortunes. They both went west together in 1739 and were well-seasoned *voyageurs* by the time the expedition started. If this is so, La Londette's first name was Édouard, not Louis.

Turning now to the rest of the inscription, we are confronted by the letters "'to jo" or "to st." These have been variously interpreted. Some claim they stand for *temoins* (witnesses); others for Louis-Joseph; and one scholar for Toussaint.[5] The

---

[5] For these various theories see Doane Robinson's articles: "The Vérendrye Plate," *Proceedings of the Mississippi Valley Historical Association,* VII (1913–1914), 244–253 (this gives Jules Jusserand's opinion on the meaning of "to st" which he believes stands for "Toussaint"), and

reader can take his choice. Since we have assumed that La Londette's first name was Édouard, the "Louy" cannot refer to him; it must refer to Louis-Joseph. If this is so then one can make a strong case for François as the chevalier, as there are no letters on the plate that can be interpreted as "Francois." Unfortunately, for this point of view, the documentary evidence, as we have shown, is so strongly in favor of Louis-Joseph that we must accept it and interpret the plate as best we can. We are inclined to believe that François was not present when the plate was buried—he may have been busy in the Indian village—hence his name does not appear on the plate. The plate was deposited by the chevalier, as the inscription shows; and we believe that the inscription was intended to read: "Placed by the Chevalier de la Vérendrye, witnesses [if that is the correct rendering of "to st"] Louis [-Joseph], La Londette, Amiotte." It may seem strange that Louis-Joseph's name should appear as a witness when he was already mentioned as the chevalier, but there may have been a reason for this which now eludes us.

———

"La Vérendrye's Farthest West," *op. cit.,* pp. 146–150. Louise P. Kellogg's interpretation of the letters "to jo" as standing for Louis-Joseph is here given on p. 147n.

Appendix B

A WORD should be said here about the compass courses recorded in the La Vérendrye narratives. The explorers carried a compass with them and occasionally noted the direction of travel in their journals. A literal translation of these courses from the original French sometimes results in English terms that have no meaning. "Sud quard de sud ouest," translated in *Journals and Letters* as "south by southwest" is an example of this. The *Vocabulaire des termes de marine,* by Daniel Lescalier, 1797, shows (plate XVI) a compass rose with the proper French names for the thirty-two points. For some strange reason west is placed to the right of north and east to the left, but this should give no trouble to one who can box the compass. "Sud quard de sud ouest" is here shown to be south by west, and by using the rose the various courses given by La Vérendrye can be easily identified. The translations in *Journals and Letters* are usually correct, but Mr. Haxo's rendering in the *North Dakota Historical Quarterly* (vol. VIII) suffers sometimes from transliteration.

It would, perhaps, be too fussy to correct La Vérendrye's compass readings for magnetic variation before applying them to a map. The variations in the localities he traversed are known today; but as they fluctuate annually there is no means of knowing what they were two hundred years ago. Moreover, the explorers did not set a course and follow it like a modern steamship; they followed a guide who led them as he saw fit, and the compass courses they recorded were more of a general direction of travel.

Appendix C

ORIN G. LIBBY, whose interpretations of the text we have followed, traces the explorers' 1738–1739 route from Fort La Reine twenty-six leagues south by west to Pembina Mountain, selecting Star Mound at Snowflake, Manitoba, as the "first mountain" mentioned by La Vérendrye. Thence he traces their route twenty-four leagues, west by north, to the second mountain, obviously some projection on the northern side of Turtle Mountain. Thus far we are fairly safe; but now we come to the side excursion to the Assiniboin village that took La Vérendrye twenty-two leagues out of his way, though he does not tell us in what direction he went. Mr. Libby believes the village *may* have been situated at the junction of the North Antler Creek with the Souris River (he says with the Assiniboine, but this is obviously an error) for at this place are to be found the remains of an earth-lodge Hidatsa village which the Assiniboins may have occupied at some time. Checking the course on a modern map, we find that it is sixty miles from Portage la Prairie (Fort La Reine) to Snowflake, the direction being south by west; fifty-eight from Snowflake to, say, Wakopa on the northeastern edge of Turtle Mountain, direction due west; and fifty-three from Wakopa to the mouth of North Antler Creek, direction slightly north of west. Taking the French league as equivalent to 2.42 miles [1]—though no one, of course, expects La Vérendrye to have been precise in his measurements—we find that these distances correspond very well with the twenty-six, twenty-four, and twenty-two leagues mentioned by him.

Assuming, then, the mouth of North Antler Creek to have been the site of the Assiniboin village, the question arises as to how far it was from this village to the first Mantanne fort, and where this fort was situated. Mr. Libby tells us that the distance between these two places was seventeen leagues. The text, however, reads differently. La Vérendrye says that it was seventeen leagues from the village to the place where the Mantannes were to meet him, a place somewhere between the two settlements. On leaving the village, the explorers and their hosts traveled very slowly. They started on November 20 and reached the rendezvous eight days later, averaging only two leagues a day. After this they appear to have proceeded more rapidly. Just what the new *per diem* rate was we cannot compute accurately, but we may examine the record to obtain a fair estimate. On the last day of the march (December 3), the day on which they entered the Mantanne fort, they started at four o'clock in the morning in order to arrive at the fort, distant seven leagues, at a fairly early hour. At noon they came to the bank of a small stream where they rested for two hours, then resuming the march reached the fort at four o'clock in the afternoon. Seven leagues, then, was considered a good day's march. This checks with La Vérendrye's statement [2] that it was 120 leagues from

[1] *J. & L.*, p. 57n.   [2] *Ibid.*, p. 312.

Fort La Reine to the first Mantanne fort, a distance he could
have covered in sixteen to twenty days had not his guide led
him far off the direct route. This means a daily march of six to
seven leagues. In computing the distance from the Assiniboin
village to the Mantanne fort, we find, therefore, that the explorers traveled seventeen leagues from November 20 to November 28 and seven on December 3, the last a forced march.
Assuming that they traveled at least five leagues a day on November 30, December 1, and December 2, three days in all,
this would make fifteen leagues, which, when added to the
seventeen covered in the first week and the seven on December 3, would make a total of thirty-nine from the Assiniboin
village to the fort.

Where, then, was the first Mantanne fort? We know from the
observation taken at this place that it was near the forty-eighth
parallel (48° 12′, to be exact) and that it was within one and
one-half leagues of a small stream. We know also that it was
within a day's march of the second fort which was situated on
the banks of the Missouri at a place where this meandering
stream flows for a short distance to the southwest. But as several
scholars have found it impossible to get Louis-Joseph's party
from the first fort to the second and back in two days, it will be
well to explain at some length the reasons that have led us to
follow the conclusions of Messrs. O. G. Libby and H. E. Haxo.[3]

According to the translation of La Vérendrye's narrative in
Journals and Letters, the Assiniboins left the first Mantanne fort
to go back to their village on December 6, and six days later
(i.e., on the twelfth) Louis-Joseph started for the second fort
on the banks of the Missouri. To make matters more confusing,
the translation tells us that he was back on the fourth, and this

[3] Orin G. Libby, "La Vérendrye's Visit to the Mandans," *Collection of
the State Historical Society of North Dakota,* II (1908), 503–508; Henry
E. Haxo, "The Journal of La Vérendrye, 1738–39," *op. cit.,* pp. 229–
271.

has led commentators to believe that the date was intended to mean January 4, thus giving Louis-Joseph time to make a long journey to the Mandans at the mouth of the Heart River.

Fortunately Mr. Haxo has solved the problem correctly. The Assiniboins left on December 6, of this we can be sure. But the phrase in the original French telling of Louis-Joseph's departure had been mistranslated. It reads: "le 6 après le depart des Assiniboilles, j'envoyés mon fils the chevalier, etc." Mr. Haxo points out that this should be rendered: "on the sixth, after the departure of the Assiniboins, I sent my son the chevalier, etc." We know, then, that Louis-Joseph left on December 6, not on December 12. Turning to the date of his return, Mr. Haxo, after a careful examination of the original manuscript, discovered that the figure "4" is actually a "7" carelessly written, a correction Mr. Burpee accepted in his comments on Mr. Haxo's article.[4] This proves that the round trip to the second fort could be made in two days, and brings the forts within twenty miles of each other.

The location of the second fort is well established by Mr. Libby. La Vérendrye tells us that his son found it on the banks of a great river flowing to the southwest by south. If we turn to a map we find that at a place called Old Crossing, near the modern town of Sanish, the Missouri takes a sharp bend to the southwest, and that high bluffs rise at the mouth of Elm Creek which conceal from the observer the eastward return of the river. It is here the government has erected on Crowhigh Butte the Vérendrye National Monument. Thus we have enough information to place the first fort with a fair degree of accuracy. It was near the forty-eighth parallel; it was one and one-half leagues from a small stream, probably the Little Knife or the Shell; and it was within about twenty miles of Sanish. In order to clinch the matter, such a spot would be about one hundred

[4] Burpee, "La Vérendrye's 1738-9 Journal," *Canadian Historical Review*, XXIII (1942), 407-411.

miles from the mouth of North Antler Creek, a figure which is equivalent to the thirty-nine leagues mentioned above.

There is, however, a fly in the ointment, and it is a rather large one. The tribe living in the vicinity of Old Crossing, as subsequent investigations have shown, were not the Mandans but the Hidatsas, sometimes called the Gros Ventres. Mr. Libby meets the difficulty by bluntly stating that La Vérendrye never reached the Mandans, despite his continual assertions that he did so. We agree with Mr. Libby, and the reader will find the matter fully discussed in Appendix D.

Appendix D

THE tribe which La Vérendrye called the Mantannes was for a long time identified with the Mandans who lived at the junction of the Heart and the Missouri Rivers where the modern cities of Bismarck and Mandan now stand. This is just below the forty-seventh parallel. This identification, so obvious on the face of it, was first made by Francis Parkman and accepted by subsequent historians without question.

Yet the obvious in this case cannot be true. Those who have brought Louis-Joseph to the mouth of the Heart River were not handicapped by a proper reading of that part of La Vérendrye's narrative which tells of the chevalier's short trip to the second Mantanne fort. They believed that he left the first fort on December 12 and returned on January 4, ample time to make a long journey. When confronted by the latitude 48° 12′, as the parallel on which the first fort was situated, some brushed it aside as an obvious error, others accepted it since they assumed that Louis-Joseph had ample time to make the long journey to the second Mantanne fort and to return by January 4.[1]

Yet, as the similarity between the names "Mandan" and "Mantanne" is too striking to be dismissed as a coincidence, it has occurred to us that the Assiniboins, in speaking of the Mantannes, may have been referring to the Mandans, without in any way weakening Mr. Libby's theory that the forts visited by the La Vérendryes were really those of the Hidatsas. La Vérendrye, during his journey, and for some time before it, was continually hearing of a tribe, possibly a nation of white men, who lived on a westward flowing river. This tribe was variously called the Ouachipouennes by the Monsoni, the Kouatheattes by the Crees, and lastly the Mantannes by the Assiniboins. The explorer, when he joined the Assiniboins on his journey to the River of the West, was handicapped by his inability to speak their language. One of his sons spoke Cree, as did an Assiniboin interpreter, and thus conversation could be relayed back and forth—ample opportunity for misunderstandings. La Vérendrye told the Indians of his desire to visit a people living on the River of the West—which seems to have been the Missouri although it does not flow westward—and his Assiniboin guide said these were the Mantannes, meaning, perhaps the Mandans proper. In his narrative La Vérendrye tells us of the excessive dilatoriness of his guide, who led him all over the country south of the Assiniboine River instead of striking out directly for the Missouri. When he was finally ready to satisfy the explorer, he led him to the Hidatsas near Old Crossing on the Missouri, who, like the Mandans, lived on the River of the West; and La Vérendrye naturally assumed them to be the Mantannes he was seeking. This is just a suggestion, and we give it for what it is worth. The problem is an intricate one and no one seems to have solved it to everybody's satisfaction.

[1] Warren Upham, "The Explorations of Vérendrye and His Sons," *Proceedings of the Mississippi Valley Historical Associations,* I (1907–1908), 43–55; DeLand, "The Vérendrye Explorations and Discoveries," *op. cit.,* 91–322; Doane Robinson, notes on Deland.

Appendix E

A WORD should be said here to explain the chronological sequence of the side trip, the importance of which will be seen in the analysis of the journey as set forth in Appendix F.

It has been generally held that the dash toward the mountains to attack the Snakes was a somewhat long-drawn-out affair, starting January 9 and ending February 9, when the French and the Bows returned to the baggage camp. That this side journey took so long a time does not seem to us likely in the circumstances, nor does it conform with the general tone of the narrative which gives the impression of rapid action taking place in a few days.

Louis-Joseph's account tells us that the explorers and their Indian friends first sighted the mountains on January 1. They then marched in a westerly direction toward them until January 8, when they halted to establish their baggage camp. This done, they, or rather the warriors among them, made a dash for the Snake encampment, traveling all the more rapidly since they were now unencumbered by squaws, children, and impedimenta. Louis-Joseph here tells us that they reached the mountains on the twelfth day ("enfin, le douzième jour nous arrivâmes aux montagnes"). If this is to be taken to mean that they reached the mountains twelve days after their departure they did not reach the Snake encampment until January 21; and if they traveled at the rate of ten miles a day—a conservative estimate for a party of warriors on horseback—they must have covered at least 120 miles. Granting this estimate as approximately correct, the question naturally arises: Could they have seen the mountains on January 1 when they were an eight days' march east of the baggage camp? Furthermore, would they have left their families and supplies at a camp to launch an attack on an enemy so far away?

All this does not seem likely, so we must look for some other interpretation of the text. The words, "le douzième jour," usually taken to mean twelve days after leaving the baggage camp, may well mean the twelfth day of January, thus bringing the Snake encampment within three days of the baggage camp. On reaching this encampment the Bows became panicky and dashed for home, traveling, in all probability, more rapidly than on the outward journey. The narrative says in speaking of their return: "Enfin nous arrivâmes des premiers au village des Gens de l'Arc, le 9 fevrier qui était le deuxième de nôtre déroute." (Here the reader will recall that the French became separated from the Indians and fell behind for a while.) The translation of this sentence in *Journals and Letters* reads: "Finally we arrived among the first [that is with the Indians] at the village of the Gens de l'Arc on the 9th of February, the second day after losing our way." If this date is correct the Indians must have taken longer (that is nineteen days) on the return journey than on the outward one, despite the fact that they were in great haste to get home.

We are inclined to believe that the solution of the problem is to be found in the correct translation of the word "déroute." English-French lexicons, and also French dictionaries, give its meaning as a hasty, disorderly retreat, especially in a military sense. The "déroute" referred to must be the panic experienced by the Bows when they found the Snake encampment deserted. The passage then means that the French and Indians were back at the baggage camp two days after their panicky flight, thus taking two days to cover the distance that had taken them three on the outward march.

All this is simple enough, but what of the date February 9. This, we admit is a difficulty. But if we are forced to choose between the date and all that it implies, namely, a long excursion taking twelve days on the outward trip and nineteen on the return, on the one hand, and the theory of a quick dash, three days out and two back, on the other, we think it wise to put the date aside as one of those errors that occasionally creeps into a narrative of this sort.

Appendix F

IF THE exact route taken by La Vérendrye presented a difficult problem, the route now taken by his sons is even more baffling. Since we have accepted Mr. Libby's location of the second Mantanne village near Old Crossing as the place where the chevalier in all probability stopped when he reached the Mantannes on his outward journey, we can do no more than accept his analysis of the route now taken; in fact, we are bound to do so, for the identification of the route depends largely on its starting point.

The chevalier, therefore, crossed the Missouri at Old Crossing and proceeded in a southwesterly direction for twenty days. He must have traveled at a slower pace than on the journey down from Fort La Reine, or perhaps he traveled at the same speed but halted from time to time for a day or so, for if he had traveled at the same rate he would have eventually gone farther west than Mr. Libby believes he did. As he progressed, his route lay along the upper waters of the Yellowstone and Powder

Rivers. The mountains near the Snake encampment were the Rockies and probably the Big Horn range, though Mr. Libby is not quite sure on the latter point. He is sure, however, that they were not the Black Hills, as some have asserted. It was here that the chevalier turned back.

Having brought his hero thus far, Mr. Libby finds it impossible to get him to the mouth of the Bad River, where the plate was buried, by March 19. The distance from the Big Horns to this place is 350 miles as the crow flies, to which he adds 100 miles to allow for detours, bringing the total distance traveled up to 450 miles, far too great a distance to be covered in thirty-five days. The trouble lies, of course, in his taking the date, February 9, as the day when the warriors returned to the baggage camp and adding five days to that, thus making it February 14 before the expedition could get under way for the return journey. In order to solve the problem, he offers the ingenious though unconvincing theory that the plate was buried somewhere else and later dug up by the Indians and carried to the mouth of the Bad River where it was found in 1913. It is not, however, necessary to resort to such an assumption as this. We have shown in Appendix E that the date, February 9, is in all probability erroneous, and that the warriors were probably back in camp by January 14. Thus the return journey began on the nineteenth or twentieth, giving the Frenchmen two months instead of thirty-five days to reach the Bad River. As further evidence that the plate was buried somewhere else, Mr. Libby points out that the chevalier makes no mention of the Missouri River on his return to the Mantannes from the place where he left the plate, although the obvious route lay along the banks of this stream; nor does he speak of the Mandan and Arikara tribes he would surely have met had he followed it. This omission cannot be accounted for except by assuming that the chevalier, having described the journey westward, felt little interest in the last phase of the return trip. Louis-Joseph was not a verbose and explicit writer; and, after all, he did not mention the Missouri when he crossed it, as he must have, on the outward march.

Charles E. DeLand offers the choice of two routes: the short journey and the long journey. According to him the expedition started westward from the Mandan village situated either at the mouth of the Heart River or at the mouth of the Little Knife and reached the mountain of the Horse Indians on August 2. This he believes, is Red Butte on the Little Missouri, thirty-five miles south of Medora, North Dakota. Doane Robinson also agrees with this identification. Red Butte forms a point of departure for both the long and short journeys. Taking up the theory of the short journey, Mr. DeLand believes the French to have started with the Beaux Hommes (Crows) as guides and traveled in a general southwesterly direction looking for the Horse Indians. Eventually they came, as the narrative tells us, to the Indians of the Belle Rivière, who were said to derive their name from the locality of their home. The party was probably near the Belle Fourche River, the northern branch of the Cheyenne in South Dakota. This would bring them just north of the Black Hills. According to this route, they never went further west than this, and from here they turned eastward and eventually reached the Missouri.

According to the long-journey theory the French moved to the south-southwest from Red Butte along the west side of the Medicine Bow Range, then going along the Little Missouri they followed the north course of the stream to the Missouri Buttes, and came to Camp Crook in South Dakota. Thence they went to Gillette, Wyoming, and then to the eastern point of the southern loop of the Powder River, a point fifty miles southeast of the place selected by Francis Parkman on the Big Horn range. Here was the baggage camp. The actual farthest west was in the vicinity of the Big Horn range. Returning, the party passed south of the Black Hills and traveled eastward until it reached the mouth of the Bad.

Doane Robinson is convinced that the chevalier did not go beyond the Black Hills. "There is not the slightest evidence," he says, "either directly or by fair inference, that the Vérendryes were ever within several hundred miles of the Bighorns." From the mouth of the Heart River he takes the chevalier to Red Butte, then almost due south to the Cheyenne, then west to the Black Hills.

Francis Parkman, whose opinion cannot be lightly set aside, favors the long journey and shows the French as starting from the mouth of the Heart and reaching the Big Horns at a spot 120 miles east of Yellowstone Park. Returning, they passed through the Black Hills. As he wrote long before the lead plate was discovered, he was not obliged to bring his party east to the Bad River. He contents himself with saying that the chevalier buried the plate somewhere along the Missouri.

John W. Smurr, the most recent commentator, rejects the Black Hills theory absolutely, and tends in general to uphold Mr. Libby. He starts the party from the modern town of Sanish and carries it in a southwesterly direction to the Big Horn range in latitude 44° 45′ N. Thence he makes the explorers retrace their steps to latitude 45° 20′ N., whence they turn eastward and proceed in a direct line to the mouth of the Bad.[1]

[1] Orin G. Libby, "Some Vérendrye Enigmas," *op. cit.*, pp. 143–160, and "Additional Vérendrye Material," *Mississippi Valley Historical Review*, III (1916–1917), 387–399; DeLand, "The Vérendrye Explorations and Discoveries," *op. cit.*, pp. 99–322, and "Additional Vérendrye Material," *Mississippi Valley Historical Review*, III, 378–386; Robinson, *ibid.*, pp. 368–377, and "The Vérendrye Plate," *op. cit.*, pp. 244–253; Parkman, *op. cit.*, II, 40–55; Smurr, "A New La Vérendrye Theory," *op. cit.*, pp. 51–64.

Appendix G

THERE is some difficulty in identifying the locations of the forts built on the various lakes west of Lake Winnipeg and assigning to them the proper dates of their establishment. This is due partly because two of them bore the name of Bourbon, evidence that they could not have existed contemporaneously, and partly because the references to them are rather casual.

Fort Dauphin, we know, was built in 1741. La Vérendrye gave his son, Pierre, orders to establish a post on Lac des Prairies, a name given sometimes to Lake Manitoba, sometimes to Lake Winnipegosis, possibly because in those days the narrow strip of land at Meadow Portage separating the two may have been submerged, making them one and the same lake.[1] The fort, however, was actually built on a different body of

---

[1] L. A. Prud'homme, "Les Successeurs de la Vérendrye," *Proceedings and Transactions of the Royal Society of Canada*, XII (1906), sec. I, 65–81.

water, Lake Dauphin, which drains northward into Winnipegosis through the Mossy River. It was near the place where
the Valley River enters the lake that Fort Dauphin was erected
in section 7, township 27, range 18. Alexander Henry says that
Peter Pond wintered there in 1775,[2] and Pond's map (see *Report
on Canadian Archives*, 1890) shows a post on a lake that can
only be Lake Dauphin. It cannot be the Northwest Company's
post, as this was situated on the Ochre River, south of Lake
Dauphin.

It was probably at this time that Pierre built the first Fort
Bourbon near the mouth of the Saskatchewan in Cedar Lake.
La Vérendrye in his Summary Journal [3] says that when he sent
Pierre to build Fort Dauphin he also gave him orders to establish Fort Bourbon. Pierre himself in his Memorandum [4] speaks
of having built Fort Dauphin at this time, though he says nothing about Fort Bourbon.

Cedar Lake is situated a short distance west of the northern
part of Lake Winnipeg and north of Lake Winnipegosis, from
which latter it is separated by a neck of land some three miles
wide. Into its western waters flows the Saskatchewan, and this
river continues through the lake to its eastern end where it
continues on its way to Lake Winnipeg. It may, therefore, be
said to have two mouths, one in Cedar Lake and one in Winnipeg. Near the Cedar Lake mouth lies a group of islands, on
the largest of which (Fort Island) Pierre built the first Fort
Bourbon. This post did not last very long, for we find that in
1748 or 1749 another fort called Bourbon was erected at the
mouth of the Rivière aux Biches (Red Deer River) which flows
into the northwestern part of Winnipegosis known as Dawson
Bay. The Fort Memorandum [5] speaks of the Fort Bourbon on
Cedar Lake as having been "abandoned for lack of provisions
in the winter." As further evidence that the one on the Red

[2] Henry, *op. cit.*, p. 263.
[4] *Ibid.*, p. 496.
[3] *J. & L.*, p. 454.
[5] *Ibid.*, p. 486.

Deer River was the second we refer to La Vérendrye's statement that the one "on the lower course of the Rivière aux Biches"
was the last one he ordered built.[6]

[6] *Ibid.*, p. 478. See also J. B. Tyrell, "Report on North-Western
Manitoba," *Geological Survey of Canada*, V, 70-E, 79-E.

Bibliography

Adair, E. R. "Anglo-French Rivalry in the Fur Trade during the 18th Century," *Culture*, VIII (1947), 434–456.

Archives des colonies. In the Public Archives at Ottawa.

The Aulneau Collection 1734–45. Ed. by A. E. Jones. Montreal, 1893.

Blegen, Theodore C. "Fort St. Charles and the Northwest Angle," *Minnesota History*, XVIII (1937), 231–248.

Bradford, Lee C. Article in *Minnesota Archeologist* (April 1947).

Brymner, Douglas. "Journal of La Vérendrye, 1738–9," *Report of Canadian Archives, 1889*, pp. 3–38.

Buade, Philippe. *Considérations géographiques.* Paris, 1753.

Burpee, Lawrence J. "The Lake of the Woods Tragedy," *Proceedings and Transactions of the Royal Society of Canada*, 1903, 2d ser., IX, sec. 2, 15–28.

——. "La Vérendrye's 1738–9 Journal," *Canadian Historical Review*, XXIII (1942), 407–411.

Calendar of State Papers, Colonial Series, America & West Indies.

Campbell, T. J. "Out of the Grave," *Bulletin de la société historique de Saint-Boniface*, V, pt. iii, 1–22.

Caron, Ivanhoe. "Pierre Gauthier de Varennes de la Vérendrye et ses fils," *Bulletin des recherches historiques*, XXIII (1917), 169–181.

Carver, Jonathan. *Travels through the Interior Parts of North America, 1766–1768*. London, 1778.

Coues, Elliott. *New Light on the Early History of the Greater Northwest*. 3 vols. New York, 1897.

Crouse, Nellis M. "The Location of Fort Maurepas," *Canadian Historical Review*, IX (1928), 206–222.

DeLand, Charles E. "Additional Vérendrye Material," *Mississippi Valley Historical Review*, III (1916–1917), 378–386.

——. "The Vérendrye Explorations and Discoveries," *South Dakota Historical Collections*, VII (1914), 99–402.

Delanglez, Jean. "A Mirage: The Sea of the West," *Revue d'histoire de l'Amérique française*, I (1947–1948), 541–568.

Documents Relative to the Colonial History of the State of New York. Ed. by E. B. O'Callaghan. 15 vols. Albany, 1853–1887.

Dunbar, J. B. "Massacre of the Villazur Expedition by the Pawnees on the Platte in 1720," *Collections of the Kansas State Historical Society*, XI (1909–1910), 397–423.

Edicts, Ordinances, Declarations, and Decrees Relative to the Seigniorial Tenure Required by an Address of the Legislative Assembly, 1852. Quebec, 1852.

Eschambault, Antoine d'. "Le Voyage de La Vérendrye au pays des Mandannes," *Revue d'histoire de l'Amérique française*, II (1948–. 1949), 424–431.

Faillon, Etienne M. *Histoire de la colonie française en Canada*. Montreal, 1866.

Fauteux, Aegidius. "Les Gaultiers de Varennes et de la Vérendrye," *Bulletin des recherches historiques*, XXIII (1917), 244–249.

Franchère, Gabriel. *A Voyage to the Northwest Coast*. New York, 1854.

Frémont, Donatien. "L'Enfance de la Vérendrye," *Le Canadien français*, 2d ser. (1937), 5–21.

Groulx, Lionel. *La Pénétration du continent américain par les Français 1783–1846, traitants, explorateurs, missionnaires*. Montreal, 1939.

Haxo, Henry E. "The Journal of La Vérendrye, 1738–39," *North Dakota Historical Quarterly*, VIII (1940–1941), 242–271.

Henry, Alexander. *Travels & Adventures in Canada and the Indian Territories between the Years 1760 and 1776.* Ed. by James Bain. Boston, 1901.

Hodge, F. W. *Handbook of Americans North of Mexico.* Washington, 1907–1910.

Kellogg, Louise P. *The French Regime in Wisconsin and the Northwest.* Madison, 1925.

La Vérendrye, Pierre de. *Journals and Letters of Pierre Gaultier de Varennes de la Vérendrye and His Sons.* Tr. from the French by W. D. Le Sueur. Ed. by Lawrence J. Burpee. (Publication of the Champlain Society.) Toronto, 1927.

Lescalier, Daniel. *Vocabulaire des termes de marine.* Paris, 1797.

Libby, Orin G. "Additional Vérendrye Material," *Mississippi Valley Historical Review*, III (1916–1917), 387–399.

——. Introduction to Haxo's translation of La Vérendrye's Journal, *North Dakota Historical Quarterly*, VIII (1940–1941), 229–241.

——. "La Vérendrye's Visit to the Mandans in 1738–1739," *Collections of the State Historical Society of North Dakota*, II (1908), 502–508.

——. "Some Vérendrye Enigmas," *Mississippi Valley Historical Review*, III (1916–1917), 143–160.

Malchelosse, Gérard. See Régis Roy.

Margry, Pierre. *Mémoires et documents pour servir à l'histoire des origines françaises des pays d'outre-mer.* 6 vols. Paris, 1879–1888.

——. "Les Varennes de la Vérendrye," *Le Moniteur universel* (Sept. 14, 1852), pp. 1408–1410; (Nov. 1, 1852), pp. 1773–1774.

Marhault, Olivier. "Où repose Pierre Gaultier de la Vérendrye," *Revue d'histoire de l'Amérique française*, VI (1952–1953), 467–469.

Massicote, E. Z. "Jacques de Noyon: Nouveaux détails sur sa carrière," *Bulletin des recherches historiques*, XLVIII (1942), 121–125.

Morton, Arthur S. *A History of the Canadian West to 1870–71*, London, New York, 1939.

——. "La Vérendrye: Commandant, Fur Trader, and Explorer," *Canadian Historical Review*, IX (1928), 284–298.

Munro, William B. *Documents Relating to the Seigniorial Tenure in Canada, 1598–1854.* Toronto, 1908.

——. *The Seigniorial System in Canada.* (Harvard Historical Studies, vol. XIII.) New York, 1907.

Nute, Grace L. "Marin versus La Vérendrye," *Minnesota History,* XXXII (1951), 226–238.

——. *The Rainy River Country.* St. Paul, 1950.

——. "The Voyageurs Highway." (Publication of the Minnesota Historical Society.) St. Paul, 1941.

Parkman, Francis. *A Half-Century of Conflict.* Boston, 1900.

——. *The Old Regime in Canada.* Boston, 1901.

Prud'homme, L. A. "Autour de Fort Saint-Charles," *Le Canada français,* ser. 1918–20, vol. III.

——. "La Vérendrye, son oeuvre," *Revue canadienne,* LVI (Mar.–Apr. 1909).

——. "Pierre de Varennes," *Bulletin de la société historique de St. Boniface,* V, 35.

——. "Pierre Gaultier de Varennes," *Proceedings and Transactions of the Royal Society of Canada,* 2d ser., XI (1905), 9–57.

——. "Les Successeurs de la Vérendrye—sous la domination française," *ibid.,* XII (1906), sec. i. 65–81.

Rapport de l'archiviste de la Province de Quebec. Quebec.

Robinson, Doane. "Additional Vérendrye Material," *Mississippi Valley Historical Review,* III (1916–1917), 368–377.

——. "La Vérendrye's Farthest West," *Proceedings of the State Historical Society of Wisconsin,* VII (1913), 146–150.

——. Notes on DeLand's "The Vérendrye Explorations and Discoveries," *South Dakota Historical Collections,* VII (1914), 91–322.

——. "The Vérendrye Plate," *Proceedings of the Mississippi Valley Historical Association,* VII (1913–1914), 244–253.

Roy, P. G. "Communication," *Le Canada français,* 2d ser., III (1918–1920), 294–295.

Roy, Regis, and Gérard Malchelosse. *Le Régiment de Carignan, son organisation et son expédition au Canada.* Montreal, 1925.

Schaefer, Francis J. "Fort St. Charles, the Massacre in the Lake of the Woods and the Discoveries Connected Therewith," *Acta et Dicta,* II, 114–133.

Smurr, John W. "A New La Vérendrye Theory," *Pacific Northwest Quarterly*, XLIII (1952), 51–64.

Sulté, Benjamin. "Au Lac Winnipeg," *Bulletin de la société de géographie de Quebec*, XIV, 140–142.

——. "The Early History of the Militia, 1636–1700," *Mélanges historiques*, I, 127–146.

——. "Au Manitoba, 1738–1743," *Bulletin de la société de géographie de Quebec*, XIV, 213–215. ˙

——. "Au Nipigon, 1727," *ibid.*, XIII, 133–138.

——. "La Vérendrye avant ses voyages au nord-ouest," *Bulletin des recherches historiques*, XXI (1915), 97–111.

——. "Pierre Boucher et son livre," *Proceedings and Transactions of the Royal Society of Canada*, 2d ser., II (1896), sec. 1, 99–115.

——. "Le Régiment de Carignan," *Mélanges historiques*. Montreal, 1922.

——. "Trois Rivières d'autrefois." Vols. 19–21 of *Mélanges historiques*. Ed. by Gérard Malchelosse. Montreal, 1933.

Tanguay, Cyprien. *Dictionnaire généalogique des familles canadiennes depuis la fondation de la colonie jusqu'à nos jours.* Montreal, 1871–1890.

Titles and Documents Relating to Seigniorial Tenure, in Return to an Address of the Legislative Assembly, 1851. Quebec, 1852.

Trémaudan, A. H. de. "Who Was the Chevalier de la Vérendrye?" *Canadian Historical Review*, I (1920), 246–254.

Tyrell, J. B. "Report on North-Western Manitoba," *Geological Survey of Canada*, V, 70-E & 79-E.

Upham, Warren. "The Explorations of Vérendrye and His Sons," *Proceedings of the Mississippi Valley Historical Association*, I (1907–1908), 43–55.

Will, George F. "Criticism of 'Some Vérendrye Enigmas,'" *American Anthropologist*, n.s., XIX (1952), 291–297.

Wilson, Clifford. "La Vérendrye Reaches the Saskatchewan," *Canadian Historical Review*, XXXIII (1952), 39–49.

Acknowledgments

THE writer expresses his thanks to The Champlain Society for permission to reprint the map facing page 4 and to quote from its edition of La Vérendrye's journals and letters. He is also grateful to *Minnesota History* for permission to use its photograph of La Vérendrye's statue, which appears in the frontispiece, and to reproduce the tablet on page 188.

Index

243

246

246

INDEX

La Vérendrye, Pierre Gaultier (cont.) 87; promise to build Lake Winnipeg post, 87, 88; conference with Monsonis at Ft. St. Charles, 88-91; at Quebec, 1734, 93-96; fur business, 98, 99

Start of 1735 journey, 100; conferences with Crees and Monsonis, 1736, 110-115; journey to Ft. Maurepas, 116-119; purpose, 120-121; council with Crees and Assiniboins, 121-125; at Quebec, 126, 127; interview with Beauharnois, 127-131; contract with De Lorme and D'Ailleboust, 131

Journey to Ft. La Reine, 131-138; journey to the Mantannes, 1738-1739, 139-156; return to Ft. La Reine, 156-158; report of white people in Far West, 162-164; difficulties with De Lorme, 165-167; at Quebec, 168, 169; final expedition, 169; peace talks with Crees and Monsonis, 171; decision not to lead expedition to Western Sea, 172, 174

Surrenders command, 192-194; difficulties with Beauharnois, 195-198; opinions about his achievements, 200-202; second courtship, 207; plans for last expedition, 207-209; death, 209; estate, 210; appraisal of his work and character, 210-212

La Vérendrye, Pierre, Sieur de Boumois, 31, 55, 91-94, 197, 213, 214, 234, 235; journey to Lake Winnipeg, 88; builds Ft. Dauphin, 173, 202; subsequent career, 203, 204

La Vérendrye, Mme. Pierre de, 28-31, 38-40, 61, 98; death, 168

Legras, Daniel, 99, 108, 109

Legras, Jean-Baptiste, 38, 98, 126, 169, 170

Lestage, Mme. Pierre de, 207, 210

Linctot, René de, 54, 66

Little Cherries (Indian tribe), 180, 185, 186, 188, 231

Little Foxes, 178, 179

Little Knife River, 147, 223, 232

Louis XIV, 5, 18, 20, 31

Louis XV, 7, 13, 15, 69, 78, 94, 96, 122, 194, 199, 200; refusal to finance La Vérendrye's expedition, 70

Louisiana, 12, 46, 152, 186

Louvière, Louis d'Amours de, 135, 137

Mandans, 43, 148, 223-226

Mantanne fort (village) I, 189, 221, 225; location, 147, 222; description, 152, 153

Mantanne fort (village) II, 175, 176, 188-190, 225, 230; location, 223

Mantannes, 42-44, 93-99, 112, 117, 121, 123, 127, 131-137, 141, 162, 167, 173, 191, 201, 208, 211, 225, 226, 230; first news of, 67-69; later news of, 80-83; found not to be like white men, 143; escort French to their first fort, 143-146; identity discussed, 148

Massacre Island, 107, 109

Maugras, Pierre Gamelin, 38, 99, 169, 192

Maurepas, Jean-Frédéric Phélipeaux, Comte de, 13-14, 40, 41, 47, 48, 58, 69, 95, 96, 102, 150, 167, 168, 173, 183, 192, 199-202; seeks advice of Charlevoix, 49-51; correspondence with Beauharnois over La Vérendrye's failure, 126-131; reinstates La Vérendrye, 194-197

Mesaiger, Father Michel, 57, 59, 61, 67, 100

Michilimackinac, 3, 11, 12, 15, 57, 61, 64, 74, 94, 99, 104, 115, 126, 132, 133, 169, 171, 203, 204; location, 58

Militia, 25, 26, 30

Ministry of Marine, 13, 15

Mississippi River, 5, 10, 12, 43, 48, 73, 232

Missouri River, 12, 13, 44, 69, 80, 121, 162, 176, 186, 187, 208, 209, 222-226; see also River of the West

Monsonis, 60, 70-76, 105, 131, 133; habitat, 35; conference at Ft. Pierre, 1734, 84-87; conference at Ft. St. Charles, 88-91; conferences with La Vérendrye at Ft. St. Charles, 1736, 110-115; wish to join Crees in attack on Sioux, 171

Nelson River, 3, 35

Newfoundland, 27, 28

Nipigon River, 39, 41-43